RECLAIMING LOCAL DEMOCRACY

A progressive future for local government

Ines Newman

First published in Great Britain in 2014 by

Policy Press
University of Bristol
6th Floor
Howard House
Queen's Avenue
Clifton
Bristol BS8 1SD
UK
Tel +44 (0)117 331 5020
Fax +44 (0)117 331 5367
pp-info@bristol.ac.uk
www.policypress.co.uk

North American office:
Policy Press
c/o The University of Chicago Press
1427 East 60th Street
Chicago, IL 60637, USA
t: +1 773 702 7700
f: +1 773-702-9756
sales@press.uchicago.edu
www.press.uchicago.edu

© Policy Press 2014

British Library Cataloguing in Publication Data
A catalogue record for this book is available from the British Library

Library of Congress Cataloging-in-Publication Data
A catalog record for this book has been requested

ISBN 978 1 44730 890 4 paperback
ISBN 978 1 44730 891 1 hardcover

The right of Ines Newman to be identified as author of this work has been asserted by her in accordance with the 1988 Copyright, Designs and Patents Act.

Cover design by Andrew Corbett
Front cover: image kindly supplied by Corbis Images
Printed and bound in Great Britain by CPI Group (UK) Ltd, Croydon, CR0 4YY
Policy Press uses environmentally responsible print partners

"Ines Newman provides a thoughtful and trenchant analysis rooted in her longstanding experience and commitment to local democracy and local government."
Lucy de Groot, Chief Executive of Community Service Volunteers and previously Executive Director of IDeA

"I very much enjoyed reading this book. It gives councillors a rare opportunity to raise our heads and look beyond the foothills."
Cllr Roger Lawrence, Leader of Wolverhampton City Council

"Rich with practical examples and proposals, this provocative new text asks 'what *should* local government do?'. Moving beyond technical fixes, Newman argues that local government has an obligation to promote social justice. The book shows how a more proactive and inclusive local democracy can generate creative responses to meeting social need. A must-read for practitioners and academics alike."
Vivien Lowndes, Professor of Public Policy, University of Nottingham

To our grandchildren who are already asking the challenging ethical questions.

Contents

Acknowledgements

I could not have written this book without the considerable support I have received from very generous colleagues and from my family. Of course, the final product, any mistakes and weaknesses are my responsibility, but there is no doubt that those who have helped me have made this a better book.

My first thanks go to my colleagues who invited me to participate in their Marxist reading group when I joined the University of Warwick (Jonathan Davis, Crispin Fuller, Mike Geddes and Madeleine Wahlberg). I would not call myself a Marxist, but the stimulating discussions in this group helped to reawaken my interest in ideas and theories and made me read the literature that provided a background to this book. Jonathan, furthermore, facilitated my appointment as a Visiting Senior Research Associate at De Montfort University, providing an essential academic base for the research, and I am grateful to the university for its support. Second, I would like to thank the four anonymous reviewers of my original book proposal and the anonymous reviewer of the typescript, all of whom made helpful suggestions for improvement.

Particular thanks go to Janet Newman. Janet is no relation, but an academic for whom I have the highest regard. She gave invaluable advice on the original book proposal and read the first draft, quickly identifying some core weaknesses and helping me to address them. The first draft was also read by Marjorie Mayo, John Stewart and Councillor Roger Lawrence. Each of them provided really useful criticism, guidance and encouragement and contributed to improving the book. Roger read the book despite having a massive workload as leader of Wolverhampton in a period of austerity and cuts. His dedication to the city has delivered one of the most progressive councils in the UK. John Stewart originally inspired me when I did my MBA at Inlogov in the early 1990s. The course was a formative experience both as a result of the quality of the teaching and the stimulation from the student body. I loved it! John took the time to read the draft very thoroughly and made the type of gentle, perceptive and thoughtful comments for which he is well known. Marj is a very dear friend and provided general support, as well as invaluable advice on the proposal and the first draft.

Several friends and colleagues have also provided me with ideas and assistance with the case studies in the boxes that illustrate the text, and helped by discussing the book with me. Thanks go to: Janet Sillett and Alan Walters at the Local Government Information Unit (LGiU); Jane Foot, whose work on asset-based approaches and discussions with me provided all kinds of leads; Mandy Cooke, who is one of our Thursday walking group where the book was discussed; Pete Challis at Unison, who is a fund of reliable knowledge on financial and housing information; Dexter Whitfield, who founded the Centre for Public Services in 1973 and has worked unstintingly and consistently to protect the concept of 'public' and promote citizen and worker engagement in public services; and Fiona Campbell, whose expertise on health inequalities and public health is exceptional. My job at LGiU brought me in to contact with a group of colleagues whose understanding of local government is outstanding. I was honoured to work with them and to learn from them. Other experts helped me via email correspondence: Allan Cox from the Department of Communities and Local Government, who clarified the statistical information on public sector procurement from the private sector; David Hall, Director of the Public Services International Research Unit, who helped me on international work on outsourcing; Mark Bramah from the Association for Public Service Excellence (APSE) who provided a wealth of information and case studies; Stuart Roden, regional organiser from Unison, who provided information on Cornwall's outsourcing; Melanie Oliver from Nesta, who provided information on their Creative Councils programme; Kathryn Rees, who updated the information I had on the Wigan social care case study; Peter Davies, who similarly updated the information on Monmouthshire County Council; and Chris Grey, whose little book on studying organisations is excellent and who helped me on management theory. Finally, Geoff Mulgan in many ways stimulated this book. He chaired a seminar, around 2000–02, on localism as defined by the New Local Government Network (NLGN), which I strongly criticise in this book. Having listened to the presentation and the discussion, I exclaimed: "But the purpose of local government is to provide for need." Geoff, as I remember it, replied: "You can't say that, Ines – need is a relative concept." This book is a riposte to that comment. Geoff himself no longer believes that need is a relative concept, as he kindly told me when I wrote to him, referring me to the Young Foundation's 2009 publication, *Sinking and swimming: understanding Britain's unmet needs*.

The publishers, Policy Press, have been terrific. Emily Watt, the senior commissioning editor, was encouraging, professional and efficient at each stage. I was very pleased with the cover design by Andrew Corbett facilitated by Rebecca Tomlinson. The rest of the team – Laura Vickers, Jessica Miles, Kathryn King, Jo Morton, Susannah Emery and Nicole Whitaker – have all been a pleasure to deal with.

I am very fortunate in having a large family who are my main support. Hannah Edmonds, Russ Bubley, Jeffrey Newman and Hannah Newman all helped to proofread the book. My nephew, David Edmonds, creator of www.philosophybites.com/, gave me cogent criticism of my original Chapter Four. Councillor Joe Caluori, my niece Amy's husband, inputted in the last chapter and provided further councillor feedback. Our daughter, Kate Newman, has a far better understanding than I do of rights and participation. I have learnt a great deal from her work in development studies. Furthermore, she commented on early drafts of the book. Her siblings, Hannah and Zack, provided moral support and encouragement.

Most important has been the support from my husband, Michael Newman. When he first did his PhD, I told him that I did not have the perseverance or volition to do a research degree but one day I would write a book that could be far more polemical and lively than a PhD. I have written many journal articles and chapters in books, and edited the work of others, but the sole-authored book remained a challenge. The rash commitment to Mike led me to complete this book, which is both my first and last. Watching him writing his numerous books and articles was a central learning process. But more important has been his general support: taking more of his share of household tasks; talking me through blocks in the writing; critically reading every chapter two or three times through various stages; cycling with me to the British Library; and having complete faith that I would produce a quality publication. Thank you, Mike.

About the author

Ines Newman has a background in town planning and local economic development. She was Head of Policy at the Local Government Information Unit (1999–2007) and Principal Research Fellow, Local Government Centre, Warwick Business School (2007–12). She is currently Visiting Senior Research Associate at De Montfort University. In 2011, Policy Press published *Promoting social cohesion: implications for policy and evaluation*, which she edited jointly with Peter Ratcliffe.

Glossary and some abbreviations

Some of the definitions contain terms that appear elsewhere in the Glossary. Terms included in the Glossary are presented in **bold** the first time they are mentioned in the main text.

Academies	Schools funded by central government and free from local authority control but must follow guidance on admissions, special educational needs and exclusions. They have greater control over staff pay and conditions, the curriculum and the length of terms and school days.
Arm's Length Housing Management Organisation (ALMO)	A fully council-owned, not-for-profit company that provides housing management and improvement services for council housing. Many ALMOs were set up following a referendum by council tenants because the government offered extra funding from 2002 to 2009 to successful ALMOs to raise the standard of council housing. This money was not available for council housing that remained under local authority management.
Big Society	The term describes the 2010 Coalition Government's intention to open up public services to new providers, increase social action and devolve power to local communities.
Best Value	The Best Value regime was introduced in the Local Government Act 1999. It placed a duty on local authorities to secure economic, efficient and effective services through reviews of each service in which: quality as well as cost were considered; consideration was given to whether the service could be better provided by the private or voluntary sector; monitoring and performance indicators and regimes were put in place; the community and business interests were consulted; and the focus was on continuous improvement.
Commissioning	A complex process with responsibilities covering: specifying services; procuring products and services to achieve specified outcomes, usually (but not necessarily) through a competitive process involving bids from private sector providers; and supporting and monitoring service providers to ensure outcomes are delivered.
Commodification	The process of turning a public or social good or service, or a good that has not traditionally been sold, into a commodity.
Communities and Local Government (CLG)	See DCLG below.
Community Right to Build	Community Right to Build orders allow neighbourhoods to propose development needed by the community without the need for planning permission, provided that the majority of local people agree via a referendum. Part of this process includes preparing a business case. Any financial benefit the development generates must be used for the benefit of the local community, for example, maintaining local facilities.

Community Right to Challenge	The Community Right to Challenge came into force on 27 June 2012. Under the Right to Challenge, local authorities must consider expressions of interest in providing a service and, where they accept an expression of interest, they must carry out a procurement exercise for the service.
Compulsory Competitive Tendering (CCT)	Compulsory Competitive Tendering was the requirement to submit local authority services to competitive tender under the Local Government Acts of 1988 and 1992. It was replaced by the Best Value regime under the Local Government Act 1999.
Council	The council is the body of people elected to run the local authority. Full council is the meeting of all the elected councillors in the area. It has statutory duties such as agreeing the budget, constitution and strategic plans.
Councillor	Elected representative in UK local government. There are around 18,500 councillors in England and Wales.
County council	The top tier of local government in areas with both district and county councils. Responsible for schools, social services, public transportation, highways, waste disposal and trading standards. There are 27 county councils in England.
Department for Communities and Local Government (DCLG)	Name of the government department for local government in England since 2010. This department is frequently re-organised and renamed. From 1970 it was called the Department of the Environment (DoE). In 1997, when Labour came to power, the DoE was merged with the Department of Transport to form the Department of the Environment, Transport and the Regions (DETR). In June 2001 the department was renamed the Department for Transport, Local Government and the Regions (DTLR). A year later the DTLR was split, with transport getting its own department and the rest going to the Office of the Deputy Prime Minister (ODPM). In 2006 DCLG was established but until the Coalition Government in 2010 it was generally known as Communities and Local Government (CLG).
Department for Work and Pensions (DWP)	The government department responsible for welfare to work and welfare reform.
Depoliticise	To render apolitical. In this book the term is used to suggest that essentially political questions about the differential impact of policy decisions on different sectors of society are obscured and not discussed. The term is not used in the book to imply that policy should necessarily be party political.
Dirigiste	Comes from the French word 'dirigisme' which denotes an economic system where the state exerts a strong directive influence over investment. A dirigiste state implies an interventionist central state that controls economic and social matters.
Discourse	A discourse is 'a shared way of apprehending the world' (Dryzek, 2005, p 9).

District council	District councils are the second tier in county areas. They can be called borough councils (but metropolitan borough councils are unitary authorities – see later). They are responsible for local rather than strategic services, including council housing, local planning, recycling and refuse collection, and leisure facilities. There are 201 district councils in England.
Early Intervention Grant	The Early Intervention Grant (EIG) replaced a number of centrally directed grants, including the Sure Start grant of £1.1bn in 2010, to support services for children, young people and families. It could be used flexibly by local authorities. In 2011/12, £2,235m was given to local authorities in England through the Early Intervention Grant. By 2014/15 the grant will be only £1,600m, as cuts have been made and funds have been removed to meet the government's commitment to early education for two-year-olds from lower-income households.
European Union (EU)	An economic and political union established in 1993 after the ratification of the Maastricht Treaty by members of the European Community and since expanded to include 28 countries by 2013.
Fordism	Fordism, named after the car manufacturer, Henry Ford, combines mass production of standardised goods (using manufacturing processes with strict division of labour, production and assembly lines) with mass consumption. The manufacturing systems produce low-cost goods and enable the employers to pay sufficient wages for the workers to afford to buy the goods.
General Power of Competence	The Localism Act 2011 introduced a new General Power of Competence. It allows local authorities to take any reasonable action they need 'for the benefit of the authority, its area or persons resident or present in its area' (Localism Act 2011, Part 1, Chapter 1, Section 1, para 4). Previously, local government could only take action if there was a specific legal power that allowed this action to be taken. The well-being power, introduced in the Local Government Act 2000, did not give many councils the confidence that the Act could be used to cover all necessary action. The General Power of Competence has been designed to give councils the confidence to act.
Greater London Authority (GLA)	Government for London with strategic powers over the area covered by the 33 London boroughs, established in 1999. Has strategic responsibility for police, fire, strategic planning and transport.
Greater London Council (GLC)	Metropolitan county authority for London abolished in 1986 along with other metropolitan counties.
Greater London Enterprise Board (GLEB)	Established in 1982 by the GLC as its wholly owned economic development company and the first Enterprise Board in the UK. Renamed Greater London Enterprise when the GLC was abolished and now owned by the 33 London boroughs and run as an independent, not-for-profit company.

Grant-maintained (GM) schools	Grant-maintained schools were state schools in England and Wales between 1988 and 1998 that had opted out of local government control, being funded directly by a grant from central government
Health and Wellbeing Board	The Health and Social Care Act 2012 established Health and Wellbeing Boards as a forum where key leaders from the health and care system work together to improve the health and well-being of their local population and reduce health inequalities. Each top tier and unitary local authority established its own Health and Wellbeing Board, which took over their statutory functions in April 2013.
Improvement and Development Agency (IDeA)	Formed in 1998 to work in partnership with all councils in England and Wales. Merged into the Local Government Association's Local Government Group in July 2010.
Inherent need	Refers 'to needs that are inherent to the human individual not only because they are a biological organism, but by virtue of their very humanity. The notion of inherent need requires a theory or idea of personhood and of what it means to be a person' (Dean, 2012, p xiv).
Interpreted need	Refers 'to needs that are constructed or attributed to the human individual by interpretation. Interpreted needs may be established by observation or analysis, or through claims or demands, but they are established or articulated concretely, or from the bottom up' (Dean, 2010, p xv).
Local Agenda 21	Agenda 21 is part of the voluntarily implemented sustainable development action plan of the United Nations agreed in Rio, Brazil in 1992. Chapter 28 recommended a local dimension, which is known as Local Agenda 21.
Local Area Agreement (LAA)	Local Area Agreements were three-year agreements on improvement priorities and targets between central government and a local area working through its Local Strategic Partnership. They were abolished in April 2011.
Local Government Association (LGA)	The LGA is a politically-led, cross-party organisation that works on behalf of councils to ensure local government has a strong, credible voice with national government. It is a membership organisation. It provides sector-led improvement and workforce support.
Local Strategic Partnership (LSP)	A non-statutory body bringing together the different parts of the public, private, voluntary and community sectors to work at a local level, with the local council in the lead role.
Mayor	In Victorian England the mayor was an elected councillor chosen by their fellow councillors to be the leader of the council. This role is now called leader of the council and mayors now mostly have a ceremonial function in British local government. There are, however, 16 directly elected mayors in England under the Local Government Act 2000 and Greater London Authority Act 1999.

Members of Parliament (MPs)	The UK public elects MPs on a constituency basis to the House of Commons. In addition representatives are elected to the Scottish Parliament, the National Assembly for Wales and the Northern Ireland Assembly.
Millennium Development Goals (MDGs)	The MDGs are eight international development goals that were officially established following the Millennium Summit of the United Nations in 2000 and are to be achieved by 2015 (see: www.un.org/millenniumgoals/).
National Health Service (NHS)	Founded in 1948. Hospitals, doctors, nurses, pharmacists, opticians and dentists are brought together under one umbrella organisation to provide services that are largely free at the point of delivery.
National non-domestic rates (NNDRs)	Also called business rates. Property tax on business based on a nominal rent for the property.
Neighbourhood	A geographically defined area within a local authority area, typically around 5,000 households but with considerable variation. The 1997–2010 New Labour administrations promoted neighbourhood renewal in the most deprived neighbourhoods, with funding allocated to Local Strategic Partnerships and attempts to involve local residents in decision-making. National statistics are produced for very small geographical areas, known as super output areas, which now makes it possible to examine trends in neighbourhoods. See: www.neighbourhood.statistics.gov.uk
Nesta (and its Creative Councils programme)	Nesta is an independent charity with a mission to help people and organisations bring 'great ideas to life' (www.nesta.org.uk/about-us). Its Creative Councils programme, supported by the Local Government Association, ran from 2011 to 2013 and was designed to support local authorities to develop and implement radical innovations.
New Deal for Communities (NDC)	New Deal for Communities was a flagship component of the Labour government's National Strategy for Neighbourhood Renewal and was designed to help close the gaps between 39 deprived areas and the rest of the country. NDCs involved 10-year funding being handed over to community-led neighbourhood partnerships to improve their area
New Public Management (NPM)	NPM was a term coined in the late 1980s to describe an increased emphasis on private sector management approaches in the public sector. The doctrines have been defined as: • Hands on professional management • Explicit standards and measures of performance • Greater emphasis on output controls • Disaggregation of units in the public sector • Greater competition • A stress on private sector styles of management practice • A stress on resource efficiency (Hood, 1991, pp 4-5). The approach has been strongly criticised for ignoring the distinctive features of the public sector (eg Ranson and Stewart, 1989; Pollitt, 1990).

New Towns

The New Towns Act 1946 allowed the government to designate areas as New Towns as a response to the housing devastation of the war. Land was compulsorily purchased and handed to development corporations, which controlled development and kept the development gain from the land. The design of early post-war new towns was influenced by the Garden City movement.

Nolan Principles

The Seven Principles of Public Life, known as the Nolan Principles, were defined by the Committee for Standards in Public Life (see: www.public-standards.gov.uk/). They are selflessness, integrity, objectivity, accountability, openness, honesty and leadership.

Overview and scrutiny committees

Under the Local Government Act 2000, councils must establish overview and scrutiny arrangements through which non-executive councillors can question and challenge the performance of the executive. The Health and Social Care Act 2001 confers on first-tier local authorities (those with social care responsibilities) powers of health scrutiny. Under the Localism Act 2011, councils can move to a committee system and decide their own decision-making structures. Authorities operating the committee system are not required to operate a formal overview and scrutiny system, but must comply with certain requirements should they decide to appoint one or more overview and scrutiny committees.

Parish councils/ community councils and town councils

Parish councils were formed in England under the Local Government Act 1894. They have directly elected councillors and the power to precept (tax) their residents to support their operations and to carry out local projects. Parish and town (local) councils in England and community and town (local) councils in Wales are the first tier of local government. There are around 10,000 local councils in England and Wales, made up of nearly 100,000 councillors. The National Association of Local Councils represents these councils in England, and One Voice Wales is the principal organisation for community and town councils in Wales.

Parker Morris housing standards

In 1961, the Parker Morris Committee drew up a report on housing space standards in public housing in the UK. In 1967, these space standards became mandatory for all housing built in New Towns, and in 1969, for all new council housing. The mandatory nature of the standards was ended by the Local Government, Planning and Land Act 1980.

Poll tax/community charge

The community charge, introduced in 1989 by the Thatcher government, replaced rates. The community charge was a fixed tax per adult living in the house with some reductions and exemptions. It became widely known as the 'poll tax'.

Private Finance Initiative (PFI)	A way of funding public infrastructure whereby private consortia raise the finance needed, construct and maintain the buildings, and often run services within the building and lease them back to the public sector for a yearly fee, typically on a 25- to 30-year contract. They are an expensive funding arrangement but attractive to the government since the capital expenditure is not on national accounts and so does not count as public debt.
Rates	Property tax until 1989 based on the rent that could be derived by letting a property.
Rate capping	Central government directive on the maximum that a council could charge through rates brought in through the Rates Act 1984. Although reformed, central government has retained some control over how much local authorities can raise through taxes.
Resilience	A 'resilient' community or local authority is one that is deemed able to anticipate threats, reduce the impact of these threats by taking pre-emptive action, respond appropriately when these threats materialise and recover afterwards.
Responsibilisation	As Speedbird says: 'It's a terrible word, but maybe a terrible thing deserves one: "responsibilisation" refers to an institution disavowing responsibility for some function it used to provide, and displacing that responsibility onto its constituents, customers, or users' (http://speedbird.wordpress.com/2009/09/22/responsibilization-and-user-experience/).
Right to bid for community assets	From 12 October 2012, parish councils (England) and community councils (Wales) and local voluntary and community organisations can nominate local land or buildings to be included in lists of community assets maintained by local authorities. In the event of a proposed sale, a process will be triggered that allows a community interest group to express an interest in bidding to purchase the property.
Securitised	A process through which financial assets are bundled together into a single debt and a linked stream of revenue that is due to meet this debt in a form that can be sold as a financial product or bond, similar to the many derivatives constructed from mortgage debt.
Select committees	House of Commons select committees are largely concerned with examining the work of government departments. The majority of select committee chairs are now elected by their fellow MPs. The book makes reference to: the Public Accounts Committee (PAC), which is concerned with value-for-money of government expenditure; the Political and Constitutional Reform Select Committee (PCRC), which considers political and constitutional reform, scrutinising the work of the Deputy Prime Minister in this area; the Local Government and Communities Committee (LGCC), which monitors the policy, administration and spending of the Department for Communities and Local Government and its associated arm's length bodies; and the Treasury Select Committee.

Social movement	Defined in the *Encyclopaedia Britannica* as a loosely organised but sustained campaign in support of a social goal, typically either the implementation or the prevention of a change in society's structure or values. Although social movements differ in size, they are all essentially collective.
Spending Review	A Spending Review, or Comprehensive Spending Review, is a UK governmental process carried out by the Treasury to set firm expenditure limits. These decisions used to happen annually, but in 1998 Gordon Brown introduced a system of three-year Spending Reviews to bring more certainty to long-term planning. In 2010, George Osborne's first Spending Review covered a four-year period. An additional Spending Review took place in 2013 to cover the year 2015/16, during which the next general election will be held.
Surplus	An amount or a quantity in excess of what is needed. In Marxist economics, surplus value is a wider term than profit. The value of a good is the socially necessary labour time to produce it. But price is not necessarily related to this concept of value and a good is usually sold for a price above its labour value. Surplus value is the value transferred to those who did not labour to produce the good (the rent, the interest paid to the bank and the profit and capital gained by the employer which may be reinvested). Surplus value therefore adds to the initial capital invested.
Sustainable Community Strategy (SCS)	Under the Local Government Act 2000, SCSs were prepared by LSPs as a set of goals and actions that they wish to promote. The strategy informs the strategic planning framework and acts as an umbrella for all other strategies devised for the area.
Teckal exemption	Falling within the exemption means that the 'procurement' falls outside of the public procurement rules and does not have to be put out to tender. The Teckal case established that, under certain circumstances, a contract awarded to a third party will not count as public procurement if 'the local authority exercises over the person [ie the company] concerned a control which is similar to that which it exercises over its own departments and, at the same time, that person carries out the essential part of its activities with the controlling local authority or authorities' (see www.localgovernmentlawyer.co.uk/index.php?option=com_content&view=article&id=12842:the-use-of-teckal-company-structures-in-public-service-delivery&catid=59:governance-a-risk-articles&q). Wholly owned council companies carrying out work for the local authority can therefore be given work without the contract being put out to tender.

Third sector   The Office of the Third Sector, which was replaced in 2010 by the Office for Civil Society, defined the third sector as made up of organisations that are: 'non-governmental, value-driven, and that principally reinvest any financial surpluses to further social, environmental or cultural objectives' (National Audit Office glossary of terms, www.nao.org.uk/successful-commissioning/successful-commissioning-home/glossary-of-terms/). The sector includes social enterprises, registered charities and social firms and co-operatives, as well as hundreds of thousands of small community groups.

Unison   Unison is a public services union with 1.3 million members. It represents full-time and part-time staff who provide public services or work in the utilities sector, whether they work in the public or private sector.

Unitary authorities   A single level of local government responsible for all local services. Can be called a council, a city council or a metropolitan borough council. There are 56 unitary authorities in England, 22 in Wales, 32 in Scotland and a further 33 London boroughs, which are effectively unitary authorities but have some powers administered by the GLA.

Note

[1] Some of the information in this Glossary is taken from LGiU (2012) and LGA (2011).

ONE

Introduction

The second decade of the 21st century is a period of unprecedented trauma for local government. Austerity programmes have left it struggling to meet the demands for local services. In this context, this book asks how local **councillors** and officers can make their way through the challenges they face. What are the fundamental principles that should guide decision-making? This work seeks to develop an ethical framework for local government. It argues that unless policymakers have a clear concept of the fundamental purpose of their actions, they will be blown this way and that.

The analysis presented here suggests that current policymaking is dominated by what a number of economists have called 'market fundamentalism' (George Soros, 1998; Joseph Stiglitz, 2001, p 518). The result is a confused focus on 'what works', the increasing marketisation of public services and a growing lack of trust in representative democracy. The book seeks to move the agenda from 'What works?' to 'What should an ethical local government do?' and 'How will its policies impact on social justice and democracy in the area?'.

The approach fundamentally rejects the relativist conception that everyone has a different moral stance, so nothing can be said about what local government should do. The investigation seeks to provide an overall framework. It asks how an understanding of universal basic needs can be used to develop an obligation on local government to meet needs for existing and future generations. It argues that if local authorities have the power to remedy an injustice, there are compelling arguments for them to do just that. And the case is made that it is not just what local government *does* that matters, but also *how* decisions are made. People's lives are enhanced by taking part in the democratic process and by being active citizens.

These are important issues of values and principles. The book is unashamedly focused on local government. But it does not deal with the dry, familiar debate about what structures and powers local government should have. It seeks to move beyond these debates and to energise all concerned to re-engage with a political and ethical approach. It asks how local government can promote social justice, how it can develop active citizens and how it can make a difference to the well-being of those in different places. I hope that it might also persuade some students to consider a role within local government, as officers or councillors.

The book draws on my working life experience as a practitioner and academic within local government and **third sector** organisations. Since it deals with general issues, it has relevance far beyond England. The book includes examples from local practice in many countries but these are only illustrations. It will be up to those involved in local politics or local policy development elsewhere to re-interpret the arguments and ideas to make them more relevant to their own practice and knowledge.

My arguments are addressed to elected representatives and officers within the local government community, as well as to the academic community. However, the book should also be of interest to activists in the voluntary and community sector. It argues that progress has been, and will be, made only when local government opens itself up to **social movements**. Local authorities must be prepared to facilitate discussion of alternative ways of thinking about public policy issues and must engage with voices that are usually not heard. So, although there is no discussion of how to build autonomous social movements,[1] local government's relationship with citizens, employees and the voluntary and community sector are fully explored.

The ethical framework seeks to outline what local government should do. The book argues that all human beings have inherent needs and, from this premise, it follows that local government has an obligation to pursue policies around social justice. The policies and actions that local authorities adopt to meet this obligation depend on a range of economic, social, cultural and environmental issues that vary over time and place. Of course, some readers will disagree with these conclusions. But the book challenges them either to propose an alternative ethical framework demonstrating the relationship between *their* values and *their* conclusions, or accept the framework in the book but argue that different means should be used to achieve the desired ends. Alternative proposals must be able to stand up to reasoned scrutiny, not just from those directly involved, but also from those not usually heard, so must be justified with appropriate evidence. If this book generates a more challenging debate on the ethical purpose of local government and more interest in local democracy, it will have succeeded in its purpose.

The argument

The book follows Jones and Stewart (1983, p 5) in arguing that: 'Local government is no passing luxury. It should be the guardian of fundamental values. It represents, first and foremost, a spread of political power.' The three purposes of the public sector have been described as: the provision of public goods and services; the development of values of democracy and citizenship; and the realisation of justice and equity (Ranson and Stewart, 1989). Jones and Stewart also argued that:

> Our system of government must have the capacity
> * to learn
> * to respond
> * to change, and
> * to win public loyalty. (Jones and Stewart, 1983, p 7)

Yet, increasingly, over the last 30 to 40 years, the preoccupation has not been on fundamental values, democracy and justice. Nor has the focus been on how local government can learn, respond, make a difference and win legitimacy. Rather, it has been on efficiency and effectiveness, on meeting targets set by central government and coping with public expenditure cuts.

Chapter Two traces this trajectory in England, starting with Birmingham, which Asa Briggs (1952, 1963) regarded as the best-governed city in the world in the 1870s and 1880s. The chapter addresses the questions of how the purpose of local government has changed over time. It describes how the conception of local government has varied, and how, in each period, there have been attempts to centralise power at the national level, combined with new opportunities to make a difference at the local level. It looks at how wider changes in local economies and society have influenced ideas and practice. It also asks whether local government continues to have the capacity to make a difference. The chapter shows that local government continues to have creative autonomy and that there is no inevitability in how it will be managed or conceived in the future. Councillors and their political vision *can* make a difference. It also reveals that as well as change, there is continuity. The chapter argues that we have lessons to learn from history: from the civic gospel of the 19th century to the failures of 'holistic' approaches since the 1960s. The chapter ends with the 2010 Coalition Government's take on local government, with the council now seen as a community leader and commissioner.

Chapter Three starts by asking what the impact has been of the cuts and the new concept of local government in England as a commissioner rather than provider of services. There has been a gradual commodification of public services and this has resulted in the market shaping the way public services are provided. The case is made that this has created greater inequality in society. Yet, the chapter draws on evidence that general well-being would be improved in a more equal society. The facts show that outsourcing and privatisation do not deliver cost savings and higher-quality services in the long term. An alternative approach is therefore needed and it is argued that local government has the capacity to pursue this. The chapter looks at three approaches that seek to put forward alternative paradigms that could inform policy and practice. These are: partnership governance; public value theory; and the relational state. It then goes on to show that they all have something to contribute in the search for an alternative, but none of them ultimately delivers a satisfactory framework for local government and the chapter concludes that a new ethical framework is required.

Chapter Four develops such a framework. It posits the argument that local authorities have a duty to support health and personal autonomy so that individuals can participate in society. It builds on this argument to make the case that local authorities also have an obligation to tackle injustice, to promote citizenship through developing concepts of the common good and to pursue policies to grant citizens equal respect and recognition. The framework is developed in the form of a set of questions that can be used to interrogate policy to see if it accords with these duties. The chapter also looks at issues emerging from our growing concern with sustainability. Day-to-day ethical issues in the delivery of personal social services are similarly discussed. By providing a clear set of questions to ask in relation to the ethical implications of policy decisions, the book aims to contribute to the work of local decision-makers who want to make a difference.

How should local government relate to social movements and the increasing demand for participation in decision-making? How do you integrate participative and representative democracy? Does it make sense to cultivate a strong strategic centre and community empowerment at the **neighbourhood** or **parish** level? What forms of engagement with council employees can support local democracy? Chapter Five seeks to answer these questions. It argues against those who see a decline in democracy and suggests instead that there has been a rapid growth in citizens playing an active role in their local area. However, it also argues that the growth in democracy has been constrained by elitist models of representative democracy that separate the councillor and politics from discussions with citizens about what should be done. It builds on the ethical framework in Chapter Four and looks particularly at the relationship between representative democracy and participative democracy across the different tiers of government that characterise the UK. It suggests that there has been an attempt to confine participative democracy to the neighbourhood/parish level, where it has influence over a narrow range of policy issues. An alternative approach is to open up all issues to bottom-up influence and to link campaigns claiming rights across tiers of government with wide participation. The chapter also highlights some of the tensions in this approach, and explores the ways in which councillors/elected representatives can increase political debate and develop really effective local democracy. It argues for strengthening and supporting the councillor role.

Chapter Six shows how the language we use and the questions we ask shape the way we think about problems and constrain the possible solutions. It illustrates the dominance of the market **discourse** and the discourse around 'scroungers' and the 'deserving poor', which distort the purpose of the public sector and smother the voice of the poor and disadvantaged. It shows how an approach that starts from values, as promoted in this book, results in very different discursive strategies. The focus is on deliberative democracy and collaboration, through which the impact of current policies on social justice can be explored. In these discussions, conflict and power inequalities need to be acknowledged. This progressive approach facilitates the emergence of some common values, or shared interests, in specific alternative possibilities for existing and future generations.

The final chapter turns to the future. It asks how the ethical framework and the approach to reclaiming democracy and developing new discursive strategies can be put into practice. It argues that local government needs to engage with other groups who are challenging injustice and fighting for their rights in order to open up possibilities for change and to further social justice. It also suggests that local government must have the capacity to respond to the alternatives that emerge from this engagement. While the use of the private sector is necessary, and even desirable, to access specific goods or specialisms, the case is made that wholesale privatisation of public services undermines citizenship and notions of the common good, and also the ability of local government to respond to new proposals. If local government is going to be able to learn, respond, make a difference and win legitimacy, it has to be more than an enabling authority. Finance is necessary to implement effective alternative policies and a strong case is made for the reform of council tax and council tax benefit. The chapter explores how local democracy can be strengthened through democratic management practices. It concludes by calling for an active relationship with citizens, building their ability to engage in local politics, facilitating their access to power both at the local and national level, and enabling them to have an impact on policy decisions. This requires: building relationships; focusing on what people can contribute rather than on their difficulties; and seeing the councillor role as linking campaigns and providing routes through to those with decisive power and influence.

The book is wide-ranging but does not claim to have all the answers. It conceptualises both local government and civil society in a more progressive way to identify spaces for more ethical action strategies. It seeks to provide a framework in both theory and practice to guide councillors, officers and civil society in exploring ways forward to pursue alternative agendas. It will hopefully encourage all those in local government in the UK and beyond to question what they are currently doing and ask 'Is this the right thing to do?'

Note

[1] There are many other excellent authors who cover this ground: Piven and Cloward (1977); Mayo (2000, 2005); Piven (2006); Barnes et al (2007); Wainwright (2009a); and Calhoun (2012).

TWO

Learning from history

During a period of austerity, when local government is significantly constrained, it is easy to dismiss local authorities, arguing that they have no potential to effect change. However, a longer perspective offers a more nuanced analysis, seeking to develop an understanding of both continuity and change in local government over time. This chapter does not seek to present a detailed history, but to deepen this longer-term understanding and to give a context to the chapters that follow. The chapter will focus on what was seen as the purpose of local government in different time periods. It will also explore how wider changes in local economies and society have influenced ideas and practice. It will seek to both explain the changes and continuities that have occurred and to look critically at them, identifying whose interests are served and whose interests are disregarded by changing conceptions of local government.

As Stewart (2000) posits, it would be easier to write about local government if the institution was the same over time and space, but local government is, by its very nature, highly diverse. If it were not, it would be mere administration. Understanding local government is not only based on an analysis of continuity and change, but also of uniformity and difference. Despite the variations, it is possible to identify key shifts in how local government has been conceptualised. The chapter focuses mainly on England and urban government, but draws on national and international literature. It shows how English local government has always been a site of conflict between forces that have different interests: national government/local government; employers/the employed; government/the governed. Critically, there is evidence over time that local government does have some autonomy and can use this if it so chooses.

History also provides learning, or should do so. Just as individuals are meant to learn from their mistakes and not repeat them, so one would hope that governments would learn from previous policy directions, building on successes and analysing why failures occurred. However, this short history shows that a cycle of failed policy has taken hold, with repeated unsuccessful attempts to: join up policy; adopt a holistic, preventative approach; turn around deprived areas; and build cohesive communities capable of tackling 'broken Britain'. We need to understand what has gone wrong if progress is to be made.

The 'good city': Victorian paternalism

City government was originally in the hands of city merchants and industrialists while county government was the domain of the landed gentry. The early history of current local government grew out of the Industrial Revolution and its associated urbanisation, with the Municipal Corporation Act 1835 setting up elected municipal corporations in the largest towns and cities. However, those writing on local government usually focus on 1873–76, when Joseph Chamberlain was **Mayor** of Birmingham and private bill legislation was used to municipalise utilities and improve the city centre.

Birmingham

Towards the end of the sixties a few Birmingham men made the discovery, that perhaps a strong and able Town Council might do almost as much to improve the conditions of life in the town as Parliament itself. I have called it a 'discovery'; for it had all the freshness and charm – it created all the enthusiasm – of a 'discovery'. One of its first effects was to invest the Council with a new attractiveness and dignity.... The November ward meetings assumed a new character. The speakers, instead of discussing small questions of administration and of economy, dwelt with growing enthusiasm on what a great and prosperous town like Birmingham might do for its people. They spoke of sweeping away streets in which it was not possible to live a healthy and decent life; of making the town cleaner, sweeter and brighter; of providing gardens and parks and music; or erecting baths and free libraries, an art gallery and a museum. They insisted that great monopolies like gas and water-supply should be in the hands of the Corporation; that good water should be supplied without stint at the lowest possible prices.... Sometimes an adventurous orator would ... suggest that Birmingham ... might become the home of a noble literature and art. (Dale, 1899, pp 401–2)

As well as these achievements, in 1869, Birmingham became the centre of the National Education League that fought for free, non-sectarian education for all children paid by both **rates** and national grants. The Education Act 1870 met some, but not all, of Birmingham's demands. Under George Dixon, who replaced Chamberlain as mayor in 1876, the Birmingham School Board became a model for educational authorities everywhere (Briggs, 1952, pp 100–6). Briggs (1952,

1963), perhaps controversially, states that, in the 1870s and 1880s, Birmingham was the best-governed city in the world.

Briggs (1952, p 67) argues that the civic revolution in Birmingham and other major cities was not the work of one man, but effectively an early social movement driven by a belief in the 'Civic Gospel', which was being preached in the Nonconformist churches at this time. Chamberlain was an active member of George Dawson's church. Dawson, originally a Baptist preacher, became Minister of the Unitarian Church of the Saviour in 1847, a church erected for him by his supporters in Birmingham. Dawson developed the concept of the Civic Gospel (Briggs, 1963, pp 184–240). He preached that 'A great town is a solemn organism through which shall flow, and in which shall be shaped, all the highest, loftiest and truest ends of man's intellectual and moral nature' (Briggs, 1952, p 100), and that 'it was the duty of those who derived their prosperity and opportunities of culture from the community to become its servant' (Dale, 1899, p 402). This Gospel was later developed further by Dr Robert William Dale, Minister at the Congregational, Carrs Lane Church in Birmingham from 1854 to 1895. Dale, as a Minister of Religion, was disqualified by law from standing for election to the council but threw himself into supporting the Liberal Party and campaigning for reform (Dale, 1899, p 404). He brought to the task a 'conviction of duty, deliberation in judgement, sagacity in counsel, earnestness in action, unreserved candour and unfaltering courage in declaring and maintaining the truth as he saw it' (Dale, 1899, p 417). He argued that 'for men to claim the right to neglect their duties to the state ... is gross unrighteousness' (Dale, 1899, p 415); service on the town council to improve the well-being of Birmingham was advocated by Dale as having moral and religious worth.

The Civic Gospel can be seen as related to the work of Thomas Hill Green (1836–82) and British Idealism, which was very important in the last quarter of the 19th century. It grew out of criticisms of the laissez-faire approach to the Industrial Revolution, underpinned by the utilitarian philosophy of Jeremy Bentham, which suggested that freedom would be maximised if the state was restricted to its minimum necessary functions. Green was an academic, active on his local town council in Oxford and on the school board, deeply religious, and concerned about the poverty and squalor he saw around him. He sought to establish a theory of ethics and of political obligation that would explain not only how people act, but also how they ought to act (Pearson and Williams, 1984, p 145). His major contribution was to substitute the concept of 'positive liberty' for the 'negative liberty' of Bentham. Negative liberty is focused on limiting the interference of the state in the actions of the individual: promoting freedoms such as freedom of conscience and free speech. Green argued that an increase in the power in the state could enlarge freedom and create positive liberty by removing obstacles to the full development of the individual.

Green believed that people are moral beings who naturally use reason to seek moral 'self-perfection' (Lancaster, 1959, pp 219, 222). However, seeking to be a better person only made sense if people had a concept of the common good – 'a permanent well-being in which the permanent well-being of others is included' (Pearson and Williams, 1984, p 145). Moral fulfilment could only flow from individuals reflecting on the common good and striving to achieve it. So, it could not be achieved in isolation, only as part of society. In an ideal state, the common good is embodied in the institutions of civil society. The state's role was to foster and protect the social, political and economic environments in which individuals would have the best chance of acting according to their conscience. However, if a state was not acting for the common good in this way, individuals should seek to reform or resist the state, although not to destroy it (Pearson and Williams, 1984, p 147). Green therefore puts forward an organic relationship between the state, society and the individual. The morality of the goals sought by the individual is shaped by society, which creates the conditions, through the state, in which the individual can seek self-perfection (Newman, M., 1993, p 38). Individuals should strive through the state to raise everyone to a level where moral action was possible.

Green, however, was clear that there were limits on state action and was concerned to ensure that his theories did not justify an authoritarian state: 'One of the first lessons of morals that everyone learned was that no-one could be made directly good by another' (Nicholson, 1985, p 85). He argued that if people did good just because the law made them do so, this destroyed individual moral capacity. He was concerned about good motives – means as well as ends. So, state action should be limited by asking whether it would contribute to the development of moral character in the individual citizen. Action should be taken only when this justification was in place.

The state, therefore, should intervene only when it could enhance positive liberty, and this required an analysis of the facts and experience. Green favoured voluntary action combined with action by the affected community itself rather than national state action, and only when this failed to remove a barrier to freedom should the national state legislate. He argued that the offer of voluntary free schooling had still left two million children without education and therefore unable to make the most of themselves, so compulsory education was preferable. The alcoholism of his elder brother combined with his perception that alcohol influenced the 1874 election result led him to argue that drunkenness stopped many people making the best use of their lives. He set up an alcohol-free community centre to provide an alternative to pubs. But when the majority of residents in Oxford petitioned for longer licensing hours, he campaigned for national prohibition laws (Nicholson, 1985). He argued that the distribution of responsibilities between central and local government should depend on particular circumstances and should enable as many individuals as possible to make their own moral decisions (Tyler, 2011 [2003]).

The model of local government that emerged from the Civic Gospel and this British Idealist philosophy opened up enormous possibilities for local industrialists to take action to improve the welfare of their area and encouraged them to stand as councillors. It was, however, an elite model. There was no suggestion that the barriers to their moral improvement should be discussed with those in poverty or with groups, such as women, who were excluded from the political process. The basic moral norms of society and social relationships were only challenged by the argument that those who had benefited from society should provide opportunities to others to do likewise. The improvements were related to what the industrialists saw as barriers to self-improvement and focused on physical infrastructure, health and culture/education. Poor relief continued to be run on the 19th-century principles of making it a support of last resort and a cause of shame for claimants so as not to endanger self-reliance (Morphet, 2008, p 3). Chamberlain was to join Lord Salisbury's Conservative government and Green defended property rights and inheritance. The assumption was that rational men would agree on the common good and the state would therefore embody this ideal purpose.

The First World War was to shatter such assumptions and reveal that, in practice, governments had no such elevated characteristics, nor did they agree about the common good (Newman, M., 1993, p 45). But aspects of the Civic Gospel and British Idealism lived on, influencing Left thinkers like R.H. Tawney and, more recently, Roy Hattersley (Carter, 2003), and shaping local government. They have also influenced recent definitions of the purpose of local government, which is seen as a multipurpose organisation promoting the well-being of an area (Lyons, 2005, p 6). Green saw local government as subservient to national government. He asserted the moral duty of the local state to intervene in a free market to enable individuals to achieve their full potential and set in place a value system to support public service. A strong belief in the benefits to the individual of public service and the importance of a concept of society remain entrenched within the politics of local government. The Victorian period is also important because it illustrates the transformative power of effective local government, as described in the box on Birmingham.

Keynesian welfare state

The origins of the state promoting universal public services are found in the radical alternative put forward by the Fabians at the end of the 19th century. They saw the possibility of what Sidney Webb called 'nationalisation of the means of enjoyment' outstripping nationalisation of the means of production and thereby developing a public sector workforce who could further socialist ideals (Stewart, 2000, p 32). Webb argued that when gas, water and markets are owned and controlled by local government, when roads and river transport are managed for 'public use', and when artisan dwellings are removed from 'the whims of philanthropy', then 'a vast army of London's citizens will be directly enrolled in London's services', have decent employment and housing, and 'will at last have been placed in a position really to take advantage of the opportunities for civilisation which life in the capital of the Empire should imply' (Webb, 1891, pp 213–14, quoted in Stewart, 2000, p 33).

Following the Second World War, the radicalism demonstrated by the election of a Labour government, rather than Churchill's Conservatives, opened the door for the introduction of Keynesian welfarism. This was characterised by embracing Keynesian economics and the belief that the state could intervene in the economy to guarantee full employment, spending in anti-cyclical ways to smooth out business cycles. The proposals made in the Beveridge Report (Beveridge, 1942) were also adopted, providing universal social protection through national insurance for the old, sick, unemployed or widowed, and establishing the **National Health Service** (NHS). So, the market was to remain as the primary driver of growth, but its negative effects would be controlled through state macroeconomic policy and through social protection for all through the welfare state. T.H. Marshall (1950) argued that the welfare state extended the concept of citizenship to include social rights and responsibilities, and that people were entitled to welfare by virtue of being citizens. This concept of citizenship has been contested ever since the post-war settlement, as governments have sought to restrict or consolidate universal welfare rights.

In the event, the welfare state settlement was not to see a transformation to socialism through municipal collective action and was a mixed picture for local government. On the one hand, many of the public services that local government had municipalised were nationalised (eg water, electricity) and the welfare state was seen as a national responsibility with only some services administered through local authorities. Furthermore, local government's role in the NHS was minimised and local authority-run hospitals were absorbed into the NHS. The local government role in the NHS was abolished under the Health Act 1973. More recently, local government has been given a role in public health and holding the NHS to account.

Local government's key role became planning, post-war reconstruction and the delivery of services (education, housing and social services) prescribed by central government (Stewart, 2000, p 35). Expenditure increased rapidly: revenue expenditure from £3,592 million in 1950 (1975 prices) to £12,253 million in 1975, and capital expenditure from £331 million to £4,075 million over the same period (1975 prices).

The period is now often characterised negatively, with the state being seen as Fordist, producing standardised products for a mass market (a rejection of this theory is given in the section on understanding change). However, real gains were made by working people through Keynesian full employment policies and the welfare state. While the Keynesian welfare state furthered capitalist interests (Cockburn, 1977, p 55) and may have reinforced unequal gender relationships, very significant gains were certainly also made by all UK residents. Elements of standardisation (eg **Parker Morris housing standards**) were highly beneficial in introducing minimum standards. The 1960s' tower blocks, which are now seen as the symbolic disaster of post–war planning, had more to do with the way the Conservative government in the late 1950s and early 1960s offered housing subsidies to local government for slum clearance than with planners and architects imposing their concepts on communities. Local government rose to the task of post-war reconstruction and did not do so in a completely standardised way.

The focus on the car and ring roads were serious attempts at place-shaping. This focus proved to be a major mistake, destroying cities like Birmingham and Glasgow for several decades. However, there were also successes and innovation, for example: **New Towns**, new schools offering comprehensive education, family social work and health centres. Local authorities took over a range of new services developed in the voluntary sector where there were calls from voluntary and community groups for wider universal services. Furthermore, expanding local government still enabled the voluntary sector to provide a range of personal, innovative social services.

The welfare state under pressure

As the rapid expansion in public spending started to slow down from the mid-1960s and local government started to address more complex issues (child abuse, drug and alcohol issues, family break-up and racial tensions), the weaknesses in the post-war consensus started to emerge. Increasingly, governments attempted to limit the role of the public sector, trying to reduce its welfare role and responsibility for full employment and push responsibility onto individuals and communities. However, this meant that poverty re-emerged as an issue in the 1960s. The oil crisis of 1973 was to exacerbate the difficulties.

Allan Cochrane (2007) argues that from President Lyndon Johnson's State of the Union address in 1964, when he declared a War on Poverty, there was a shift to an increasing focus on place- and area-based policies. The paradigm was to coordinate the multiple initiatives in deprived areas in order to increase opportunities and change the attitudes, values, motivations and lifestyles of the poor. In this way, individuals would be able to pull themselves up by their bootstraps and residents in poor areas could support each other to lessen inequality. This has been termed a 'social pathology approach', which seeks to get families to recognise that they are failing and to articulate a need for, and encourage families to engage in, self-help (Cochrane, 2007, p 112). Katz (1989), while seeing the War on Poverty as part of a discourse that highlights differences between people in poverty and thereby weakens the universal nature of the welfare state, also notes that the War on Poverty generated significant social reform in the USA: 'Between 1965 and 1972, the government transfer programmes lifted about half the poor over the poverty line' (Katz, 1989, p 113). Programmes like Headstart (preschool education for poor children), Job Corps (for adolescents) and Upward Bound (preparing disadvantaged young people for college) were very popular.

In the UK, a parallel change was occurring. Already in the 1960s, 'joining up' and 'efficiency' were becoming the new mantra. Cockburn sees the new emphasis on larger local authorities (the Conservative government set up the Maud Commission in 1964 and the Conservatives legislated for re-organisation in 1972 [Cockburn, 1977, p 23]), coordination and corporate management as a move to govern more effectively and intrusively in the interests of capital (Cockburn, 1977, p 12). Others argue that corporate management was essential in the attempt to control the baronies into which large council departments had evolved under old-style Town Clerks, and also to push through new policies. Cockburn sees the rise of public participation and community development as a complementary process to the rise in corporate management, as local councillors tried to increase legitimacy and paper over the cracks that were appearing in the early versions of **Big Society** and the move towards self-help rather than state provision (Cockburn, 1977, pp 107–8). However, she also recognises that community action was opening up new areas for collective action, particularly for women, in schools, housing estates and in the family.

Making the local

While the national and local state took over from many local community and 19th-century charities, there was also a growth in local activism by the 1960s. Janet Newman characterises the community action that started to develop in this period as 'making the local'. She notes the way social movements of the late 1960s and early 1970s – including, but not restricted to, feminism – created new resources and capacities, for example: local playgroups and other resources for children; women's health groups; co-operative and collective housing; community arts and education projects; free schools; women's refuges; and other alternative forms of provision (Newman, J., 2012, p 848). Some of these outcomes led to new services being developed within local government and by social housing providers.

These social movements to 'make the local' were developing in parallel to workplace action for higher wages and better living conditions (Cockburn, 1977, p 158). They continue to shape local government today.

Two further changes were to impact on local government. First, linked to the growing involvement of women in local government was a growing concern about equalities, made more urgent by the increasing racial tensions in the period. Second, the costs of industrial restructuring on the inner city (in terms of unemployment, derelict land, decline in business rates and undermining community solidarity) was becoming more significant as companies moved manufacturing plants to greenfield sites with lower labour costs, often assisted by both the national and local government. In this context, the simple focus on holistic policies at the neighbourhood level was to come under attack from both the New Right and new urban Left. The problems were perhaps best exemplified by the Community Development Project (CDP) (see following box) and will be explored further in the following sections on the New Right and new urban Left.

Contesting the local: Community Development Project

The CDP was launched in 1969 to some extent 'out of concern with the assimilation of newcomers to the city' (Marris and Rein, 1972, p xvi) following Enoch Powell's 1968 speech on immigration, where he declared that British inner cities would be transformed into alien territories: 'Like the Roman, I see the River Tiber foaming with blood.'[1] The projects were set up by the Home Office, rather than the department responsible for local government, and sought a coordinated, holistic approach to solving poverty. The local holistic approach, however, was constrained by turf wars in Whitehall that remain to this day. The strategy may also have reflected a deliberate attempt to increase government power by the incorporation of the voluntary sector in areas of existing or potential unrest (Lawrence, 1983).

The CDPs were established in 12 neighbourhoods of social deprivation with populations between 3,000 and 15,000. They had a strong research focus, which was meant to gather local information 'as a means of creating more responsive local services and of encouraging self-help' (Loney, 1983, p 3).

In 1979, a working group of the conference of socialist economists, called the London Edinburgh Weekend Return Group, produced a pamphlet *In and against the state*. The pamphlet discussed the experience of working-class people employed within the public sector in the late 1970s, or relying upon it as service provider, and the contradictions that were revealed. They described the CDP project as follows:

> The Home Office CDP was an interesting example of a state programme, whose intention in this respect was diverted by the workers in it. Many were socialists, and many more became so as a result of what they learned during the course of the project. They were appointed to twelve different local authorities around the country, mainly, though not exclusively, in areas of inner city decline.
>
> They were expected to study and analyse the problems within their respective communities and try to develop community self-help to overcome them. Instead, they rejected the definition of 'community' proposed by the state and its implied boundaries, and compiled joint reports, comparing and analysing on a national level so that the problem of each area came to be seen for what it was – a product not of misfortune or fecklessness, but of capitalism. (London Edinburgh Weekend Return Group, 1979/80, ch 6)

The New Right

In 1979, a Conservative government was elected, influenced by the New Right ideas of economists such as Eltis (Bacon and Eltis, 1978) and Friedman (1962), by political economy theorists such as Hayek (1973, 1976), political philosophers such as Nozick (1974), and public choice theorists such as Buchanan and Tullock (1962) and Niskanan (1973). All these authors emphasised the primacy of the individual over collective rights. As Margaret Thatcher argued: 'The role of government is limited ... if you extend democracy into every single sphere of life, you are denying personal liberty' (*Independent*, 8 June 1987, quoted in Gyford, 1991a, p 157). They emphasised how the freedom to make individual choice is best organised through the market to allocate goods and services in the most efficient and effective way. In contrast, they suggested, local government has a built-in tendency to oversupply: the bureaucrats' incentive to maximise their empire is aligned via the committee system with the politician's incentive to buy votes (spreading costs to future generations), and both of these are supported by pressure groups of the beneficiaries of state expenditure. Hayek argued that liberal-democratic institutions 'necessarily lead to a gradual transformation of the spontaneous order of a free society into a totalitarian system conducted in the service of some coalition of organised interests' (Hayek, 1973, quoted in Gyford, 1991a, p 157). In order to counteract these trends, Nicholas Ridley (then Environment Secretary with responsibility for local government) proposed that the local state should be an enabler, not a provider: 'We should always question whether it is right for the public sector to do a job when private individuals or companies could and would compete to do the job themselves' (Ridley, 1988, p 29). His concept of the 'enabling' state related to a minimum state that commissioned, rather than delivered, services. Moreover, he argued that in the remaining services delivered by the public sector, monopoly supply should be broken up, bringing in competition and quasi-markets and making the service more responsive to the 'customer' or user, rather than 'the producer' or council worker.

This ideology was to have a marked impact on local government. First, local expenditure was to be curbed since expansion was seen to have crowded out investment in the private sector (Bacon and Eltis, 1978), as well as curtailing personal liberty. Controversially, the amount of money that could be raised by councils through the rates was capped, limiting local government's ability to raise revenue, while borrowing and capital expenditure were controlled. Budgets were 'ring-fenced', making them available only for specified services and enforcing central priorities. The proportion of local authority expenditure supported by central government grant also fell by around 15% during the Thatcher governments to nearly 40% of local revenue expenditure by 1989/90 (Adam et al, 2007, p 16). But then, legislation was passed to introduce the **poll tax/community charge** (a tax on each individual living in a property, replacing rates, which were a property tax) in 1990/91 and to nationalise business rates. In 1991/92, there was a large increase in central government grant as the new Major government sought to lessen the impact of the poll tax. Local authorities became increasingly dependent on central government finance, which peaked at just under 80% of local finance in the early 1990s (Adam et al, 2007, p 16). Local authority financial management was forced to shift from a demand-led approach to a cash-limited approach with a focus on economy, efficiency and effectiveness.

In understanding the impact of the New Right on local government, it is also important to analyse how their ideology affected internal management and the performance culture. The restriction of finance was accompanied by the development of '**New Public Management**' (NPM) and the growth of inspectorates. These changes continue to influence local government today and will be discussed further in subsequent chapters. Hood (1991) defined these changes as the New Right ideology – the freedom to choose – being combined with the scientific management movement – the freedom to manage. The latter involved a stress on private sector styles of management, a focus on performance, output and target controls, and a greater professionalisation of management. Forms of management were developed from the private sector, and the public sector failed to take account of the distinctive nature of the public domain and develop a management approach for public and ethical purposes. Pollitt (1990) argued that managerialism itself became an ideology. He criticised the focus on efficiency and managerialism, arguing that it lacked coherence because it omitted the ethical and legal base of public service. This issue is central to subsequent chapters. Pollitt also suggested that since new managerialism did not deal with the distinctiveness of the public sector, it would fail. The private sector's simple target of maximising profit is not available in the public sector, which depends upon the quality of service and developing relationships and trust. Goodhart (a former director of the Bank of England) devised a law which stated that numerical measurement will always be inaccurate if it is used to control people (Boyle, 2011). Staff will always be clever enough to subvert the results. Targets shift the focus from user and citizen to managers. For example, Mid Staffordshire Hospital met all targets set by the government for performance and yet had 400 unnecessary deaths during 2005–09 (Francis, 2010).

A further problem with new managerialism is that it attempts to separate out the political process from the management process (Stewart and Walsh, 1992, pp 12–13). This can lead to increased inequalities (Pollitt, 1990) and a reduced capacity for learning and adaptability (Stewart and Walsh, 1992, p 25). Finally, the growing use of private sector language undermines the values of a public service, an issue picked up in Chapter Six of this book.

The creation of quasi-markets in local government through the local management of schools, **Compulsory Competitive Tendering** (CCT), the removal of further and higher education from local government influence and a focus on contracting out community care and residential care for the elderly have all also led to increased fragmentation of local government and an increase in the discourse around governance and partnership. These trends are not specifically British and can be seen in many other countries in slightly different forms. They have also led to the dominant discourse claiming that the purpose of local government should not be direct service delivery, but **commissioning** and place-shaping to further the well-being of the whole community: the concept of 'community leadership'. This will be discussed further in the following section on New Labour. First, though, the chapter looks at the growth of the new urban Left and then seeks to explain why radical movements of both Right and Left occurred in local government.

Creative autonomy and the new urban Left

While the 1980s and 1990s are best remembered for the rise of the New Right, they also saw an increase in the politicisation of local government, experiments in policies devised by new urban Left activists and significant creative autonomy at the local level. From the mid-1970s, the new urban Left drew from the debates around municipal socialism and the 'nationalisation of means of enjoyment' discussed earlier. Their policies were not restricted to the social sphere, but were also concerned with what was happening in the production sphere: the industrial decline in the cities first evidenced by the CDP project and the new managerialism in the public sector.

In the early 1980s, some local authority managers led by radical council leaders concentrated on creative accounting and other methods of avoiding the increasingly stringent financial controls. In England, expenditure actually rose in real terms by around 13% from 1981/82 up to 1989/90 (Cochrane, 1993, p 33). But as loopholes closed, campaigns against **rate capping** increased. In 1983, radical councils established their own network and campaign support body called the Local Government Campaign Unit (in 1997, renamed the Local Government Information Unit [LGiU]).

Atkinson and Wilks-Heeg (2000, p 2) 'reject the notion that local government under the Conservatives became a defenceless victim of an all-powerful central government'. They suggest that although local authorities had to concede some autonomy, they found a variety of ways of protecting and expanding their independent policymaking capacity in other areas. They highlight: local economic development; experiments with decentralisation in Walsall, Islington and Tower Hamlets; the focus on equal opportunities and participation; the engagement with the **European Union (EU)** in an attempt to bypass national government and raise finance; and innovations on environmental policy. These latter initiatives followed the voluntary action plan, **Local Agenda 21**, issued by the United Nations (UN) in 1992 and agreed at the Rio summit, which called for a local authority role to *promote* sustainable development. As Atkinson and Wilks-Heeg (2000, p 193) suggest: 'Within the EU, the UK has the most explicit response to Agenda 21 of any member state' (O'Riordan and Voisey, 1997, p 2). Furthermore, 'By far the most vibrant institutional innovations were taking place at this level, most notably in the UK' (O'Riordan and Voisey, 1997, p 19), pushed by 'the desire of local authorities to reassert and develop their role in an area where many responsibilities have been removed from local government control' (O'Riordan and Voisey, 1997, p 46).

To some extent, politicisation was a reaction to the New Right attack and the increasing importance of locality, which will be discussed further later. It was also a function of the 1968 generation emerging from protest movements and moving into politics in the 1970s at the local level; and of increasing demands on local authorities as unemployment and industrial decline spiralled in the early 1980s. As already discussed in relation to the CDP project, the pamphlet *In and against the state* (London Edinburgh Weekend Return Group, 1979/80) was very influential among socialists in local government and played a role in clarifying the purpose of those on the Left working in this sphere. It suggested that the development of party control over local authorities and the increasing use of manifestos, group meetings and caucusing could change the nature of local government, ensuring that it served the interests of those who were disadvantaged (Gyford, 1985; Widdicombe Report, 1986).

The Left has always been active at the local level, where there was often significant working-class representation with deep roots in the local community and the local trades council. In 1919, the Labour-controlled Poplar Council, under their Mayor George Lansbury, paid 'higher wages to its workers and higher rates of unemployment relief to its poor and [refused] to collect rate precepts for other local authorities until a more equitable distribution of income had been introduced between rich and poor authorities' (Bassett, 1984, p 86). Thirty councillors, including six women, were jailed in 1921 but were released after six weeks and a rates revision was achieved. In 1956, Labour Left councillors in the old London borough of St Pancras lowered council rents, were expelled from membership of their own Party and were surcharged. In 1972, in Clay Cross, Labour councillors refused to implement the rent increases imposed under the Housing Finance Act 1972; they were also surcharged, and dismissed by the government and replaced by an appointed commissioner.

These earlier protests and Birmingham's radicalism under Chamberlain were very much in mind in the early 1980s. As Cllr David Blunkett, leader of Sheffield City Council at the time, suggested, radical initiatives by local authorities were:

> Not an entirely new approach, but a return in a sense to earlier years, when people saw local government as a very positive tool for making progress, for establishing democracy in its truest sense with people actually participating in decisions as to how their resources were to be used. There has been a shift away from seeing local councils as local administration, to seeing them again as local government.... Sheffield and elsewhere are doing so from a socialist perspective. We are saying it isn't good enough simply to run services in their present form, reduced to fit parameters set by central government. We really have to decide what we are doing in the local community and how we can build on this. (Boddy and Fudge, 1984, pp 243–4)

In 1983/84, Liverpool refused to set a rate and ultimately the government found some £20 million extra funding for housing in Liverpool. This was subsequently seen as a successful fight and by mid-1984, some 40 local authorities decided to join a rate-capping campaign, agreeing that councils whose budgets were capped would refuse to set any budget at all for the financial year 1985/86, requiring the government to intervene directly in providing local services, or to concede. Fifteen councils, including Sheffield, were affected. Eventually, under threats of legal action, all but Liverpool and Lambeth capitulated. These two councils were subjected to an extraordinary audit, which resulted in the councillors responsible for not setting a budget being required to repay the amount the council lost in interest, and also being disqualified from office.

Many commentators saw the end of the rate-capping campaign as the collapse and defeat of socialism in local government and the hegemony of central government and the market. It was followed by the abolition of the **Greater London Council** (GLC) and the metropolitan councils and the election of a Thatcher government for a third term in 1987. However, the battle was far from over. While the GLC was abolished, it was generally agreed that Ken Livingstone, the GLC leader, had won the campaign (Mackintosh and Wainwright, 1987) and he was to re-emerge as the Mayor of the replacement body (the **Greater London Authority** [GLA]) in 2000 following a referendum on setting up the GLA in May 1998. The poll tax riots showed that community protest was still a force to be reckoned with, and contributed to the demise of Margaret Thatcher. Many urban authorities emerged from the 1980s completely reformed from within, with corruption destroyed, a workforce that reflected the local community and councillors and officers who sought wider public engagement with disadvantaged and discriminated citizen groups. All this shows that there is nothing inevitable in the dominance of the market, and new managerialism and the direction of local government remains contested, while local government has considerable capacity to re-invent itself. Furthermore, the period (as the following case study also shows) saw the move of policy at the local level into the productive sphere and whole new areas for local influence around local economies, environmental policies and equalities.

The Greater London Enterprise Board: 'restructuring for labour'. Governing the local

The **Greater London Enterprise Board** (GLEB) was established in 1982 as the key instrument in the socialist response in London to the massive restructuring of capital in 1970s and 1980s. This restructuring followed: the rising oil prices; the decreasing competitiveness in manufacturing of the UK; mergers and takeovers consolidating international capital; capital investment replacing labour; and the ability of capital to move to where costs were cheaper and labour less militant without having to pick up any of the costs for the social devastation that was left behind. The CDP (Benington, 1976), the Joint Docklands Action Group (Newman, I. and Mayo, 1981) and others had documented how industrial decline in the inner city had led to rising unemployment, increasing dereliction and growing local campaigns to ensure redevelopment was in the interest of remaining residents and trade unionists rather than property development.

Previous local authority economic development policy had focused on providing sites for companies, attracting inward investment and offering some small soft loans (Boddy, 1984, p 161). These actions had furthered industrial restructuring. The GLC adopted a very different approach, arguing that in order to restructure for labour rather than capital, the state had to intervene in the production process and gain control of this process through ownership or equity investment:

> Only a large scale investment programme aimed at key sectors of London's industry will rescue the capital's manufacturing economy from total annihilation. The public sector will have to take an active role in such a strategy. GLEB is the instrument of that active role for the private economy. (GLC, 1985, p 40)

The GLC overestimated the power of one local authority in a capitalist system with a hostile national government (Newman, I., 1986). The GLC's industrial strategy (GLC, 1985) assumed that companies that needed to restructure would seek local government support and that the council, through GLEB, could negotiate benefits for workers in exchange for equity investment. In the event, most of those companies seeking help were going bust and there was no scope for restructuring for labour in these circumstances. GLEB also pursued investments in support organisations for industrial sectors, which were supposed to make the sector more competitive while increasing social control and improving working conditions. Initiatives such as the Hackney Fashion Centre tried to improve productivity and assumed that this would 'trickle down' into better working conditions, which failed to materialise (Davenport and Totterdill, 1986).

The result was to show the limitations of socialism in one local authority. However, the experience was not a total failure. Analysis showed that traditional interventions in the local economy often merely benefited capitalist interests and led to worse conditions for the employees. It focused attention on interventions in the production process that could benefit workers and strengthen their power to negotiate. The importance of addressing these would underpin the growth of local economic development policies and a raft of policies around training, equal opportunities, the living wage, contract compliance, support for co-operative and community enterprise, development trusts, planning gain, family-friendly employment policies and support for unionisation. Local government was not just about service delivery, but also about intervening in production to defend and improve the working conditions of its residents. GLEB's successor body, GLE, owned by the 33 London boroughs, continues to operate as an independent, not-for-profit company.

Why did this change happen?

This section briefly examines three theories that contribute to our understanding of the increased influence of the New Right and new urban Left and the changing role of local government. It serves as an introduction to Chapter Three, which will provide a critique of current conceptions of local government. While market influence grew, the preceding description of change has already focused on contestation and the opportunity for creative autonomy. The theories seek to explain these conflicts. As Atkinson and Wilks-Heeg (2000, p 33) suggest, we need theories to help us to assess why changes have happened and to help distinguish trends. The following section does not seek a full analysis of the theories but provides a simplified summary: readers who are interested can follow up the references to explore the issues in more depth. This section draws on the theories to start to explain: first, why the New Right emerged and why they promoted marketisation, NPM and contracting out of public services; second, why local authorities became more politicised and the growing importance of locality or place; and, finally, why, despite centralisation in the UK, national government was unable to squash the creative autonomy of local government.

Fordism/post-Fordism/regulation theory

This set of theories, inspired by Marxists seeking to explain the survival of capitalism and then applied to explain changes in local government, suggests that prior to the 1960s, there was a **Fordist** regulatory regime, or accommodation between capital and labour, brokered by the state in industrialised countries. This accommodation rested on Fordist modes of mass production of standard goods produced by a strict, hierarchical division of labour, underpinned by the Keynesian welfare state, which sustained mass consumption and effective demand. However, the crisis of profitability in the mid-1960s led to the breakdown of this consensus and to companies moving from mass production to differentiated consumption and a focus on luxury goods. It also led to public sector expenditure cuts and the nation state having less power, as power shifted to both the global and local level. Post-Fordist, multinational organisations concentrate on batch production and are characterised by small flexible units, flattened hierarchies, devolved decision-making and the contracting out of non-core functions. Similarly, it is argued, post-Fordist public services moved away from standardised mass services thereby seeking to provide more choice. They also changed from corporate management practice into flattened hierarchies, decentralisation and the contracting out of services.

An effective critique of this theory is given by Cochrane (1993, ch 5). He argues that the shift from Fordism to post-Fordism is of questionable validity within the private sector. Here, many post-Fordist companies (eg MacDonald's, Tesco) are organised with staff having strictly controlled tasks within a hierarchy, and these multinational companies are replacing smaller family-run businesses, which were clearly not Fordist. But the theory is particularly inappropriate for the public sector. There never was a simple Fordist state. While some administrative functions, such as benefit administration, can be cast as routine, professional teachers and social workers never fitted into a Fordist organisational framework but were products of the welfare state. Lipsky's (1980) detailed study of professional workers also shows that public services involve decisions about people and discretionary intervention. Although there is pressure to standardise, a one-size-fits-all approach is not possible in the public sector. The importance of this critique is that it questions the inevitability of flattened hierarchies, decentralisation and contracting out in the public sector and suggests that organisational change implemented by the New Right remains contested and subject to the political process. While regulation theory can be useful in providing some insights into the management change that has happened, the critique indicates the continuing importance of the political process in determining the future of local government.

Regulation theory has influenced dual welfare theory. Here, the analysis is that the universal minimum standard services of the Keynesian welfare state have now been replaced by a Schumpeterian/enterprise workfare state (Jessop, 1994). In the latter, social policy is subordinated to the needs of the market and a dual welfare system is developed with the weak reliant on minimum welfare and the better-off with access to higher-quality private and public provision. The dominance of the market in welfare policy and in local government policymaking is a theme that is explored in more detail in Chapter Three.

Locality

The origins of current emphases on 'localism' can be found in the locality literature, usefully summarised by Gyford (1991b). This literature claims that uneven development, with capital flowing into areas where it can make the most profit, has resulted in growing economic, political and social diversity. Urry (1987, quoted in Gyford, 1991b, p 13) has suggested that decreased labour mobility and the increased significance of the home as a financial asset (or liability!) has resulted in the growing importance of place as a symbol of identity and the organisation of civil society around issues of property, as well as gender, race and religion. Other forces, such as the effect of history on place and destruction of town centres through changes in retail business, have also impacted on local interest in locality. Gyford contended that questions concerning 'whose space?' and 'who manages the space?' were becoming increasingly significant, as was evidenced by the new urban Left. He indicated that powerful coalitions of those who see place as a source of identity and as a marketable commodity may have interests that are incompatible to those less powerful groups who are interested with minimum standards and access to services. He saw opportunities in the growing importance of locality for a new conception of the role of local government and this is discussed in the following section on New Labour and is also picked up in Chapter Three.

Centralisation and policy networks

Rhodes (1988) provides one explanation for why central government was unable to dominate the policymaking process at the local level. Rhodes explores the limitations of both state and market systems to meet the challenges of modern society. He defines policy networks as 'a structure of resource-dependent organisations' (Rhodes, 1997, p 24). He emphasises the importance of policy networks (such as the education network, linking the middle class, the local professionals and the civil servants who negotiate over delivery of services). Network theory introduces the concepts of governance networks (that is informal involvement of the public, private, voluntary and community sectors in the process of policy decision-making) replacing local government (that is the formal governmental system involving the exercise of particular powers, duties and public resources under clear procedural rules involving statutory relationships between politicians, professionals and the public) (Guarneros-Meza and Geddes, 2010, p 115). Network theory is the subject of a wide range of literature in different policy fields, with a variety of views around why networks are formed, whether it is an inevitable or a desirable process that government is replaced by governance, and the extent to which networks replace hierarchical public administration with more dispersed forms of power. Chapter Three will look at local authority partnerships in more detail as part of this debate.

Here, it is just worth noting how Rhodes saw the post-war period as one of a 'dual polity', with central government isolated from local political elites and separated from local issues and details of implementation. He saw the New Right trying to replace this dual polity with a command code: central government telling local government what to do. Rhodes argued that because central government does not understand the importance of policy networks, this has not led to unified, centralised policymaking, but to 'a policy mess'. Such a mess is characterised by politicisation and the growing new urban Left at the local level as local elites challenge the centre instead of negotiating via networks. Rhodes's work is important in that it provides one explanation for the increasing politicisation of local government in the 1980s and the fact that while the New Right at central government level destabilised local government, it failed to control it.

What do these theories tell us?

The preceding theories are useful in that they help us to understand the changing purpose of local government and why simple stories around the dominance of global capitalism or centralisation and the end of local government only provide a partial picture. New regimes open up new areas for contestation and new opportunities. For example, the post-war Keynesian settlement can be seen as an attempt to confine local authorities to the sphere of welfare provision – with no legitimate role in the direct production sphere (this has been well illustrated in Turok's [1989] book on Bracknell New Town). The collapse of the Keynesian welfare system allowed the growth of local economic development units and has led to local government having a major role in the economic agenda. Similarly, globalisation has reinforced the importance of the local level and opened up the European level for local authorities in Europe.

The chapter now turns to look at the New Labour period from 1997, where the contradictions and opportunities in central government policy towards local government became increasingly evident.

New Labour

In opposition, New Labour had argued for devolution and stronger local government. Progress was clearly made with regional structures and devolution to London, Scotland and Wales (and Northern Ireland following the peace process). Local government in the devolved nations has developed in very different ways and this book focuses on England, while making occasional references to wider experience in the UK. There were also a series of positive reforms for local government, including:

- the prudential borrowing regime, which made capital spending more flexible;
- the power to do anything that was not illegal that furthered the well-being of the community;
- **Sustainable Community Strategies,** which were strategic frameworks that supported engagement;
- **Local Strategic Partnerships** (LSPs) of the key stakeholders in the locality, in which local authorities were given a clear leadership role;
- obligations on public sector partners to seek to deliver the **Local Area Agreements** (LAAs) or multi-agency targets agreed locally through LSPs;
- a scrutiny role regarding health services;
- the replacement of CCT with the **Best Value** regime;
- reforms to contracting out legislation to ensure that transferred staff not only had the same salary, but also the same conditions and pensions;
- improved payment and pensions for councillors;
- and stronger equalities and consultation frameworks.

All these reforms were significant and welcomed by those who wanted greater powers and flexibility for local government and support for partnership-working.

Most significantly, local government was supported through an increase in expenditure. In 1997/98, central government financed 50% of revenue expenditure through grants of £25,291 million (CLG, 2009). By 2007/08, grants for revenue stood at £51,658 million, covering 56% of revenue expenditure. This was a significant real increase (although it should be noted that the lion's share was taken by education and social services and passed through local authorities direct to schools or absorbed by the growing number of elderly people, and, furthermore, a decreasing proportion of this grant came from the business community through non-domestic rates[2]). In real terms, capital spending also increased by 25% between 2004/05 and 2008/09 (CLG, 2010, p 4). At the end of the New Labour period, there was no doubt that the quality of the built environment and the quality of public services had massively improved. Estimates from the Office for National Statistics suggest that public services improved considerably over the period from 1997 to 2007, with measured outputs suggesting a one-third increase in the quantity and quality of public services (Chote et al, 2010, p 1):[3]

> The pace and scale of reform in local government always seems unremitting to those close to it. For a long period before 1997, the reforms all appeared to be focused on reducing the power and central role of local authorities, both in their democratic leadership of their communities and in being the first point of contact between citizen and government. The changes since 1997 ... are seen to be leading somewhere, stages on a journey that could take local government back to the point of local leadership, co-ordination and direction. (Morphet, 2008, p xi)

Managing the local

> Those who had used the oppositional spaces of the GLC, left leaning local authorities, the CDP programmes and other opportunities to full effect often moved into the new invited spaces of governance under New Labour working in neighbourhood renewal projects, policy action teams, local strategic partnerships, either directly employed or, more usually, as consultants, trainers and development workers on part time/short term contracts. Others created and mobilised new forms of 'outside' space – advocacy groups, local audit projects, tenant groups, advice centres, and even local streets – which became the focus of new and creative forms of opposition. But across these categories women were drawn into the wider governance shifts introduced by New Labour, including policy networks and partnership bodies. These were both spaces of influence and spaces in which multiple rationalities and resources could be assembled and recombined. (Newman, J., 2012, p 851)

Others moved into influential positions in central government (as **Members of Parliament**, think-tank experts, etc) and tried to control local government from above.

Many analysts, however, would disagree with Morphet's analysis. The significant reforms just outlined were conceived within the context of New Labour's 'modernisation' programme for local government. This involved the growth of central government intervention, with new political structures, targets, inspections and prescriptions. Centralised control was reinforced by the use of new technology and monitoring frameworks. The reforms fell short of the socialism that underpinned much of the Labour-controlled local councils' thinking in the 1980s. It was also dominated by the ideology of the 'Third Way'. The Third Way, as Giddens (2004) explained, was a label to cover all attempts to find a 'revisionist social democracy'. However, it allowed the interests of the market to continue to dominate policymaking.

Wilks–Heeg (2009) has argued that New Labour succeeded in successfully implementing failed Conservative, market-dominated policies. He gives four examples, which are summarised and updated as follows:

• The Education Act 1988 sought to introduce **grant–maintained (GM) schools** and, later, City Technology Colleges were created. In January 1998, there were 15 City Technology Colleges, 508 GM primary schools in England, 667 GM secondary schools and 21 GM special schools.[4] GM status was abolished by the Labour government but City **Academies**, also independent of local authorities, were legally created by the Learning and Skills Act 2000, which amended the section of the Education Act 1996 relating to City Technology Colleges. In 2010, there were over 200 secondary academies.[5] The 2010 Coalition Government drove the policy forward and by September 2012, there were 2309 academies.[6]

• The Housing Act 1988 promoted the Large-Scale Voluntary Transfer (LSVT) of council housing estates to housing associations; however, by 1992, only 1.9% (15 authorities) had transferred their stock. In contrast, in 2006, 148 authorities had transferred their stock. On 1 April 2000, local authorities owned 3 million dwellings; by April 2010, this had fallen to only 1.8 million dwellings. This decline has been associated with the Right to Buy (RTB) and LSVT of local authority stock to registered social landlords.[7]

• The Local Government Act 1988 introduced CCT but 80% of service provision remained in-house. Under Labour's programme of comprehensive performance assessment and Best Value, privatisation accelerated. By 2007, local government spent £42 billion on external contracts[8] – over 40% of all local government expenditure (HM Government, 2011a, p 47).

- In 1992, the Conservatives introduced the **Private Finance Initiative** (PFI). The scheme was implemented in health and transport but only one local authority signed a PFI scheme under the Conservatives. In total, 34 PFI schemes were agreed in the 10 years between 1986 and 1996, worth £2 billion. New Labour revamped the scheme and in the following 10 years (1996–2006), 549 PFI schemes were agreed, worth £51 billion, including many local authority PFI schemes. Over £260 billion of PFI commitments were accrued by the time Labour left office, for buildings valued at around £60 billion (Huitson, 2012, pp 68–9). PFI proved a very expensive way of financing capital expenditure and involved privatising the management of new facilities. It will be further discussed in Chapter Three.

Stuart Hall saw New Labour as centralising and technocratic despite their discourse around devolution and decentralisation. He argued that New Labour had taken Thatcher's attempt to install 'the enterprise culture and "market forces" at the heart of society' as its 'platform' (Hall, 2007, pp 119–20). Even if this critique is too strong, it is evident that the focus on the market, choice and the target culture led to more and more contradictions in policy development. On the one hand, New Labour was championing community engagement, innovation and devolution; on the other hand, it was trying to ensure that local government did what central government wanted it to do through performance targets and opening up public services to the market. Furthermore, while the argument for 'subsidiarity' (the principle that political power should be exercised by the lowest possible level of government) grew, it did so within the concept of the 'enabling' local state first proposed by Ridley (1988).

In 2000, the New Local Government Network (NLGN) – a think tank set up by key figures close to the Labour government to promote Labour's ideas on local government – together with the Institute for Public Policy Research (IPPR) – the main Labour Party-sponsored think tank at the time – published *Towards a new localism: a discussion paper* (Filkin et al, 2000). This was followed two years later by *New localism: refashioning the centre–local relationship* (Corry and Stoker, 2002). Both pamphlets argued for local government to be a community leader rather than a service delivery body, although these roles are not in conflict, as will be explored further in this book. They made the case that direct service delivery was a distraction from the community leadership role and that community leadership could exist without any direct service delivery function. They called for a 'genuine localism',

—
31

which they characterised as a strategy aimed at devolving power and resources towards front-line managers, local democratic structures, local consumers and communities (note the order).

In 2005, a government commission on local government, chaired by Sir Michael Lyons, produced its interim report and argued that local government's role was 'place-shaping'.

Place-shaping

The strategic role of local government, one we might term 'place-shaping', encompasses:

- Building and shaping local identity;
- Representing the community, including in discussions and debates with organisations and parts of government at local, regional and national level;
- Regulating harmful and disruptive behaviours;
- Maintaining the cohesiveness of the community and supporting debate within the community, ensuring smaller voices are heard;
- Helping to resolve disagreements, such as over how to prioritise resources between services and areas, or where new housing and development should be located;
- Working to make the local economy more successful, to support the creation of new businesses and jobs in the area, including through making the area attractive to new investment and skilled workers, and helping to manage economic change;
- Understanding local needs and preferences and making sure that the right services are provided to local people through a variety of arrangements including collective purchasing, commissioning from suppliers in the public, private and voluntary sectors, contracts or partnerships, and direct delivery; and
- Working with other bodies to respond to complex challenges such as dealing with natural disasters and other emergencies.

(Lyons, 2005, p 6)

The highlighting of the wide, legitimate democratic leadership role was widely welcomed. However, it is notable that in this broad definition of local government, the purpose of meeting needs, central to the Victorian concept of local government, comes towards the bottom of the list. Direct service delivery is also the last option as the way to meet local needs. Lyons does not go as far as the NLGN in arguing that delivery for need had a negative impact on community leadership. However, the moral framework of the Victorians and the universal welfare state are no longer apparent – this is a more utilitarian definition of local government based on maximising satisfaction (Lyons, 2007, p 57). Furthermore, it is strongly influenced by the market and conceptions of welfare that divide the deserving from the undeserving poor. Lyons' definition includes supporting the private sector but does not include intervention in the economy to ensure employers consider the interests of workers. It does not suggest that the role of local government is to promote equality, target support on those most in need or reduce child poverty. It suggests that there is a role to 'regulate' anti-social behaviour but not necessarily to tackle the causes of such behaviour. It contains relatively little about the sustainability agenda or obligations to future generations, except to locate housing appropriately. The focus on 'place-shaping' supports the concept that one of the key roles of a local authority is to make its area attractive to inward investment and mobile 'skilled' workers in a context of competition between locations for growth and private investment. The conception of local government had shifted again.

Although New Labour's intent was not necessarily to pave the way for increased privatisation, their policies were to lead seamlessly into the 2010 Coalition Government's localism agenda.

The 2010 Coalition Government and localism

The discourse of the 2010 Coalition Government has been around the failure of New Labour and its target-driven approach and the need to 'free' local government. As the Localism Act 2011 was passed, the Secretary of State, Eric Pickles, claimed:

> Today marks the beginning of an historic shift of power from Whitehall to every community to take back control of their lives.
>
> The Localism Act pulls down the Whitehall barricades so it will no longer call the shots over communities – bug bears like housing targets and bin taxes are gone.
>
> For too long, local people were held back and ignored because Whitehall thought it knew best. That is changing for good.[9]

In terms of formal powers, there were gains and losses for local government. The Labour proposal that, from 2010, local authorities would be re-involved in the running of further education was revoked. Local government was to progressively lose control over schools, as the academies and free school programmes were expanded. However, it was to gain control over public health and, as regional structures were abolished, regional planning and economic development functions. Local government was given the **General Power of Competence** that had long been sought. National indicators were slashed and the Audit Commission and LAAs were abolished. However, reporting on indicators remained, value for money auditing through the National Audit Office was extended and payment-by-results funding bringing in even tighter national controls was significantly increased. Some powers were passed direct to residents rather than local authorities. On the whole, although much trumpeted, these were minor powers. Local residents could draw up local neighbourhood plans but these had to fit into the local authorities' strategic planning strategies and could only add, not remove, developments. The residents had a **right to bid for community assets** and had a '**Community Right to Build**', but both of these powers required the ability to raise funds. The '**Community Right to Challenge**' opened up a service to a procurement process, which could result in privatisation rather than greater community control. An authority that wished to propose a council tax increase that exceed that allowed by the Secretary of State had to put this proposal to a referendum. In effect, the referendum process will be used to enforce a council tax framework based on principles set by central government (LGiU, 2012). However, none of this was as significant as the public expenditure cuts and the reform of public services, which are discussed in detail in Chapter Three.

The 2010 Coalition Government's definition of the role of local government in their White Paper has subtle differences to the place-shaping role in the Lyons report:

Local government's role as defined by the Coalition Government

We will want to explore the opportunities for local authorities to:

- be the people's champions for all public services in their area, irrespective of whether they are directly accountable for those services;
- be empowered to shape their local area through greater local freedoms on planning, finance, regulatory powers and infrastructure;
- be as financially self-sufficient as possible;
- be able to integrate the full range of public resources to solve complex social, economic or environment issues, such as the needs of people on housing estates who have multiple disadvantages;
- benefit from the maximum possible decentralisation of central government services to the local level;
- champion direct democracy and transparency of public data;

- act as the principal representatives for their communities;
- actively decentralise power to individuals and neighbourhoods and inspire successful responses to these new opportunities;
- be excellent and open commissioners of those services which cannot be devolved to individuals and communities; and
- combine forces with neighbouring local authorities and lower-tier councils within their area to improve the success of the wider area.

(HM Government, 2011a, p 50)

In the *Open Public Services* White Paper (HM Government, 2011a), which relates to local authorities in England only, it is clear that services are to be handed over to the voluntary sector or commissioned, rapidly pushing forward a trend that was started in the early 1980s (Lawrence, 1982). Local authorities in England are no longer expected to deliver any services themselves. They are to be community champions but their power will be limited since they no longer control the day-to-day provision of services. They are to be excellent commissioners with no way of learning how to improve services, as knowledge, expertise and power over service delivery moves to the private sector. They are to provide accountability as services move out of their control and across political boundaries. They are to be financially self-sufficient in an era of massive public expenditure cuts. They are to solve the problems of multiple disadvantage, although the areas of multiple deprivation have been hardest hit by the public expenditure cuts.

Chapter Three will deal in more detail with the role of the state and the impact of public expenditure cuts and opening up public services to the market. Here, it is enough to note that the struggle between central and local government continues, as does the trend towards the privatisation, commodification and fragmentation of local services. Within this framework, new bottom-up community initiatives are developing and consolidating, from the Occupy movement and Citizens UK through to community development trusts and the joint campaigns between unions and residents to stop major outsourcing. These will be discussed further in Chapters Five and Seven. The local authority role remains contested. The Trades Union Congress (TUC) has put the opposition case clearly:

> Public services are not discretionary commodities. They are public goods that provide benefits to both individual service users and wider society.
>
> The TUC believes that the founding principles of public services, namely universal access, delivery according to need,

services free at the point of use, and services delivered for the public good rather than for profit should be at the heart of any model of service delivery.

It is our view that through its democratic accountability, unique funding mechanism and long-term integrated approach, the public sector is best placed to provide public services that meet the criteria above. (TUC, 2011, section one)

Conclusion

It is clear from the discussion in this chapter that there was never a golden age of local government; the Victorian reforms operated in the context of paternalism and the Poor Law and the role and purpose of local democracy has always been contested. The perceived purpose of local government changes over time and reflects fundamental changes in the economy, society and ideology. The chapter has shown five different interpretations of local government: as a provider of infrastructure to allow citizens to lead a good life (the Victorian era); as a provider of welfare services (the Keynesian welfare state); as an intervener in the economy to ensure that restructuring considers the interests of workers as well as capital (the urban new Left); as a place maker (New Labour); and as a community leader and commissioner (from the New Right to the present Coalition Government). It has shown how concepts of local government have changed and how local public services are increasingly marketised.

However, despite change, there is also continuity. We still have much to learn from Victorian paternalism. The enabling council of Nicholas Ridley still informs Coalition policy. The focus on community engagement and the coordinating role of local government can be traced back to the 1960s. The critique made by the CDP staff of the failure of such approaches to tackle the root causes of poverty and unemployment, still holds good today. The rationale for traditional public administration to provide high-quality public goods fairly, consistently and accountably has not disappeared as a result of the focus on NPM. And many of the initiatives that started at the local level have gone on to influence national policymaking, sometimes taking powers up to the national level but building on local authority inventiveness and experience.

The chapter has also emphasised that there is no inevitability in the new managerialism or in centralisation. Politicians do have choices as to how and where to focus local resources. And despite continual pressure to centralise policy at the national level, there are always spaces for creative autonomy and innovation at the local level. Local authorities, and the professionals working within them, are particularly good at identifying these and moving forwards. They do this because local government is close to its local community and there will always be pressure from social movements within the local area. The role of the activist councillor, resident and local authority employee will continue to be explored throughout the book.

Notes

[1] BBC, 20 April 1968, http://news.bbc.co.uk/onthisday/hi/dates/stories/april/20/newsid_2489000/2489357.stm

[2] Over this period, the percentage of revenue financed by redistributed **national non-domestic rates** (NNDRs) dropped by five percentage points from 25% to 20% (CLG, 2009).

[3] If productivity had increased in line with expenditure, the quality and quantity of public services could have risen by a further 16% for the same cost (Chote et al, 2010, p 1).

[4] See: http://discovery.nationalarchives.gov.uk/SearchUI/details?Uri=C15654

[5] See: www.bbc.co.uk/news/10161371

[6] See: www.education.gov.uk/inthenews/inthenews/a00213703/huge-increase-in-academies-takes-total-to-more-than-2300

[7] GLG, 'Local authority housing statistics, England, 2009/10', November 2010. Available at: https://www.gov.uk/government/publications/local-authority-housing-statistics-for-england-2009-to-2010

[8] This figure comes from a survey, by the then Regional Centres of Excellence, of procurement contracts (Roots, 2009, p 6). Government revenue expenditure figures show an even higher percentage, with £51.868 billion expenditure on local authority procurement in 2006/07. The £42 billion expenditure is quoted in HM Government (2011a, p 47) as the correct figure for external contracts, rather than procurement, but is likely to be an overestimate. There is a lack of accurate data on outsourcing: the data sometimes conflates different geographic areas, for example, England and the UK; the extent of outsourcing is exaggerated by the outsourcers and public service defenders alike; and there

is a lack of clarity in categorising goods, services, capital expenditure and grants/contracts to the voluntary sector when the data are used.

[9] News release dated 16 November 2011. Available at: www.communities.gov. uk/news/newsroom/2030130

THREE

Injustice

This chapter starts by looking at the 2010 Coalition Government's policies, which have inflicted an exceptional assault on local government. It then makes the case that the injustice caused by this assault harms *everyone* in society. It argues that the attack results from the domination of the interests of the market but that this is not inevitable. Councillors have some capacity to pursue alternative approaches; as the last chapter showed, they did so very actively during the Thatcher era. To drive forward other courses of action, it is necessary to develop alternative concepts and theories that support different policy approaches. The final section of this chapter looks at three such approaches that have been used and suggests that they all provide some insights. The case is made, however, for an ethical framework, which is developed in Chapter Four.

Current government policy

As Chapter Two made clear, the Localism Act 2011 and other reforms passed by the Coalition Government have simultaneously tightened central government's grip on local government and opened up new opportunities for local innovation and action. However, these reforms took place in the context of the immediate attack on public services following the accession of the 2010 Coalition Government to power. The local government expenditure reductions are dramatic and unprecedented. The cuts in the five-year period of the Coalition Government to 2014/15 were estimated in 2011 to be three times the level of the cuts in the UK between 1978 and 1985 and two-and-a-half times the level of those in the US in this earlier period (Jones et al, 2011; Talbot and Talbot, 2011). The local government sector experienced a real decline of income from central government of 11.8%, or £3.5 billion, from June 2010 to November 2011, and it was calculated that the sector would experience a 26% reduction in central government support by 2014/15 (Audit Commission, 2011, p 10). These cuts were increased in the autumn statement 2012 and an additional reduction in funding of £220 million was introduced for 2014/15 in the March 2013 Budget. The cuts had now risen to over a third of council budgets (LGA, 2012b). In May 2013, the Public Accounts **Select Committee** published a report warning that some

12% of local authorities may prove financially unviable (Public Accounts Select Committee, 2013, p 8).

Yet, in the **Spending Review** in June 2013, the Chancellor announced that the local government resource budget will be reduced by a further 10% in 2015/16 (although some funding was redirected from the health budget to join up health and social care). It is now clear that over the period May 2010–May 2015, the term of the Coalition Government, the cuts are even greater. Sir Merrick Cockell, the Conservative Chairman of the Local Government Association, told *The Guardian*:

> This cut will stretch essential services to breaking point in many areas. While positive steps have been taken to target NHS [National Health Service] funding and social care, the fact remains that some councils will simply not have enough money to meet all their statutory responsibilities. Services such as culture and leisure facilities, school support, road maintenance and growth-related programmes will bear the brunt of these cuts.[1]

Furthermore, the fall in funding was forced through in a context of rising demand for services for the elderly, increasing numbers of children being taken into care and a 10% increase in pupil numbers in maintained nursery and state-funded primary schools.[2] There were additional hidden cuts in some powers passed to local government, such as the administration of Council Tax Benefit and the pooling of early intervention funding streams into the **Early Intervention Grant**. Here the 25% cut in 2011 was accompanied by an unfunded commitment to future 'free' nursery provision for two year olds (Studdert, 2013, p 28). Overall, the level of cuts means that efficiency and incremental savings cannot balance budgets on their own. Even financial changes, such as extending loan terms or refinancing long-term debt, cannot plug the gap. Local authorities will have to decide not to fund services that up until now have been deemed worthy of support (Talbot and Talbot, 2011), and, as the Public Accounts Select Committee makes clear, they may not be able to fund their statutory duties.

The decline in public expenditure also needs to be seen in relation to cuts in the welfare budget. The income of households in England claiming benefit will be on average lower in real terms by £1,615 a year – or £31 a week – in 2015/16 compared to May 2010 as a result of welfare reforms. This excludes the impact of Universal Credit. The average claimant household incomes in London will be lower by £1,965 per year because of high housing costs (Wilson et al, 2013, p 4). The increasing poverty will place additional demands on local authorities. The decline also needs to be seen in terms of the government policy of quantitative easing, which is leading to higher commodity prices, a rise in asset values and a redistribution of wealth from those with savings, fixed and low incomes to wealthy asset-holders, mortgage borrowers, the banks and the government itself (Treasury Select Committee, 2013).

The slashing of public spending was justified in terms of countering increasing public debt, but it was a political as well as an economic choice. Both David Cameron and George Osborne have made it clear that they are in favour of a smaller state, Osborne stating: 'I have an innate faith in individuals and communities being in charge of their own destiny, not a big central government prerogative' (Eaglesham, 2008). In the US, President Obama in similar economic circumstances chose a stimulus bill and higher public spending and has achieved higher economic growth and job creation. Blinder and Zandi (2010) estimated that without the US government's stimulus package, 'GDP [Gross Domestic Product] in 2010 would be about 11.5% lower, payroll employment would be less by some 8½ million jobs, and the nation would now be experiencing deflation.'[3]

The cuts in the UK were accompanied by a further drive to open up public services in England to competition predominantly from the private sector. In the *Open Public Services* White Paper (HM Government, 2011a, p 29), the 2010 Coalition Government made it clear that: 'In the services amenable to commissioning, the principles of open public services will switch the default from one where the state provides the service itself to one where the state commissions the service from a range of diverse providers'. Effectively, the service role of local government in England is being commodified and privatised. This is being done in the name of equality, efficiency and effectiveness: 'The better our public services, the more we are helping those most in need' (HM Government, 2011a, p 5).

However, there is plenty of evidence that the public expenditure reduction is impacting most severely on the most disadvantaged areas (Hastings et al, 2012; Whitfield, 2012; SIGOMA, 2013; Studdert, 2013, p 32[4]), and particularly on women, as redundancies are made in local government and local services are reduced (Green, 2012; Stephenson, 2012). The Public Accounts Select Committee expressed concerns that those councils more reliant on government grants – which serve poorer and more vulnerable communities with higher demands on services – are experiencing the greatest spending reductions (Public Accounts

Select Committee, 2013, p 9). Chapter Six will also explore in more detail how services have been **depoliticised** by handing them over to the private sector, looking at 'what works' and reducing decisions into technical judgements about efficiency and efficacy, rather than exploring who benefits and who loses and what values underpin the decision. All of this disempowers those who are poor or disadvantaged by categorising and prioritising those who are in most severe need of help and thereby masking collective interests.

While the private sector has always played a role within public services and will continue to do so, it is the extent of its dominance that is now causing concern to many councillors and their residents and employees. The UK leads the world in the privatisation of public services and the use of Public–Private Partnerships (PPPs; which include the Private Finance Initiative [PFI]) for financing infrastructure (Whitfield, 2012). However, the increased privatisation or outsourcing of public services is not just a UK phenomenon. The privatisation of public services is achieving greater importance and has been gaining speed since the early 1980s in most countries worldwide (see for example, Henke, 1989; Olmedo et al, 2012; on privatisation in Sweden, see also Karlsson and Montin, 2013).

Taking public services first, Chapter Two already highlighted the level of funds that flowed to the private sector under New Labour and the fact that there is no accurate data for local authority outsourcing of services to the private sector. Total procurement (which includes everything from the purchase of stationery or outsourcing contracts to other local authorities and the third sector, to major private sector outsourcing contracts on public services) in 2011/12 was £57.635 billion (58% of total revenue expenditure), down from the high in 2010/11 of £61.442 billion (58.89% of total revenue expenditure) as local authority expenditure was cut (DCLG, 2012, p 6). It is clear that the private sector now has a major stake in local authority expenditure and although this has also been hit by public expenditure cuts, the proportion of local authority expenditure going to the private sector is likely to rise.

Turning to public sector infrastructure, there has been a decline in investment as a proportion of GDP in most countries over the past 30 years, but public infrastructure investment has been privatised to an unprecedented degree in the same period (Whitfield, 2010, p 13). By June 2009 in the UK, PPPs had been used to finance 900 projects, with a capital value of £70 billion, not counting the additional £1.4 billion investment in health centres through the Local Improvement Finance Trust (LIFT) programme and the investment in Building Schools for the Future (Whitfield, 2010, p 149). All these schemes mean that the contracts are 'off the books', although they are listed on departmental spending; Huitson (2012) states that if they were listed on the National Accounts, it would add an additional 2.5%, or £35 billion, to the national debt. They are less accountable and more complex to procure: 'democratic accountability, economic development, sustainability, social justice and other public interest matters are marginal to the financial assessment of risk and "whole life" costs' (Whitfield, 2010, p 16). They are also much more expensive in the long term (Huitson, 2012, p 69). They are a way of financing current capital expenditure that results in future generations being saddled with the costs. Future generations will therefore have greater problems in financing their necessary current expenditure as more and more expenditure goes to meet past PPP commitments (Whitfield, 2010, p 149).

Local Government Funding Agencies

There are alternatives to PPPs. For example, Local Government Funding Agencies (LGFAs) are found in the four Nordic countries and in New Zealand and are joint local (and regional) authority institutions formed to raise capital for infrastructure. They have central government support. They issue bonds on the domestic and international bond market to fund the construction and maintenance of infrastructure, replicating the relatively low cost of borrowing delivered by the government bond market. The activities of all the LGFAs are restricted to providing credit exclusively for the municipal sector. LFGAs do not seek to maximise profits, but to remain profitable and sustainable over the long term. LGFAs now provide local government in other countries with a source of secure long-term financing for basic infrastructure, which is far cheaper than PFI (Andersson and Anderson, 2012). Other options are possible, including the changing of Treasury rules on what counts as public debt. This has long been advocated in housing finance, where a change would open up many different options for council house-building programmes. The House of Commons **Communities and Local Government Select Committee** has argued:

> We are not convinced that the existing accounting treatment, or the cap, is justified. A change of rules would bring the UK in line with other European countries and enable councils to borrow on the same terms as housing associations. (Independent Commission on the Future of Council Housing in Southwark, 2012, p 31)

Furthermore, the PPP debt is sold on in various secondary markets, together with streams of public revenue that have been **securitised** (eg student loans and housing rents), raising:

some concern that, under such an arrangement, those ultimately owning the PPP debt may become so remote from the actual operation, and the debt instruments so bundled, that they are unable to form a true assessment of the actual risks involved. (Whitfield, 2010, pp 206–7)

Williams (2012) points to the private equity firms that now dominate children's services and adult social care. Accountability quickly becomes obscured:

[In children's services] Sovereign and 3i are the big contenders, but it is hard to pinpoint which firm owns what; their waters seem to be in perpetual motion, as they buy one another and take one another over, and offload assets. Advanced Childcare was England's biggest operator, with 143 homes and 1,400 staff; it was bought in 2011 by American private equity house, GI partners, having previously been owned by Bowmark Capital. Advanced Childcare went on to purchase Continuum Care and Education, which was previously owned by 3i. Castlecare, in Northamptonshire, runs 40 children's homes; it was bought by Baird Capital Partners Europe for £9 million in 2004. The company has expanded by buying two smaller childcare companies, Quantum Care and Sovereign Care, for £1 million and £1.3 million respectively. (Williams, 2012, p 31)

There is also the issue of private sector providers becoming too big to be allowed to fail, with the public sector being unable to fill the gaps in provision in the short term:

For example, Serco operates public transport services such as the Docklands Light Railway and Barclays Cycle Hire Scheme. It manages laboratories including the National Nuclear Laboratory. It runs prisons and young offenders institutions, provides a range of security services to the National Borders Agency and other clients, such as accommodation and detention services for asylum seekers; it also supplies electronic tagging systems. It provides maintenance services for missile defence systems and military bases; it provides air traffic control services, facilities and management for hospitals, as well as pathology services.

It manages leisure services, administers government websites including Business Link, provides a range of IT services and operates waste collection services for local councils. It also manages education authorities on behalf of local governments. Its failure would cause extreme turbulence in public services. No business should be too big to be allowed to fail. (Williams, 2012, p 10)

It is not surprising that this power is abused, as is illustrated by the case of Serco and G4S being investigated for £50 million fraud gained by charging the taxpayer to monitor non-existent electronic tags, some of which had been assigned to dead offenders.[5]

The preceding discussion suggests that it is not only the direct impact of cuts on services that are of concern, but also the issue of the redirection of public spending to suit private interests as they gain an ever-greater foothold in making money out of public services. The prison example from the US described in the following box is an extreme example, but it indicates some possible worrying trends.

The prison–industrial complex

The following is an edited version of an article by Eric Schlosser in *Atlantic Magazine* in December 1998.

Over the past twenty years [1978–1998] the State of California built twenty-one new prisons ... and increased its inmate population eightfold.... The state holds more inmates in its jails and prisons than do France, Great Britain, Germany, Japan, Singapore, and the Netherlands combined....The enormous increase in America's inmate population can be explained in large part by the sentences given to people who have committed nonviolent offenses....

The prison boom in the United States is a recent phenomenon.... The United States has developed a prison–industrial complex – a set of bureaucratic, political, and economic interests that encourage increased spending on imprisonment, regardless of the actual need....Since 1991 the rate of violent crime in the United States has fallen by about 20%, while the number of people in prison or jail has risen by 50%....

Prison jobs have slowed the exodus from small towns, by allowing young people to remain in the area....The job brings health benefits and a pension. Working as a correctional officer is one of the few ways that men and women without college degrees can enjoy a solid middle-class life there.

What was once a niche business for a handful of companies has become a multibillion-dollar industry with its own trade shows and conventions, its own Web sites, mail-order catalogues, and direct-marketing campaigns.... The prison–industrial complex now includes some of the nation's largest architecture and construction firms, Wall Street investment banks that handle prison bond issues and invest in private prisons, plumbing-supply companies, food-service companies, health-care companies, companies that sell everything from bullet-resistant security cameras to padded cells available in a 'vast color selection.'

The line between the public interest and private interests has blurred.... Fundamental choices about public safety, employee training, and the denial of personal freedoms are increasingly being made with an eye to the bottom line.... Private prison companies are the most obvious, the most controversial, and the fastest-growing segment of the prison–industrial complex.... The nation's private prisons accepted their first inmates in the mid-1980s.... [In 1998] at least twenty-seven states made use of private prisons, and approximately 90,000 inmates were being held in prisons run for profit.... The private-prison industry usually charges its customers a daily rate for each inmate; the success or failure of a private prison is determined by the number of 'man-days' it can generate.... The interstate commerce in prisoners, like many new industries, developed without much government regulation.

From 1963 to 1972 the number of inmates in California had declined by more than a fourth, despite the state's growing population.... More than any other state, California was dedicated to the rehabilitative ideal, to the belief that a prison could take a criminal and 'cure' him, set him on the right path. California's prisons were notable for their many educational and vocational programs and their group-therapy sessions....

The extraordinary demand for new prison and jail cells in California has diverted funds from other segments of the criminal-justice system, creating a vicious circle. The failure to spend enough on relatively inexpensive sanctions, such as drug treatment and probation, has forced the state to increase spending on prisons. In 1998, the state Department of Corrections estimates that it will need to spend an additional $6.1 billion on prisons over the next decade just to maintain the current level of overcrowding. (Schlosser, 1998)

Williams (2012, p 14) argues that this American experience is being transferred to the UK, where the private sector runs 12 prisons, accommodating 13% of the nation's prisoners, the highest percentage in Europe. She also points out that in 2006, the value of prisoners' work in the US reached $6 billion with some prisoners being paid as little as 23 cents an hour and that this benefit to private providers is now being built into the bidding price (Williams, 2012, p 41). This trend is also transferring to the UK, where in HMP Oakwood, run by G4S, wages for working prisoners are between £7 and £9 a week (Williams, 2012, p 41). Staff pay is also lower in private prisons – 40% lower on average. There were also 25% more prisoners per officer in privately run compared to public prisons (see: www.howardleague.org/public-slams-private-prisons).

The prison example shows that the private sector is gaining increasing control over public services, creating a set of problems around accountability, control of the policy direction of services and future poverty as wages and pensions are reduced. Yet, there is no substantive evidence that services contracted to the private sector are cheaper or better. In the area where there has been most research – welfare to work – the basis for privatisation is very shaky indeed (Newman, I., 2011). As Hasluck and Green (2007, p 145) put it: 'There is little robust evidence that the nature of the provider of services, be it Jobcentre Plus, a private sector provider or some other organisation, has a systematic impact on effectiveness.' Peter Whilby (2012, p 34) quotes the US's non-partisan Project on Government Oversight, which found that in 'over 550 outsourced services, the federal government paid, on average, almost twice as much to contractors as it would have paid its own employees and in one case, five times as much'. In the short term, savings can often be generated, and in services like waste management, there are economies of scale. However, as private sector oligopolies emerge, the long-term costs grow and the risks of failure increase.

Fife: insourcing

In Fife, Scotland, electrical repairs were brought back in-house after they had been outsourced. This saved funds and improved the quality of services: 'Operating the service in-house has meant it can be more fully integrated with other aspects of housing services and avoid duplication' (APSE, 2011, p 22).

There is growing international evidence that contracting out services fails to deliver cost savings unless the wages or working conditions of those delivering the service are cut, while procurement costs and the increased risk of failure in the long term outweigh any benefits (eg Deloitte Consulting, 2005; APSE, 2009; Wainwright, 2009b; Unison, 2011; Jeffreys, 2012; Whitfield, 2012; Williams, 2012; Queensland Audit Office, 2013 We own it, 2013;).

Effects of contracting out public sector tasks: a major Danish and international study, 2000–11 (Petersen et al, 2012)

This comprehensive research drew on 3,893 international publications and 80 studies completed since 2000. It first looked at the impact on price and quality of contracting out. The research found initial minor cost savings. However, 'the administrative, legal and transaction costs may be considerable and should self-evidently be taken into account when assessing any cost savings in an area, but the research review shows that this is rarely the case'. Furthermore, 'studies analysing the financial advantages of contracting out over longer periods tend to show that the relative advantage of using private companies disappears over time'. The research also documented a lack of research on service quality, so could not come to any conclusions as to whether the initial cost savings had been at the expense of quality or whether the quality had also improved.

The research also shows that while there was evidence for initial cost savings in technical areas like waste management, there was no evidence for claiming that savings have been made by contracting out social services. Finally, the research found that 'contracting out can lead to lower job satisfaction, lower wages and poorer employment terms, and increasing stress and absenteeism'.

The research concluded that there should be a level playing field, with in-house tenders facilitated, and that employee perspectives should be included in any future impact analyses of contracting out. There is also a need to evaluate quality as well as price over time.

Dunleavy (1986) suggests that outsourcing is clearly not a rational policy but is pursued like other irrational policies (the 1960s' system-built housing; the 1970s' and 1980s' out-of-town shopping centres) because a section of private interests have lobbied and their interests have coincided with government ideology. Exaggerated claims about the success of the new policies are made[6] and managers in the public sector see an opportunity to increase their status, power and income through policy changes.

Furthermore, the policy of reducing the size of the state is likely to fail. Brown and Jacobs (2008) have shown that overall public spending increased twice as fast under President George W. Bush compared to Clinton. They argue that utopian ideas about how the market can solve all problems lead to market failures and greater regulation. The commissioning and regulation of privatised services, combined with the state trying to control the lives of people who are negatively affected by growing inequality (tackling issues such as anti-social behaviour, unemployment, obesity, depression and crime), create additional burdens on the public purse. Austerity has had an impact on growth and tax revenues, leading to a rise in government debt and higher costs in servicing this debt. While public debt remains high, these trends mean that the budget deficit can only be reduced by slashing public spending (and/or raising taxes significantly). Under the Coalition Government, a greater proportion of public spending: will flow into the private sector; will fund expensive infrastructure (from High Speed Rail links to free schools in wealthy areas); will be used to fund inspection and regulation (particularly in the NHS); will go into debt servicing; and will fund services that address the social problems that are being created by austerity itself, such as long-term youth unemployment. Less public funding will be used to reduce inequality and provide universal services, from early years support to youth clubs and respite care. The Coalition Government will take 'government consumption of goods and services – a rough proxy for day-to-day spending on public services and administration – to its smallest share of national income at least since 1948' (Office for Budget Responsibility, 2013, p 7), a year when the UK was in the grip of post-war austerity.

So, current policy is enforcing a reduction in the welfare goods and services of local government and privatising and marketising public services but is unlikely to significantly reduce overall public spending. Chapter Six will discuss how the discourse of the 'deserving poor' is being used to undermine universal welfare services and to individualise the causes of social problems. This discourse aims to encourage people to take responsibility for their own problems and reduce the support for welfare by 'othering' those who need state aid. Here, we look at why the assault on local government matters and why it has occurred.

Injustice

Ask any councillor why they have gone into politics and the usual reply is that they want to make a difference and improve the well-being of their residents; the Civic Gospel, with or without the religious aspects, remains a strong motivator. Remedying the injustice that acts as a barrier to individuals meeting their full potential is central to local government.

The report that established the welfare state (Beveridge, 1942) identified five evils: Want, Disease, Ignorance, Squalor and Idleness. It is of concern to local authorities that while the welfare state had a major impact on reducing these evils in the period from the end of the Second

World War to the mid-1960s, they are now re-emerging. Want remains, even in the UK, with the Joseph Rowntree Foundation evidencing that the minimum income needed by families for an acceptable living standard is getting harder to earn in these harsher economic times. The gap between the incomes and needs of the worst-off households in the UK is widening, especially for families with children (Davis et al, 2012). Fifty senior welfare experts have estimated that welfare reforms, combined with previous tax, benefit and public expenditure cuts, will result in a further 200,000 children in poverty and the poorest 10% of households losing the equivalent of around 38% of their income in April 2013 (Guardian Letters, 28 March 2013, p 53). Health inequalities in the UK have grown, with people living in the poorest neighbourhoods in England, on average, dying seven years earlier than people living in the richest neighbourhoods and spending more of their lives with a disability – an average total difference of 17 years (Marmot, 2010). Compared with other countries in the Organisation for Economic Co-operation and Development (OECD), those of low educational attainment in the UK have lower literacy and work skills and there is evidence that the traditional voluntarist approach to skills training in the UK is keeping those with low educational attainment (both employed and unemployed) in 'ignorance' and poverty (Paull and Patel, 2012). Squalor is likely to increase as Housing Benefit in England is capped, a bedroom tax is imposed for those on Housing Benefit with a 'spare' bedroom and families are forced into insecure private rented housing in low-cost areas, effectively ghettoising the poor and particularly lone parents (Vickery, 2012). Rising rates of youth unemployment are increasing 'idleness' in the UK and across Europe, with 20% of young people unemployed in the UK and 55% in Spain in the last quarter of 2012.

The re-emergence of Beveridge's evils has a major impact on local authorities as demand for services increases. Inequality is also reflected in spatial terms. The North–South divide has been well documented, as investment flows into London, in particular. This creates all kinds of problems: the overheated housing market in London; reduced opportunities for young people growing up in the North; and the fragmentation of social and family networks placing additional demands for social care on local government. There are also divisions within local authority areas that are now being boosted by housing and education policies, creating ghettos of the wealthy around schools with good reputations. An inner London estate agent will tell you that being in the catchment area of a good state secondary school will add £100,000–200,000 to the value of a house. This leaves local authorities having to tackle the impacts of area deprivation, where individual poverty is reinforced by disadvantage in the wider community.

It is important to recognise that growing inequality[7] is a result of political choices and is not bound to happen. The share of all income received by the richest 1% in Britain fell *consistently for over 50 years* from just over 18% in 1920 to around 6% in the mid-1970s but then rose rapidly to over 16% by 2005 (Dorling, 2011, p 191). This rise since the mid-1970s has been presented by those who benefit from it as natural: there is no alternative to paying bankers salaries of £1 million, 38 times the average wage in the UK, as this is the salary set by the market. Nor, it is claimed, is there any alternative to cutting the income of the poorest 10% of households by 38% since the 'tax burden' of the welfare state is 'unacceptable' and many of them are in any case 'scroungers' who need an incentive to stop being reliant on welfare benefits. Danny Dorling's powerful book, *Injustice: why social inequality persists* (Dorling, 2011), shows how inequality is now being recreated and supported by five new sets of beliefs: 'elitism is efficient, exclusion is necessary, prejudice is natural, greed is good and despair is inevitable' (Dorling, 2011, p 2). These beliefs are interrelated. He draws on detailed statistical analyses to show how the beliefs are false and how they promote injustice:

> Elitism suggests that educational divisions are natural.... Elitism is the incubation chamber within which prejudice is fostered. Elitism provides a defence for greed.... It perpetuates an enforced and inefficient hierarchy in our society.... The exclusion which rises with elitism makes the poor appear different, exacerbates inequalities between ethnic groups and, literally, causes racial difference.... The prejudice that rises with exclusion allows the greedy to try and justify their greed and makes others think they deserve a little more than most. The ostracism that such prejudice engenders further raises depression and anxiety in those made to look different.... In turn despair prevents us from effectively tackling injustice. (Dorling, 2011, pp 309–10)

Dorling argues that the failure to deal with social inequality rests on the powerful in the economically affluent and unequal countries, not just the UK, propagating these five new sets of beliefs as natural and long-standing, whereas, in fact, they are relatively new constructs. Dorling's five beliefs work in a vicious circle to maintain elites and reduce social mobility. Elites capture the political system, using their power to propagate beliefs that alternatives are not possible. Inequality in income and resources is reinforced by power inequality.

The issue for local councillors who are concerned about the well-being of their constituents is that inequality is detrimental to everyone. To many, this may seem counter-intuitive: surely the rich do not suffer in an unequal society? But there is increasing evidence (eg Wilkinson and Pickett, 2009) that whether you classify people by education, social class or income, in each category, people are healthier (and have higher literacy scores) if they are in a more equal society than people in the same category of income, education or class in a less equal society. At any given level of personal income or education, someone's quality of life will be higher if he or she lives in a more equal society. Obviously, greater equality would make most difference to the least well-off, but it still produces some benefits for the well-off. The reasons for this are still being researched but are likely to be linked to Dorling's fifth evil – despair. Societies that promote competitiveness and inequality and that reduce the safety barriers of welfare support put all their citizens under greater stress. This will clearly have an impact on health and well-being. Around one in five people in the UK experience mental health problems at some point in their lives. The number of prescriptions for anti-depressant drugs increased from 9 million in 1991 to 34 million in 2007 (Young Foundation, 2009, p 8).

Yet, despite the benefits to everyone of living in a more equal society (and the fact that far greater equality existed in the early 1970s in the UK and continues to exist in economies such as Japan, the Nordic countries, France and Germany), inequality in the UK, the US and many other countries continues to increase. To understand this, and its implications for local government, it is necessary to look a little deeper into neo-liberalism and the ability of local government to make a difference.

Neo-liberalism and the autonomy of the local state

Chapter Two looked at dual welfare and regime theory, which suggested that social policy has been subordinated to the needs of the market. This has been described as the development of neo-liberalism and most authors agree that it is the dominance of neo-liberalism since the mid-1970s that has increased inequality.

The concept of neo-liberalism is complex, diverse and contested (eg Brenner and Theodore, 2002; Leitner et al, 2007; Fuller and Geddes, 2008). There is a major debate as to whether neo-liberalism constitutes a 'rolling back' of the state or whether it should be regarded as a 'roll-out'. A 'roll back' perspective regards deregulation (such as the reduction in development planning controls), public expenditure cuts, the privatisation of public services and the reduction in public services (such as social care) as a means of releasing productive capacity for private capital accumulation.[8]

However, there are elements of the previous Labour Government's policy and of the 2010 Coalition Government's policy that can be better described as the roll-out of the state. Here, some services and state regulation are increased to maintain the legitimacy of neo-liberalism by managing the socio-spatial contradictions and tensions that have arisen. Fuller and Geddes describe the concept of roll-out neo-liberalism as follows:

> Roll-out interventions that seek to embed and extend neoliberalism include state spatial strategies and projects geared towards 'cohesion and inclusion' and 'citizenship and community', led by a **'dirigiste'** state ... [and employ] various techniques associated with the emergence of neoliberalism that ensure agents adhere to state objectives: state setting of strategic objectives, targets and spatial jurisdictions, and monitoring of activities, expenditure and 'delivery' through audits, performance management and evaluation. (Fuller and Geddes, 2008, pp 275–6)

Some government policies can be better understood as roll-out interventions. These include the attempt to radically extend the level of activation in the labour market by mandating more of the unemployed into the private sector-run Work Programme and embedding a consensus that life should be shaped by work. They also include the work of the 'nudge' unit or Behavioural Insights Team in the cabinet[9] and the increasing use of payment-by-results funding.

Neo-liberalism is taken generally in this book to reflect the trend to prioritise market forces and competitiveness over a universal welfare state and redistribution. Harvey (2005, p 19) argues that neo-liberalism should not be understood as a bundle of characteristics, but as a political project, a *process of neo-liberalisation* 'to re-establish the conditions for capital accumulation and to restore the power of economic elites'. As Brenner and Theodore (2002, p 14) put it, neo-liberalism is a 'framework of disciplinary political authority that enforces market rule over an ever wider range of social relations throughout the world economy'. It is a project that has successfully consolidated the power and wealth of the rich and has, as Harvey has argued, been 'masked by a lot of rhetoric about individual freedom, liberty, personal responsibility and the virtues of privatisation, the free market and free trade' (Harvey, 2011, p 10). However, the extent to which this prioritisation is successful in the future will depend on organised opposition (Leitner et al, 2007, p viii).

Margaret Thatcher said not only that there was no such thing as society, but that she sought to change the way we understand the world and think about it: 'Economics are the method; the object is to change the heart and soul '(Butt, 1981). She was successful. As Nobel economist Joseph Stiglitz (2001) and others have argued, we are now in the grip of 'market fundamentalism'. Part of the purpose of this book is to gain recognition of this dominance and the negative consequences of market-driven local policy, but also to question its inevitability. Can local government, therefore, make a difference?

Marxists have devoted considerable attention to the role of the state within capitalist economies and have debated the extent to which it can challenge market forces. Ralph Miliband (1969; see also Newman, M., 2002, ch 6) argued that the capitalist class rarely actually governed the state, which had some autonomy and would not always act in the interest of large-scale capitalists. The state was not a tool that the capitalist class could use as it liked. However, the autonomy of the state was reduced by the extent that business interests had penetrated the government and the fact that the social class that held power in government was overwhelmingly the same social class as the business elite. Within the local state, the closer links between the interests of business and government since the mid-1960s reflected a similar capture of the state (Cockburn, 1977, p 19).

Poulantzas agreed with Miliband about the autonomy of the state but was to go further, putting forward a structuralist theory suggesting that the structure of the state tended to reproduce and stabilise capitalism irrespective of the class backgrounds of those in government. He saw the state as representing the long-term political interests of the dominant classes while having autonomy to occasionally implement policies that were against their immediate economic interests. So, a structuralist would argue that the welfare policies or regulation of the banks have been implemented so that capitalism is able to survive in the long term and be seen as legitimate even if these policies are not in the immediate economic interests of large-scale capital.

The problem with the structuralist school of Marxism is that it ultimately becomes almost tautological. Since capitalism has survived, every policy is seen as in the political interest of capital and any kind of reformism is seen as unable to achieve a fundamental change. Newman and Clarke make a similar critique of authors who see neo-liberalism as hegemonic. Such accounts, they argue, 'leave little room for politics, and tend to add "resistance" on as an afterthought or rhetorical closing paragraph' (Newman, J. and Clarke, 2009, p 181). Miliband was extremely critical of Poulantzas, arguing that his theory was unable to identify any real analytical distinction between different liberal states (eg Norway and the US) or even between a liberal-democratic state and a dictatorship (although Poulantzas was clear that fascism was a distinct phenomenon; see Newman, M., 2002, p 211).

The work of structuralists was very influential and there was a tendency in the 1970s for Marxist academics to describe local government policies as all tending to reinforce capitalism. The structuralist solution focused only on organising struggles against capitalist interests and the local and national state as a way of building a more equal society. More recently, Harvey has also seen state power as defending capitalism, particularly finance capitalism, and has argued that this can change only when people 'rise up and say enough is enough' (Harvey, 2011, p 12). However, he suggests that the distinction between reformism and revolution is never as sharp as some Marxists maintain (Harvey, 2000, p 85).

My conclusion from this discussion is to reaffirm the fundamental point that both central and local government have some autonomy, although the state in a capitalist society is certainly under pressure to comply with business interests and market forces. This is necessarily a limitation on local government in a capitalist society. A local authority cannot create a socialist island in the middle of capitalist Britain, as the Greater London Council (GLC) example in the last chapter demonstrated. However, local government is not powerless. Chapter Two also referenced the work of the London Edinburgh Weekend Return Group (1979/80). This group looked at those on the Left working in local government and other local public sector agencies and argued that they had to work in and against the state, refashioning the state to build a sense of change that would lead to a more just world. This issue is not the Conservative/Labour discussion of more or less government, but of the type of government and social relationships we want in our society. The extent to which a local authority can modify the dominance of market interests will depend on its history and on the values of its councillors and residents and their ability to build coalitions to resist market-driven policies. Marxists writing on the state are also clear that progressive change cannot occur without the support of government. Party and agency are essential and need to be combined with social movements. This issue will be discussed further in Chapters Five and Seven.

The inadequacies of current solutions

So far, this chapter has critiqued the impact of neo-liberal policies, arguing that reliance on the market increases inequality, which affects everyone. It has also argued that vital services that provide social protection are being cut and that the private sector is starting to dominate policymaking in the public sector to further its interests. However, the simple rejection of neo-liberalism is not enough and local government does have some ability to make a difference. Those who reject the New Right need to find other ideas and concepts if they are going to persuade anyone to change track.

This book seeks to develop a framework that will help councillors decide which policies to pursue to further well-being. It is clear from the earlier discussion that such a framework must be able to illuminate how policies impact on inequality. There is also the issue as to how policy is decided. The prison example was given to show how the market can distort policymaking. The discussion of neo-liberalism has emphasised that although the state has some autonomy, it is under strong pressure to adapt to market demands. A framework that seeks to open up alternatives has to recognise this limitation and address power inequalities. Lukes (1974) argued that powerful elites have the ability to shape the very wants, preferences and values of subordinate groups so that their resistance to exploitation is reduced. Workers without power, through accommodation and assimilation, enact scripts that fit in with the needs of the dominant elites. It is not enough, therefore, to be guided by focus groups. A framework needs to be supported by a process that empowers the powerless and opens up alternatives for them to consider.

The rest of the book will develop this framework by looking at the ethical underpinnings of policy and democratic processes. This section of the chapter looks in more detail at three approaches that are taught on public administration courses and purport to influence local political practice and change the way the state operates. First, there is the advocacy of partnership and joined-up governance. Second, there is the belief that an analysis of 'public value' can provide guidance in prioritising local expenditure. Finally, there is the argument from the Centre/Left for a so-called 'relational state', by which they mean that 'rather than attempting to engineer outcomes through "command and control"', governments should focus on crafting the conditions for a variety of agents involved in a given problem to solve it themselves' (Cooke and Muir, 2012, p 6). I have picked these three approaches because they do provide some insights and are relevant for rest of the book. They are therefore worth looking at briefly, but I argue that each fails to provide a secure ethical base or to address fully the issues of power in society. Ultimately, therefore, they do not provide satisfactory guidance for local action and policy and the following chapters put forward my preferred approach.

A common fallacy

All three theories present a myth of the sequencing of regimes. They present the Keynesian welfare state as a period of traditional public administration. This period, it is claimed, delivered standardised public services and goods but was unable to cope with declining resources, longer-term sustainability issues, the growing diversification of public demand and the increasing complexity of social issues (Talbot, 2009; Osborne, 2010; Benington and Moore, 2011). This, they suggest, was replaced by New Public Management (NPM), which is seen as increasing fragmentation and risk. It led to the failed outcome-focused target culture of New Labour. NPM now needs to be replaced with an approach that recognises the plural nature of the state (Osborne, 2010, p 9) and the increased complexity of society; otherwise, the 'debate will remain stuck on familiar tracks, leading to a tired politics' (Cooke and Muir, 2012, p 4).

Chapter Two argued that there is continuity and evolution in local government based on social, economic and historical factors rather than a sequence of different regimes. It posited that services in the Keynesian welfare era were not standardised and Fordist, but dominated by professionals who exercised some discretion. Elements of this regime remain, as do the more standardised aspects of traditional public administration, such as ensuring refuse collection, salary payments and fairness in the allocation of resources. Nor are Benington and Moore (2011, p 257) correct in arguing that the wholesale assault on government as a socially-productive institution experienced in the era of NPM is now over and that NPM is no longer dominant in local government. The contract culture, which has been reinforced by the rise in commissioning, continues to be driven by targets and outcomes. Private sector styles of management, with an emphasis on performance monitoring, are ubiquitous (Manson, 2012).

This would all suggest that councillors need to be wary of those who preach new managerial paradigms. Grey argues that, for all the talk about new paradigms, contemporary organisational theory and managerial methods focusing on instrumental rationality and control remain unchanged from their classical roots. However, contemporary management is justified through the discourse of 'change management', which has become the new mantra. Grey (2005, p 102) concludes: 'change is a crass theology, but a theology it is'.

The approaches, discussed in the following three sections, do not have to be adopted by decision-makers because academics and others argue that there are changes in society. Policy is driven by politicians, who exercise influence and choice over how their world can be. So, a far more nuanced approach can be pursued by councillors: seeking to learn from what has been done in the past; considering the alternatives; and listening to the experience and knowledge of their constituents and employees to understand how different options will impact on different interests.

Partnership and joined-up governance

Chapter Two discussed the fragmentation of local government and the shift to governance, with the local authority acting as the community leader across partnerships rather than as local government responsible for direct administration and delivery. It is unclear whether much of the literature that describes the growth of governance and partnership is a description of trends or an ideology that promotes partnership as a better way of governing. Certainly, under New Labour, partnership was promoted as the solution. It has been estimated that in the UK in 2001/02, there were 5,500 partnership bodies at the local and regional level, stimulated or created by the government (Sullivan and Skelcher, 2002, p 26). While the 2010 Coalition Government has abolished the statutory base of many partnerships, from Regional Assemblies to Local Strategic Partnerships (LSPs), it has created new partnerships around 'troubled' families and economic development (Local Enterprise Partnerships).

Partnerships for policymaking and implementation in the public sector, and particularly at the local level, have been promoted by the argument that they join up public services from different public agencies and provide a more 'holistic' approach. Such an approach encourages agencies to focus on prevention (the fence at the top of the cliff) rather than crisis management (the ambulance at the bottom of the cliff). It has also been suggested that partnerships open up local authorities to new ways of working and facilitate greater community engagement. These are worthy aims, as is the focus on inter-organisational relationships and trust and the governance of processes rather than just outcomes.

The reality is that there is a great variety of partnerships created for different reasons. Some are useful, building on synergy and creating win–win benefits for all concerned. Others are instrumental, for example, established to bid for some funding, and may or may not be successful in achieving their goal. The long-term evaluation of LSPs found that there was some improvement in quality on specific targets but little evidence of cost savings through partnership (European Institute for Urban Affairs et al, 2010). Few partnerships, however, are really transformative, delivering a holistic approach and improved outcomes, developing wider engagement and saving money. There is a failure in much of the literature to analyse the power relationships that underpin such partnerships or the policy content that the partnerships are seeking to implement and whom such a policy benefits. The National Audit Office reviewed 181 publications on joined-up working and found that only 10 past evaluations had assessed impact on service-user outcomes. Seven of the 10 reported a lack of robust evidence that joint or collaborative working improved outcomes (NAO, 2013, p 8).

Chapter Two already raised issues with the 'holistic', 'joined-up' paradigm. Cochrane (2007, p 33) argues that various attempts to address problems holistically are examples of what David Harvey (2000) has identified as utopian thinking: seeking to identify key moments in which to intervene in the system in order to shift it from a self-sustaining cycle of decline to a self-sustaining cycle of success. Such utopian thinking cannot succeed because the fundamental causes of the problems are not addressed (Atkinson, 1999). Furthermore, as the number of partnerships proliferates, the process is self-defeating as 'the generation of still more complex semi-autonomous schemes, each ultimately responsible to a different branch of the state, is as likely to encourage incoherence as complex solutions' (Cochrane, 2007, p 34).

Community Budgets or the 'troubled families' programme

Community Budgets are a classic and current example of the attempt to develop partnerships to bring together public agencies in providing a holistic, preventive approach, in this case, for families who make the most demands on public services. The programme evidenced families having over 30 assessment visits from different public agencies. It is clear that some simple joining up would generate savings and improve relationships with clients.

However, in the programme, the problems that the families face around the lack of secure jobs paying a living wage, benefit cuts, childcare support, poverty and inequality are marginalised and the families are made to feel that a change in behaviour alone can resolve all their issues. As such, the programme has the feel of a government-driven project whose primary aim is to reduce costs by making families behave as the state wishes they would behave (Newman, I., 2012). Furthermore, following the riots in the summer of 2011, the programme turned into the 'troubled families' programme, although there was no empirical relationship between the riots and 'troubled families'. The programme focused on payment-by-results funding from government based on five measures: getting children back into school; reducing their criminal and anti-social behaviour; setting parents on the road back to work; and reducing the costs to the taxpayer and local authorities. While, no doubt, the targets will be partially met (DCLG, 2013), such programmes are likely to have a number of perverse effects, not least the 'parking' of those with the most serious problems, less attention being paid to single adults with problems and saving money around one policy area while deepening long-term social costs through cuts in other areas.

Fragmentation of local government's ability to do preventive work is being increased with the promotion of free schools, privatisation of the probation service and commissioning in the NHS. Meanwhile, the level of local authority and government expenditure cuts means that a range of preventive services run by local authorities and the voluntary sector (on, for example, mental health, ex-offender support, youth services and children's centres) are actually being reduced. Families are experiencing higher stress as benefit levels are cut; they are placed into temporary housing; they are moved away from social networks; and they are pressured into low-paid employment.

Davies (2011) draws a useful distinction between 'networked governance', which he describes as new forms of trust that can lead to inclusive policymaking (one could take the transition town of Totnes as an example), and 'governance networks': partnerships between institutions, such as LSPs, which aim to deliver improved services usually at lower costs. He argues that governance networks do not live up to the promise of networked governance as they replicate the hierarchies, exclusions or inequalities of traditional forms of government, with increasing tokenistic citizen participation. Managers have more power and knowledge than community activists and dominate the discussion, while community members are trapped in a medium of social control making adversarialism taboo (Davies, 2011, pp 70–1).

Fuller and Geddes (2008), in their evaluation of New Labour's LSPs and **New Deal for Communities** (NDC) programme, conclude that such partnerships were weakly established, tightly controlled by national government and subordinated to core market-led policy objectives. The picture is reinforced by an article by one of the employees of one NDC, ECI in Islington, London (Kessler, 2012). She looks at what makes it so difficult to transform deprived places for residents. Some lasting change in the built environment was achieved through partnership, funding, a timetable, team-working and employees passionate about the well-being of the residents they served. Ultimately, however, the area was not transformed. Lack of trust, a compartmentalised approach, constant restructuring at local authority level and so-called 'strategic managers' meant that the programme 'achieved little, but kept the lid on things and, through effective spin, was able to placate both central government and the local authority' (Kessler, 2012, p 195). Kessler concludes:

> The idea that, as resident-led organisations, the NDCs would effectively meet the needs of residents was beguiling, but the concept was woolly and ill defined. By establishing these partnerships as being 'resident led', and giving the impression that residents would be in control of budgets, expectations were raised that could never be fulfilled, especially since the pressures, and control, from central and local government were so stringent. (Kessler, 2012, p 193)

Partnerships also present a number of accountability issues for councillors. When partnerships evolve into company structures, board representatives are meant, under company law, to act in the best interests of the company rather than the wider community interest that they represent as councillors. Even in looser partnerships, it becomes difficult to ensure that the full council and the executive are kept informed about the work that is being done and its wider implications. The new executive structures of local government mean that those with the power to make decisions are in high demand within partnership structures. Apart from time constraints, this can result in other members feeling that they are excluded from powerful forums where the key decision-makers from all public agencies get together, making decisions that should be the prerogative of the full council. Often, these decisions are ratified by the full council and can be scrutinised by scrutiny committees but this is a weaker role in decision-making than being directly involved in the original debate. For members of the public, partnership accountability is particularly confusing, often leaving very unclear roots to protest and redress for unpopular decisions.

In summary, it is clear that if partnerships can bring trust, inclusive policymaking and preventive action, they are beneficial. The focus on partnerships is helpful in that it highlights that the governance of processes is as important as outcomes, and subsequent chapters will be looking at how citizens are involved in local policymaking. Councillors will want to continue to use partnerships where appropriate and where such partnerships can further their objectives: 'Local authorities have to turn the transformatory pressures to their own advantage, establishing an active strategic role, rather than letting the partnership process contribute to other pressures for increased internal fragmentation and secrecy' (Mackintosh, 1992, p 222).

However, the focus on joining up and new partnerships is not ultimately a guide for councillors that can deliver new policy directions; it is an attempt to bring in a technical fix to fragmentation and to downplay the fundamental causes of complex problems. If fragmentation were the main issue, bringing local services back into the local state and giving users more powers to work with local authority staff to shape services might be the solution: that is, more government and real empowerment rather than governance and partnerships. As it is, this option is rarely discussed at central government level. Neo-liberalism, which favours competition, choice and fragmentation, has dominated ideas about policy, discouraging ideas about more powers for local government.

Health Action Zones

New Labour announced the Health Action Zone (HAZ) initiative in June 1997. An invitation to bid was published in October 1997. The guidance stated that the objectives of HAZs were to:

> identify and address the public health needs of the local area, to increase the effectiveness, efficiency and responsiveness of services and to develop partnerships for improving people's health and relevant services, adding value through creating synergy between the work of different agencies. (DH, 1997, p 145)

HAZs were successful in addressing some of the health issues specific to their local areas; however, they failed to bring about the change anticipated (Matka et al, 2002) and were merged into the work of Primary Care Trusts. In April 2013, local government finally took over direct responsibility for public health following the Localism Act 2011. This is a rare case of addressing aspects of the fragmentation through increasing the powers of local government after the partnership route has been shown to be ineffective.

Public value

This theory is a normative approach to policy guidance which argues that public managers should seek to create public value (Moore, 1995). To be able to create public value, Moore argued, managers have to specify strategic goals and public value outcomes, ensure that they have support and legitimacy for pursuing these goals and ensure that the organisation has the capacity to deliver. These three processes (Moore's strategic triangle) have to be aligned for success.

The ideas were developed by Benington and Moore (2011), with Benington attempting to sharpen the definition of public value and make it less individualistic, defining it not just in terms of 'what does the public most value?', but also in terms of 'what adds value to the public sphere?' (Benington and Moore, 2011, p 22). This reformulation, they believe, helps managers examine their decisions. It helps them to challenge the public to make painful choices and trade-offs between competing priorities (Benington and Moore, 2011, p 14). The public value approach, they claim, also emphasises the longer-term interests of the public and future generations of citizens yet unborn (Benington and Moore, 2011, p 22). Benington defines the public sphere as:

> a web of values, places, organisations, rules, knowledge and other cultural resources held in common by people through their everyday commitments and behaviours, and held in trust by government and public institutions. It is what provides a society with some sense of belonging, meaning, purpose and continuity, and which enables people to thrive and to strive amid uncertainty. (Benington, 2011, p 43)

He posits that the role of government is to develop 'shared vision or common purpose' and to negotiate and mobilise coalitions of interest to achieve communal aims (Benington, 2011, pp 36–7).

Public value theory has many positive aspects. It advocates a greater role for the public in decision-making and for the need to find out what the public wants (Horner and Hutton, 2011, p 121), although this is not necessarily the same as adding value to the public sphere. Benington and Moore (2011, p 272) suggest that its biggest impact is to redirect attention to creating 'a public': a sense of community identity and public purpose. They believe that only an articulate and engaged public can act as the appropriate arbiter of public value and that the theory correctly focuses on legitimacy and support. It is important also in its promotion of the concept of public value, rather than market forces, competition and choice, as a guide to action: 'It is not only about the performance of the public sector and legitimisation of public institutions, but also a more general quest for values framing our understanding of society' (Meynhardt, 2009, p 215). It highlights processes, outcomes, the importance of citizenship and the concepts around the common good, rather than materialism.

However, the theory fails both as a guide to managers and as a conceptual tool for understanding public service evolution. Although it deals with legitimacy, it does not deal adequately with power and conflict. It is assumed that one 'public' view can be generated and that policymakers can harness the commitment and resources of all three spheres (state, market and civil society) jointly behind specific shared 'public value' goals. Although most of the authors promoting the concept are clear that determining what constitutes *the* public interest in a given community or society is a mission impossible (Van der Wal and Van Hout, 2009, p 227) and that creating public value depends upon a deliberative process within which competing interests and perspectives can be debated (Benington, 2009), the theory is unable to prioritise one value over another. It also never seriously addresses the practical issue of how to ensure that the views of the most powerful do not dominate the definition of what constitutes public value.

Similar problems arise around trying to measure public value. Mulgan (2011) starts by arguing that the public are divided on what they value and social impact economic models, such as cost–benefit analysis, are often inadequate to illuminate choice, partly because we do not have the evidence about what causes lead to what impacts. He tries to adopt a reverse utilitarian approach, not calling for the greatest happiness of the greatest number, but arguing that something should be considered to be of public value if citizens – either individually or collectively – are willing to give something up in return for it (eg more communal security but at the expense of less individual freedom). However, he fails to adequately address the issue of inequality here. If you are on the breadline, your time and energy is spent surviving and any change can lead to chaos. Questions probing what low-income residents are prepared to sacrifice (Would you rather have free food or a job? Would you rather we built a library or a swimming pool?) are framed by policymakers and contain their own assumptions and are likely to be so hypothetical to the poor as to fail to generate very meaningful answers to guide decision-makers. How the information on what people are prepared to sacrifice is used hits the same problems as traditional utilitarianism. How do you weigh the preferences of people with different incomes? How do you compare Shakespeare and the Simpsons when you prefer watching the Simpsons but think that Shakespeare is more worthwhile (Sandel, 2009, pp 56–7)? Analyses of happiness, pleasure and sacrifice are unable to rank public policy choices such as: 'Is there a greater public value and should more public funds go to the popular opera than a show in a prison?' We will return to this issue in Chapter Four.

It also remains unclear as to whether it is a management theory, an empirical attempt to weigh the benefits of different options or a theory about what local authorities should be doing in relation to improving the well-being of their residents (Rhodes and Wanna, 2007, p 408). Different exponents of the theory, therefore, view it in different ways. So, the public values described by Van der Wal and Van Hout (2009) are all around good administration (honesty, openness, etc). Moore and Hartly (2010) argue that because public money is being used together with the authority of the state, any initiative should be evaluated in terms of the degree to which it promotes justice and the development of a society. Benington (2009) sees public value as lying in the identification of social needs that have not been satisfied by the private competitive market or by the state. He argues that it incorporates ecological value, political value, economic value and cultural and social value. Public value raises some important issues, but if it is to be a useful concept, it will need to be backed up with a firmer theory about justice, the common good and social need. These concerns will be addressed in Chapter Four.

The relational state

In 2012, the Institute for Public Policy Research (IPPR), the think tank closest to the Labour Party, produced a publication on the relational state, presenting a new paradigm and providing a guide to policy and action (Cooke and Muir, 2012, p 3). The publication built on previous work by the Young Foundation (2009) and Stears' (2006) work on the evolution of the British Labour Party.

The two main authors in the publication, Geoff Mulgan and Mark Stears, have different views of the relational state, but both are seeking a less dominant role for the state, both emphasise the importance of means (processes) as well as ends (outcomes), and both highlight the importance of the relationship of care between the professional and the client. This latter emphasis is not new (Walsh, 1989, p 67).

Mulgan's view of the relational state suggests that once material needs are 'substantially met' (Mulgan, 2012, p 22), the state needs to shift from a linear delivery model to a two-way relationship with citizens. The state should build the capacity of citizens to collaborate and take responsibility for their own needs, thereby meeting their psychological need to control their own lives and their relational values. Mulgan's analysis posits three levels. At the first level is the individual as a consumer, with wants and individual skills and assets, as well as attitudes and dispositions. Their **'resilience'** is therefore personalised and their failure is related to personal inadequacies. At a second level, he emphasises the importance of family and friends, networks of support that 'help us get by' (Young Foundation, 2009, p 19). It is only at the third level that systems and structures in society impact on power. His writing implies that the first two levels can and should be tackled on their own, independent of the third level; although he strongly supports a fairer society and recognises the importance of external factors in shaping lives.

The model has been adopted by the London Borough of Newham in their strategy *Quid pro quo* (Newham London, 2011). This has led to some innovative initiatives, which will be highlighted in Chapter Four. However, the approach also has some serious flaws. The assumption that material needs have been substantially met and that the critical issues of welfare have become as much about psychology and relationships as about material things is highly disputable. Yet, if poverty and deprivation cause difficulties in accessing support, psychological need and a lack of supportive networks (Laurence and Heath, 2008; Dorling, 2011), inequality needs to be tackled *before* relationships can be improved (Ratcliffe and Newman, I., 2011). This does not mean that capacity and solidarity are not important and should not be addressed. However, the evidence is clear that significant progress cannot be made on relationships unless more fundamental structural factors have been addressed. The focus in the relational state paradigm on psychological need and the assumption that basic material needs have been met downplays the importance of the state tackling inequality as a prior condition for progress on relationships. It also runs the danger of playing into the rhetoric that poverty is a result of personal inadequacy. The very title of the Newham report – implying that one should not get something for nothing – plays into the language of the deserving poor and scroungers and can undermine the case for universal welfare provision. This will be further explored in Chapter Six. In fact, the

Newham approach strongly supports universal welfare services and they seek to differentiate their approach from those that attack the welfare state, but the dangers are illustrated in the quotes from the report in the following box.

Quid pro quo: London Borough of Newham (adapted from Newham London, 2011)

Our personal skills, experiences and upbringing are essential to our resilience but these are intertwined with the resilience of the communities we live in and the economic circumstances we face. On the flip side, it is vital also to recognise the importance of character and personal responsibility and to ask more of people as citizens. There must be give and take, or a quid pro quo, for a fuller offer of support from the welfare state. (p 20)

We believe a lack of resilience keeps our residents poor. (p 5)

[Furthermore,] some have had their personal capacity undermined by the well-intentioned structure of the welfare state. (p 9)

Of course, we need to provide a safety net for people who have hit bad times. But we can't allow them to become entangled in it. (p 5)

We must no longer be in the business of managing poverty. Instead we must challenge and support people to change their lives and make sure we are really doing our bit to put the conditions and opportunities in place that will make this possible. (p 9)

On housing, the report argues that 'faced with the scarcity of social housing many local authorities, for well-motivated reasons, and in line with national legislation, prioritised the neediest' (p 13). They have thereby 'rewarded failure' (p 14) rather than reflected 'the norms of reciprocity and fair reward for contribution' (p 12). The Council is now proposing to give priority for social housing to those in work or who contribute through activity like foster caring or serving in the army, 'creating the right incentives for people to improve their personal situation' (p 37).

What this means for those in housing need without a job is very unclear. They are presumably to be offered a safety net but not priority to desirable social housing, which goes to those 'making a contribution' in order to incentivise behaviour that the council considers desirable. But how does local government assess such contributions? Is a lone mother in a job making a bigger contribution to society than a lone mother looking after her children? Is a foster carer making a greater contribution than someone whose mental health has made it difficult to access employment and who is volunteering at the local community centre? These are invidious distinctions, which is why concepts of need are used in housing allocation and why the focus should be on greater social housing provision for those in need (ie a structural change seeking to meet universal need prior to a behavioural change).

Stears' concept of the relational state is also problematic. Stears puts forward the case for a state that supports relationships between citizens rather than a relational state and sees the term 'relational state' as an oxymoron. He argues that the state is a 'complex of agencies, including the government, that come together to standardise the social experience in a way that responds to the particular demands of place, time and dominant ideology' (Stears, 2012, p 38). A state, he suggests, can standardise in different ways: there is room for a 'left' standardisation that focuses on material equality, or a 'right' standardisation that focuses on the terms of contract and exchange (Stears, 2012, p 38). However, the drive to standardise is built into a state, which is therefore unable to deal with difference, contingency and unpredictability, which are central aspects of relationships. The state, therefore, should not focus on transforming its own relationships with the public, but on creating the conditions for citizens to relate better to one another. He suggests that a state should therefore build the conditions in which relationships between citizens can flourish and this requires four factors: spaces and *places* for relationships to flourish; *time* to build relationships; *organisations* that can sustain collective relationships; and the *power* and ability for groups of citizens to effect change.

The identification of four factors to support relationships is useful, particularly the focus on the power and ability for groups of citizens to effect change. However, the analysis fails fundamentally to explain what relationship people should have with the state (apart from applying pressure to it) to ensure that the state standardises in the way that furthers any common good, or can be justified through any ethical framework. Stears argues that where standardised treatment is of the essence, the state should provide services or regulate, rather than non-state agencies, and has to do so within an audit culture. His model in these situations is accountability to the public rather than deepening democracy. In these circumstances, he provides no guidance as to how citizens can be involved or how a councillor could seek to ensure that the views of those without power help to shape the standardised services provided by the council. This theory could be called the non-relational state, with the role of the councillor merely to facilitate participative democracy rather than engage with it.

Furthermore, Stears fails to deal with multi-level governance. At what level are we talking about the state standardising? If a small commune in France standardises in a different way from an adjacent commune, is the state therefore able to deal with difference and relationships within its area or would he argue that this is impossible since both communes are merely local government within the context of a uniform French state? Such a statement would be hard to defend empirically. Local government is usually justified through its ability to meet the different needs of citizens in different places and to provide a check on a more standardised, centralised state (Phillips, 1996). Its core rationale is dealing with difference, contingency and uncertainty. Local authority employees and professionals seek to deliver universal public services in a way that responds to the individual needs of residents. The caring professions, in particular, revolve around some emotional engagement and compassion and a sense of shared humanity (Hugman, 2005, pp 49–51). While relationships remain central in the delivery of local authority services, Stears's view of the relational state is of limited use within local government.

The relational state discussion is feeding into the development of Labour Party thinking and policy commitments. It emerges from Stears's belief that a state cannot just impose radical change. To develop a genuinely progressive democratic politics, you need to build a consensus in support of progressive values and to craft new institutions that will shape public attitudes and allow progressive conceptual goals to be realised (Stears, 2006). The fact that the paradigm of the relational state recognises the importance of giving those who are dependent on the welfare state more agency to challenge and to effect change is very welcome; hence the need to build capacity and organisations that can sustain collective relationships. But to be successful, this will need to be done within the context of a state that is actively pursuing greater equality. The language of resilience, quid pro quo and the argument that the relational state is essential because governments no longer have recourse to public spending to plug the gap (Pearce, 2012, p 46) – as if this is a permanent situation and not subject to political decision-making – all play into discourse about a smaller state rather than a more active state. Another approach needs to be found that links a state that pursues the reduction of inequality together with a deepening of democracy and voice for those without power. The following chapters will be seeking to develop this approach.

Conclusion

This chapter began by highlighting how neo-liberal policies of cuts in services and privatisation are creating inequality, which is to the disadvantage of all of us. It further argued that the private sector is becoming too dominant within the public sector and is starting to shape public services in its own interest. Moreover, the risk of failure and PPP modes of financing infrastructure will cause major problems for future generations. It was argued that in order to further well-being, it is necessary to change the way the local state is working so that issues of power and inequality are addressed.

It then argued that in developing alternatives to the New Right, it is not sufficient just to draw attention to the problems caused by neo-liberalism or to argue that nothing can be done within capitalism, it is also necessary to put forward alternative ideas, concepts and principles that support an alternative policy approach. Three paradigms were explored, each of which saw the state playing a different role:

- forging alliances in partnerships, acting as a community leader and joining up fragmented services through holistic policies;
- developing public value by focusing on what the public wants and what adds value to the public sphere;
- creating the conditions to allow those outside the state to have an equal chance to effect change over issues where relationships matter.

While none of these paradigms provided firm guidance for local authorities and all were flawed in some way, they have all raised useful issues.

The focus on relationships remains an important aspect of local public service: providing a care service where resources are limited and where the relationship between the carer and client is crucial is very different from providing a service in the private sector, where relationships matter but are underpinned by the aim of maximising sales. While partnerships between public agencies with targets from central government are often an obstacle to 'networked governance' or new forms of trust and bottom-up working that can lead to inclusive policymaking, the latter remain necessary for real democracy. And public value theory has raised the importance of values and principles in politics.

Public value theory does start to ask what society values and, as such, draws us back to questions asked by T.H. Green and discussed in Chapter Two. Is there a theory of local government that can be used to argue why local authorities should address inequality and social justice?

Chapter Four starts to provide this theory, building on the problems in practice and understanding that this chapter has identified.

Notes

[1] *The Guardian*, 26 June 2013. Available at: www.theguardian.com/ local-government-network/2013/jun/26/spending-review-2013-local-government

[2] See: www.education.gov.uk/researchandstatistics/statistics/a00201305/dfe-national-pupil-projections-future-trends-in-pupil-numbers-december-2011

[3] Fitch Ratings and Oxford Economics (2011) *Gauging the benefits, costs, and sustainability of US stimulus* suggests that the US policy response to the recession increased aggregate GDP by more than 4%, two and three years after the trough of the last crisis. See: www.oxfordeconomics.com/my-oxford/projects/128929

[4] See also the Guardian Datablog, 14 November 2012. Available at: www. guardian.co.uk/news/datablog/2012/nov/14/council-cuts-england-detailed

[5] *Independent*, 12 July 2013. Available at: www.independent.co.uk/news/uk/ politics/g4s-and-serco-face-50-million-fraud-inquiry-8703245.html

[6] For example, see Oxford Economics (2012). The savings made on privatising 1.8% of housing management services are projected to the full stock, and a largely unsubstantiated claim is made that £675 million savings could be made by outsourcing the whole stock to the private sector. APSE (2011) provides several examples of insourcing housing management to save money and improve quality. Both Basildon and Ealing local authorities have abandoned using **Arm's Length Management Organisations** for administering their housing stock, and each expects to save around £1 million on their budgets annually (APSE, 2013, p 31).

[7] Inequality actually declined in the first two years of the Coalition Government, driven down by falling medium incomes and a drop in the income of top earners. However, the Gini coefficient remains high at 0.34, the same level as 1990 (Cribb et al, 2012, p 2), and is likely to rise sharply from April 2013 as benefit cuts bite and the 50% income tax rate is cut.

[8] The ability of private capital to extract surplus value and profit.

[9] See: https://www.gov.uk/government/organisations/behavioural-insights-team

FOUR

An ethical framework for local government

This chapter seeks to develop an ethical framework that can act as a guide for action for councillors, municipal leaders and officers in any local government context. Unless policymakers have a clear concept of the fundamental purpose of their actions, they will be blown this way and that – following the latest central government initiative. It is rather like pilates: the body politic needs a core strength to be able to operate effectively and sustainably. This chapter will argue that **inherent need** can provide that basic strength. The concept of need 'connects an understanding of our *interdependency* as human beings with arguments about the *rights* that we can assert against each other' (Dean, 2010, p 2, emphases in original).

The ethical framework that I develop here brings together a number of interrelated concepts around needs, rights and social justice. As a whole, they provide a set of challenges that councillors and other policymakers can use to interrogate a policy proposal to see if it accords with the ethical framework. The chapter is organised as a series of challenges that can be used to question local authority policy. Some of these challenges have already been identified in Chapter Three. The importance of addressing inequality, both of resources and power, is a central theme in the ethical framework. Other elements of the framework are introduced in this chapter: for example, the task of dealing with diversity and with future generations.

The ethical framework in this chapter is my personal answer to tricky questions of what local authorities should be doing. Others with differing political views will want to try and prioritise, or to add challenges or remove them. There is plenty of scope to interpret how these challenges should be addressed: I neither want to, nor am I attempting to, limit political debate. Clearly, also, moral norms are different in time and place. The issues of future generations and social rights, for example, have risen to greater prominence over the last 40 to 50 years. So, the challenges may change over time, but my attempt to develop a framework from a strong philosophical and ethical base presents a task for those who do not agree with the conclusions reached. I am reflecting on values and principles and what can be 'systematically deduced to be right' (Dean, 2010, p 172). If readers disagree that these normative challenges are of fundamental importance, they need in their turn to reflect on their own values and principles and derive their own ethical framework. And any ethical framework has to stand up to reasoned scrutiny and debate, including with those whose voices are not usually heard. The ethical framework is presented in the following box before being elaborated within the chapter.

The ethical framework's challenges

- Does the policy rest on a firm ethical foundation?
- Does the policy reinforce mutual obligations through universal provision?
- Does the policy address rights?
- Does the policy address distributive justice?
- Does the policy lead to a deeper understanding of citizenship and the common good?
- Does the policy address recognition and emancipation?
- Does the policy help professionals deal with day-to-day ethical problems?
- Does the policy consider future generations and promote sustainability?

Does the policy rest on a firm ethical foundation?

The word 'need' is used in a variety of ways, covering wants or **interpreted needs** (needs that we claim or argue for) and basic needs or inherent needs (needs we have because we are human beings). Dean (2010) starts his book on *Understanding human need* with 30 definitions of need and there are those that argue that the word 'need' is used in so many ways, both as a noun and a verb, that it can serve no purpose. In today's consumer society, when we talk about needs, we are usually referring to wants or perceived needs: the need for new clothes, a holiday or a mobile phone. We may be talking about psychological needs, the need for love and relationships. Or, we may use the language of normative needs, arguing that a young person needs to stay out of trouble or get a job.

Here, I will be using the concept of inherent need as a noun, arguing that all human beings have the same basic needs. A theory of human needs can therefore underpin moral action, providing a reason why local decision-makers should take certain actions (Doyal and Gough, 1991). There is, however, a relationship between inherent and interpreted needs, which will be further discussed later.

Doyal and Gough (1991) start by looking at all the relativist theories of need. Some liberal theories suggest that only individuals can decide their priority needs, so there are no such things as collective or social needs that can provide a justification for public services. Other relativist authors, like Townsend (1987), state that deprivation is relative in time and space and therefore need is relative and subject to disagreement. Doyal and Gough show how all the theories actually presuppose what they purport to reject – namely, that it is possible to identify objective and universal human goals that individuals must somehow achieve if they are to be able to take advantage of life chances. Since physical survival and personal autonomy are the preconditions for individual action in any culture,[1] they constitute the most basic human needs. Basic needs are therefore defined as those needs that must be satisfied to some degree before actors can effectively participate in life to achieve any other goals they want to pursue (Doyal and Gough, 1991, p 54). The authors clarify that, in our current world, physical survival can be seen as supporting health, and personal autonomy consists of some level of understanding or ability to make informed choices about what should be done and how it should be done. For this understanding, both cognitive skills and mental health (cognitive and emotional capacity) are required, as are the freedom and opportunities to participate. Their theory around the necessity to enable personal autonomy has parallels with that of T.H. Green discussed in Chapter Two.

For Doyal and Gough, these basic needs are cross-cultural and cannot be seen as relative. Most societies have rules and institutions that seek to satisfy these needs: stopping people harming each other; providing some basic facilities, such as clean water, shelter and basic health care; and supporting child-rearing and socialisation. How you satisfy these needs, however, depends on culturally specific factors: how wealthy the country is; how the society's rules for production, distribution and consumption are agreed and organised; and how social policy is developed. So, the policies that are used to meet the needs vary in time and place. But this does not mean that you cannot say anything about obligations and duties and what 'ought' to be done.

The attraction of this approach is that it provides a clear argument about why local authorities should be delivering basic services:

> All collectively provided services are deliberately designed to meet certain socially recognised 'needs'; they are manifestations, first, of society's will to survive as an organic whole and, secondly of the expressed wish of all people to

assist the survival of some people. (Titmuss, 2001 [1955],
p 62, quoted in Dean, 2010, p 3)

People who have poor health and no personal autonomy cannot help
themselves. We ought therefore to seek to address these issues as best
we can through collective provision or regulation, so that no one is
prevented from accessing the same level of needs satisfaction as we
ourselves claim. If, for example, we believe we have a basic need for
clean water to survive, we should support policymakers in ensuring
everyone has clean water. Furthermore, since basic needs are predicated
on us being human beings, we should support action both nationally
and internationally: 'Just as everyone has a strict duty to support the
collective provision of welfare within their own national boundary so
we have the same obligation internationally' (Doyal and Gough, 1991,
p 107). Similarly, human beings in future generations will have the same
basic needs as ourselves, so we need to protect environmental resources
to ensure that future generations can address their basic needs:

> To so damage the environment as to jeopardise the long
> term survival of a form of life which we believe embodies
> the good is to renounce our commitment to that good – no
> more and no less. If we believe a form of life to be good, then
> its story should continue. (Doyal and Gough, 1991, p 145)

Inherent needs therefore provide a firm foundation for local authority
action, but this still leaves open a significant debate around how to
prioritise satisfaction of different needs in our current society and in
different local authority areas. Councillors, whose role involves deciding
which needs should be addressed and how they should be addressed,
move from the concept of basic needs to interpreted needs. They are
contributing to a social construction of needs. This raises a key question
of how to achieve a common or agreed understanding of human needs.
To assist in this debate, further dimensions of the ethical framework
have to be developed.

Does the policy reinforce mutual obligations through universal provision?

The preceding discussion of basic needs placed an obligation on the
state to meet such needs. If this obligation is to be met, it is important
that we deepen our understanding of mutual obligation. Chapter
Three showed how market fundamentalism was increasing inequality

and marginalising those in need, thereby weakening society's sense of mutual obligation. In this context, it is helpful to look at the theorists who have dealt with the commodification of public services.

Polanyi (2001 [1944]) argued that attempts to dis-embed markets from social relationships and look for self-regulation by liberalising control over how land, money and labour are used are self-defeating and will always create a crisis and a subsequent movement calling for social and environmental protection. Polanyi wrote his book, *The Great Transformation*, towards the end of the Second World War and argued that the Industrial Revolution had led to the disintegration of communities, ruptured solidarities and despoiled nature. The attempt to liberate markets had made 'fictitious commodities' of social, ecological and public goods, which could be bought and sold without any regard to the human, social or natural consequences. He argued that the resulting movement for social protection culminated in Germany with fascism. But he suggested that there were others ways to 'defang' markets – removing their sting without destroying them altogether. His work foreshadowed that of Esping-Andersen (1990, 1996), who argued that de-commodifying services and limiting market forces through the creation of the welfare state not only opened up services for those in need and provided social protection, but also strengthened the position of the less powerful in society, enabling them to bargain more effectively for social rights and social justice agendas (Mayo, 2014).

Polanyi's (and Esping-Andersen's) argument is that the **commodification** of social relationships and ecology actually *depletes* fundamental resources, such as family and community support or air and water quality. The commodification leads to a dysfunctional society that will ultimately make more demands on national and local government services, as we have seen in the previous two chapters.

Some powerful examples of commodification and its impact have been given more recently by Michael Sandel (2012a, 2012b). In the US, you can currently buy: a prison-cell upgrade for $90 a night; the services of an Indian surrogate mother for $8,000; your doctor's mobile phone number from $1,500 per year; or immigration rights for $500,000. You can earn money to pay for these privileges by: selling space on your forehead to display a tattoo advert for $10,000; fighting in Somalia or Afghanistan for a private military contractor for up to $1,000 a day; and by queuing overnight on Capitol Hill to reserve a place for a lobbyist who wants to attend a congressional hearing for $15–$20 an hour. Sandel concludes that market values have come to play a greater and greater role in social life, corroding the way we value public goods and increasing inequality.

The implication of this argument for local government is that in order to meet basic needs and underpin the mutual obligation and attachment that people have for one another, it is necessary to de-commodify and provide universal public services. Chapter Three criticised the way the London Borough of Newham had used its policy to reinforce concepts of the deserving and undeserving poor. The Newham approach is, however, contradictory and, at the same time, recognises the importance of universal services. Their analysis has identified the lack of a good start in life as a key factor in reducing the ability of residents to make the most of life chances. In the language of Doyal and Gough, this means that widening educational support in the early years becomes a basic need for future personal autonomy. By making such services universal, the council is reinforcing solidarity and support for such interventions.

Meeting universal needs

The London Borough of Newham has argued that many current welfare services are only delivered to the very poor and fail to meet the needs of those on low incomes (Newham London, 2011). Its analysis focuses particularly on the early years and the need to build what they have called the 'resilience' of the local population. The council believes that 'universal services are a vital way to ensure all children get the best start in life. They have a broader reach and don't stigmatise recipients' (Newham London, 2013, p 19). The following initiatives have been taken:

- Newham is one of a handful of local authorities in the country to offer universal free school meals for all primary school children, supporting 3,300 households with children living in poverty who were not eligible for them under the national scheme in 2012. Evaluation has found that pupils made between four and eight weeks more progress over a two-year period than similar pupils in other areas as a result of this provision (Newham London, 2013, p 18).
- The Every Newham Child a Reader guarantee enables the universal teaching of phonics in participating schools. The scheme offers one-to-one support for children who are falling behind their peers. In addition, children are supported by reading volunteers drawn from local businesses – like Westfield, John Lewis and London City Airport – the council and the local community. Results for schools participating in phase one are up 15% and are now on average 11% ahead of the national average (Newham London, 2013, p 22).
- The Every Child a Musician scheme offers a free musical instrument and music tuition to all children in Years 5, 6 and 7. It has been taken up by 91% of children across participating schools. An evaluation by the Institute of

Education found that tuition is of high quality and that children are enjoying learning and have high levels of social inclusion, health and happiness. By the summer of 2013, around 10,000 children had received free music tuition (Newham London, 2013, p 23).
- The Every Child a Sportsperson scheme has been developed from a successful pilot with 2,000 children in 2012. From April 2013, all Year 7 pupils could choose to participate in a range of 20 sports. They are encouraged to join a club for the activity that best suits their talent, thereby driving up activity and helping kids stay healthy (Newham London, 2013, p 41).

Does the policy address rights?

The need for personal autonomy is clear, but it would mean very little in a society like North Korea, where the state is so repressive and information so tightly controlled that there is no awareness of alternatives. Doyal and Gough therefore argue that people must have critical autonomy that goes beyond personal autonomy. They define critical autonomy as the opportunity to engage in action and debate to change the moral norms and institutions of the country in which one is situated (Doyal and Gough, 1991, p 68). This entails the capacity to compare cultural rules, to reflect upon the rules of one's own culture, to work with others to change them and, in extremis, to move to another culture if all else fails (Doyal and Gough, 1991, p 187). To do this, one needs freedom, agency and political freedoms (such as free speech, freedom of conscience, free movement).

A very similar argument is put forward by Amartya Sen (2009), but he uses the language of capabilities instead of need. Sen defines capability as the capacity of a person to be able to choose between different combinations of being and doing and to achieve his/her own way of living. In other words, like Doyal and Gough, Sen argues that people must be free and enabled to live as they choose. So, capability involves ability, freedom to choose and achievement. The concept addresses personal capacity, the wider society that supports the freedom to choose and, finally, power differences that will affect achievement. All three elements need to be tackled to achieve justice.[2] Sen argues that capabilities generate obligations: the duty to reduce inequalities in the overall opportunities and advantages of individuals in society to enable them to lead flourishing lives. The capabilities concept rests on the idea that there are things to do and be that the individual will choose and that these will emerge from reasoned debate and a sense of injustice. Sen argues that the duty to make a difference rests on the understanding that if you have the power and ability (capability) to reduce injustice, there are strong and reasoned arguments for doing just that (Sen, 2009, p 269). He draws a parallel to the obligation of a mother to the powerless child. Where there is an asymmetry of power, the person with power has responsibilities (Sen, 2009, p 205). And addressing capabilities generates obligations that can lead to demands for universal rights and entitlements and institutional change (Carpenter and Speeden, 2007, p 173). Local authorities, with some power to make a difference, should have a reasoned debate about how they should be reducing injustice and increasing capabilities.

Meeting needs and developing capabilities therefore requires some basic rights to be accepted by society. Furthermore, rights add two additional dimensions to the discussion of need. First, some rights have legal status and therefore bring institutional backing and legitimation to a 'need'. Second, rights imply an entitlement and have become a rallying call for groups of citizens (women, the poor, trade unions) trying to codify needs as a universal legal right; the use of the term 'rights' has a motivational force.

There remains a debate as to whether rights are naturally given or socially constructed; whether they are inalienable or culturally defined (Newman, K., 2012, p 42). It is clear that recognised rights are evolving over time and recently claimed rights can be seen to be more closely related to what Dean has called 'interpretative needs'. Some authors argue that there are four generations of rights that have evolved over time, while noting that this classification does not signify a hierarchy of rights.

The first, 'natural rights', belong to man 'in right of his existence' and 'civil rights' belong to man 'in right of his being a member of society' (Paine, 1791/92, p 2). These reflect basic needs but also include liberal rights such as free speech, free movement and freedom of conscience.

The second generation are economic, social and cultural rights. In 1948, in the aftermath of the Second World War, there was a shift from seeing rights as a way of protecting the individual against the state – the 'negative freedoms' involved in natural rights – to providing the comprehensive social and welfare rights that are required to provide an equal opportunity to participate in civic life (positive freedoms). The United Nations (UN) adopted and proclaimed the *Universal Declaration of Human Rights*. This was institutionalised through two covenants: the International Covenant on Civil and Political Rights (ICCPR) and the International Covenant on Economic, Social and Cultural Rights (ICESCR), which was created in 1966, and came into force in 1976. The Council of Europe agreed the European Convention on Human

Rights (ECHR) in 1950, which has subsequently been incorporated into domestic law, and EU law also defines and protects rights in such areas as employment and gender equality. While many countries have only ratified one of the two UN covenants, no country has explicitly rejected the Declaration.[3] At the Vienna Conference in 1993, where 171 countries participated, it was proclaimed that:

> human rights are universal, indivisible and interdependent and interrelated. The international community must treat human rights globally in a fair and equal manner, on the same footing, and with the same emphasis … it is the duty of States … to promote and protect all human rights.[4]

In all the treaties, the primary contract is between the state and its citizens – with the citizens as 'rights-holders' and the state as 'duty-bearer' (Newman, K., 2012, pp 46–7).

The focus on the individual as the rights-holder has led many to criticise the rights approach. It has been argued that not only does legal redress provide a tortuous and relatively weak way of addressing economic and social inequality (Dean, 2010, pp 151–6), but also that it fails to deal with the structural reasons that cause infringements of rights in the first place. So, the Convention for Elimination of All Forms of Discrimination Against Women (CEDAW) in 1979 may have led to stronger laws against rape, but by focusing on individual women, the structural causes of violence and oppression were still ignored (Newman, K., 2012, p 51). A rights approach can lead to reform of the wider society being neglected (Newman, J. and Clarke, 2009, p 157).

There is now a move to claim the third generation of rights, collective rights. Collective rights promote solidarity and can be used to mobilise particular groups of people. The UN Declaration of the Right to Development in 1986 is an example of a collective right that recognises the impact of unequal power relations at the global level, and had it had stronger legal backing than a declaration, it would have obliged, rather than just encouraged Northern governments to support Southern populations. These collective rights are clearly not universal, in that they apply to specific groups of people in specific cultural contexts and are dynamic, changing over time. Collective rights usually stem from a bottom-up group challenge to the existing society. They are drawn from basic needs but are claims by groups of people for a specific obligation from their government. The right of indigenous peoples is a further example. This type of collective right is discussed later in this chapter in relation to social justice. The fourth generation of rights relates to sustainability, which is discussed in the final section of this chapter.

A focus on rights in policy development and implementation, or rights-based practice, has advanced further in international development policy than in local government policy. Increasingly, local government in the global North is drawing lessons from rights-based and participative practice in the South, in areas such as action around the **Millennium Development Goals** (MDGs), reflective practice (which will be discussed more in Chapter Five) and participatory budgeting. There is evidence in development literature that the use of rights terminology has both strengthened international development work at the local level and enabled development activists to broaden their practice, focusing on the systemic causes of poverty and inequality (Newman, K., 2012, p 57). Rights-based projects have considerably more success in 'attaining impacts that will lead to sustained positive change ... They link citizens and state in new ways and create systems and mechanisms that ensure that all actors can be part of accountable development processes' (Crawford, 2007, pp 8–9, quoted in Newman, K., 2012, p 57).

So, although there are debates on how to prioritise and operationalise all the rights that are contained in international human rights treaties and conventions and around how new collective rights fit into the legal framework, there is clear evidence about the advantages of rights-based practice in public policy. It has motivated important struggles, from the suffragettes, to the civil rights movement, to gay pride. Such struggles focus on participation, with groups of individuals who feel their rights have not been recognised or have been abused working together to change the dominant culture and claim their rights. Those who claim their rights and challenge existing society are demonstrating the critical autonomy that Doyal and Gough see as necessary, in addition to meeting basic needs. This people-centred approach is complemented by a focus on the importance of government accountability. Rights-based approaches are not just about engaging beneficiaries, but also about challenging existing power relationships and calling on governments to act. But a rights-based campaign must also tackle power inequalities:

> Unless local people are able to determine which rights to fight for, ascribe content to the right and make the link between their context and wider causes of inequality it is likely that rights discourse will be co-opted by the powerful and used to expand a specific view, to rescue the 'victims' of uncivil regimes. (Newman, K., 2008, p 16)

So, in a UK context, unless council tenants have a role in defining the right to a home and challenging the inequality in the housing market, those in power can define such a right as the Right to Buy or a minimum requirement for shelter, with no right to a spare bedroom or accommodation near family, social support structures and available jobs.

This suggests that the *process* of securing these rights is as important as the outcome itself. The process must enable culturally specific and appropriate ways of implementing rights in practice; moving from the conception of human rights as minimum standards of a life with dignity, to creating space and skills for people to articulate additional rights, relevant to their specific context. Councillors have an important role in facilitating these processes and creating the spaces for rights to be discussed by disadvantaged groups.

From a local authority point of view, working on rights is not just about engaging with legal frameworks, but involves exploring power relations and giving content to rights in specific contexts, for specific groups of people. This could include refocusing on ideas of 'peoples' rights', in addition to universal human rights.

The rights of the child

There have been campaigns by non-governmental organisations (NGOs), often linking in with local authorities, to improve early years provision (see the Children's Rights Alliance for England at: http://www.crae.org.uk). In 1989, the world's leaders officially recognised the human rights of all children and young people under 18 by signing the UN Convention on the Rights of the Child. The Convention says that every child has:

- The right to a *childhood* (including protection from harm).
- The right to be *educated* (including all girls and boys completing primary school).
- The right to be *healthy* (including having clean water, nutritious food and medical care).
- The right to be treated *fairly* (including changing laws and practices that are unfair on children).
- The right to be *heard* (including considering children's views).

All UN member states, except for the US and Somalia, have approved the Convention. The UK signed it on 19 April 1990 and it came into force in the UK on 15 January 1992 (see: www.unicef.org.uk/UNICEFs-Work/Our-mission/UN-Convention/). Research has shown that high-quality investment in Early Childhood

Education and Care from birth is essential to ensure that the UN Convention on the Rights of the Child is implemented for young children.

The Scottish National Party (SNP) in Scotland stated in their election manifesto: 'We will set out the steps we need to take to increase childcare support here in Scotland to match the best elsewhere in Europe'. The Scottish government, together with local authorities in Scotland, are now moving to give content to the rights of a child, learning from an existing scheme in Norway. Like Norway, they are proposing a universal scheme with subsidies related to parental income and a cap on parental contributions to childcare. They argue that: 'Universal early childhood services have many of the same advantages as universally available, government-funded primary and secondary school: bringing together children from different backgrounds, commanding broad and sustainable public support and engendering greater public concern for quality' (Children in Scotland ,2011a, p 1).

Norway has developed a fully integrated Early Childhood Education and Care system since 1995. In 2003, a legislative amendment to the existing Day Care Institution Act made the provision of early years services a legal duty of local authorities. The local authority: keeps a register for use by national insurance offices for calculating and disbursing cash benefits; administers grants for private and voluntary kindergartens; and is responsible for a coordinated admissions policy and process intended to ensure 'equal treatment of children and equal treatment of municipal and privately-owned day care institutions' (Children in Scotland, 2011a, p 2). From 2009, there has been a legal entitlement for all children to a subsidised full day place in childcare following the end of paid maternity/paternity care at 12 months.

Norwegians continue to rely on families and informal services, but 75% of children aged one to two years are cared for in the regulated services offering flexible part-time and full-time care. Of children aged three to five, 96% attend these settings, with 52% attending for more than 30 hours per week (Children in Scotland, 2011a, 2011b).

Does the policy address distributive justice?

Needs and rights are individually based. Can we go further than a theory of need and establish the institutions for a just society and what they should do? And can we do this in a way that deals with existing unequal power relationships in society? As Sen (2009, p vii) says: 'What moves us, reasonably enough, is not the realization that the world falls short of being completely just – which few of us expect – but that there are clearly remediable injustices around us which we want to eliminate.' It was this realisation that drove the Victorian radicals and continues to motivate councillors today. But what is meant by a just society and what is injustice? My position is that a just society requires attention to three aspects, which will be looked at in the next three sections: distributive justice; the development of citizenship and an attempt to define well-being and the common good; and recognition and emancipation. Here, we start with distributive justice.

Chapter Three has emphasised the injustice of inequality, both of power and resources. It was this injustice that Rawls (1971) sought to address when outlining the principles that should be contained in a social contract that governed our collective lives. He was concerned that our concept of justice should not be dominated by vested interests and by those with the most power and argued that any social contract had to be based on fairness. He suggested that if people got together to work out the principles of justice through a 'veil of ignorance', which meant that they did not know which position they would occupy in the world (eg whether they were rich or poor, black or white, male or female) and so had no vested interests, they would come up with two principles of justice to inform the social contract. These are:

1. Each person has an equal right to a fully adequate scheme of equal basic liberties which is compatible with a similar scheme of liberties for all.
2. Social and economic inequalities are to satisfy two conditions. First they must be attached to offices and positions open to all under conditions of fair equality of opportunity; and second, they must be to the greatest benefit of the least advantaged members of society. (Rawls, 2011 [1982], p 5)

There is plenty of criticism of Rawls' theory, the social contract approach (Sen, 2009) and particularly of his second principle (eg Cohen, 2008; Sandel, 2009, ch 7). However, the theory is very useful in promoting his concepts of liberty, defined around freedom in personal life and removed from the market and private property rights, entitlement or meritocracy. It no doubt influenced Doyal and Gough's concept of personal autonomy. Rawls' concept of justice stems from fairness and objective reasoning based on his principles, rather than reasoning biased by one's position in the world. He affirms that people have moral powers: they have a sense of justice and a conception of the good (Sen, 2009, p 62).

The Greater Manchester Poverty Commission

Initiated by a small group of Greater Manchester Members of Parliament (MPs), the Commission includes representatives from key sectors, such as: community and faith; advice and welfare; trades unions; social housing; business; a councillor who is chair of the police authority; and the media. The Bishop of Manchester is the independent chair of the Commission. It published its findings on 15 January 2013. The Commission found that those living in poverty face hunger, isolation, fear and frustration. The largest group, living on the lowest incomes, are families with children and home-owners. Many of those living in poverty are in part-time work, low-waged, suffer from fuel poverty and food poverty and have reduced access to basic services, such as transport and technology.

1. Food, fuel and finance
The Commissioners called for the introduction and development of social enterprises in the banking, food and energy sectors, suggesting that local authorities and others be encouraged to set up their own energy provider companies, credit unions and bulk food purchase 'supermarkets/foodbanks'. This would see shareholder profit replaced with reduced prices, social responsibility and greater benefit to the local community.

2. Access to key services
The Commissioners called for steps to be taken to improve access to key services for those living in poverty. This includes the expansion of free transport, affordable broadband, free legal services and quality childcare.

3. Jobs and growth
The Commissioners called on the private and statutory sectors to promote the adoption of a living wage rather than minimum wage and argued for a Social City Deal with the government to give more control to local authorities over a local welfare agenda.

4. Monitoring – moving forward
The Commissioners wished to see the establishment of an ongoing poverty working group and the development of a Greater Manchester Index, so that the extent of poverty across Greater Manchester can be known and understood (see: www.povertymanchester.org/).

There are some concerns that Rawls' theory is too abstract and takes no account of actual behaviour, which is inevitably influenced by the current distribution of power and personal and societal contexts

(Sen, 2009, pp 65–9). However, there are circumstances where local authorities could promote a discussion around the content of a policy area that addresses inequalities, asking participants (a scrutiny committee, a partnership or a user group) to act as if they are covered with a 'veil of ignorance'. The Greater Manchester Poverty Commission (see preceding box) is an example of such an exercise. A further example would be in developing local authorities' new public health role. The reality is that individuals do not know what position they will occupy in relation to their future health and can therefore more easily grasp the social justice of targeting resources at health inequalities.

Good health and emotional well-being have already been identified as basic needs that must be met to enable people to participate in life and meet their goals. The Victorian councillors were well aware of this and sought to tackle issues of water, sewage, cleanliness, open space and education. Yet, health inequalities remain and are increasing (Campbell, 2010). The World Health Organisation (WHO) and the review of health inequalities in the UK in 2010 (the Marmot Review) have both made the case for action to address the social determinants of health (Campbell, 2010, p 5).

Local authorities can have an impact on the social determinants of health through a range of powers: from education to environmental regulatory power; from speed limits on local roads to promoting active lifestyles through leisure and sports facilities; and from addressing fuel poverty to supporting those with mental health issues. Tackling health inequalities requires recognition of the fact that black and minority ethnic groups, especially those of Pakistani and Bangladeshi origin (being among the most deprived), have the worst health and the lowest life expectancy. It also involves recognition of the 'inverse care law' (Dorling, 2010, p 16): the fact that parks and access to doctors, schools and other services are all better in wealthy than poor areas. When local services are not very good, they both help maintain inequalities and can increase them.

The following case study is one of many that can be found on the Local Government Association website. It has been selected because it demonstrates a number of elements that are relevant here: the need for evidence on health inequality in access to resources and services; the role of local authority scrutiny in exposing health inequalities; the importance of inclusive debate where issues of justice and policy details can be established; and monitoring and building an evidence base to support a long-term inclusive process.

Darlington Borough Council open space strategy

Darlington has significant health inequalities, particularly within the urban area. The council's scrutiny committees prioritised further investigation of the health inequalities between groups of children and young people. This highlighted that people living in deprived parts of the town were less likely to be close to high-quality spaces. In 2007, the council thus adopted a 10-year open space strategy, which was followed by a play pitch strategy and a sport and recreation facilities strategy. The strategies set out the potential for reducing health inequalities through better access to quality open spaces. Eleven wards were prioritised based on their levels of deprivation. These areas were the first to receive funding to improve the quality of open spaces, with the emphasis on facilities and improvements that would appeal to young people. However, local people were first involved in decision-making since play spaces can be unpopular as they can attract teenagers in the evenings. In March 2010, the council, in association with the residents' group 'Friends of the Denes', made a successful bid to the Parks for People Lottery Fund. Work on sustainable travel and cycling has also helped to provide funding to put walking and cycling paths through some of the open spaces in the borough. The council is monitoring the use of open spaces, and draws on a strong network of friends' groups as well as Rangers' views for anecdotal evidence on site use (see: www.local.gov.uk/web/guest/health/-/journal_content/56/10171/3510714/ARTICLE-TEMPLATE).

Does the policy lead to a deeper understanding of citizenship and the common good?

Political theorists from Aristotle through to Michael Sandel (2009) have argued that politics does not merely have instrumental value. It is not just about achieving certain ends, such as, for example, new roads and schools, or some redistribution of wealth. It also has intrinsic value. People's lives are enhanced by taking part in the democratic process and by being active citizens. The purpose of politics is threefold: to enable people to reason in public; to form good citizens; and to teach people how to lead the good life. This search for the common good was also a fundamental aspect of Green's philosophy, discussed in Chapter One.

I am not suggesting here that one concept of the common good can ultimately be agreed. There will be questions about: the imposition of majority views of the good life on minorities; obligations to family, for example, trumping the individual rights of women; and traditional conceptions of conventions and institutions being favoured rather than bringing in views from a variety of cultures. Sen (2009) argues against the attempt to define the perfectly just society, suggesting that the definition is neither necessary nor sufficient to provide a guide to a reasoned choice of policies, strategies or institutions designed to enhance justice. It is not necessary because you can have reasoned debate about how to reduce injustices, such as famines or torture, without a definition of the perfectly just society. It is not sufficient because the definition of a just society does not allow you to compare different policies, which will only yield partial solutions. But even if a complete concept of the good society will not be agreed, reasoned debate about social justice and the common good can strengthen democracy and give purpose to deliberation. Sen (2009) also argues that such a debate should involve a diverse range of people with input from those outside the normal group, 'the impartial spectator', thereby reducing the dominance of entrenched tradition and culture. This has implications for local authority scrutiny committees, where councillors from different backgrounds can engage in debate and also ensure that they receive input from those whose voices are not always heard.

The destructive impact of commodification on notions of the common good has already been discussed. Commodification combined with inequality makes it difficult to cultivate a sense of community and understanding of the common good or the partnerships and new forms of trust that were discussed in Chapter Three. It also results in residualisation. This is the process by which the affluent withdraw from public services, leaving them to those who cannot afford anything else. This leads to poorer services as the wealthy are unwilling to support them with their taxes, invest in them themselves or campaign for improvements. It subsequently leads to a reduction in public investment, as highlighted in Chapter Three. Public services become stigmatised. The process has been most evident in housing, with the commodification through the 'Right to Buy', followed by a decline in investment in new council housing. This commodification has led to ghettos of the poor on council estates and fewer places where people from different backgrounds interact: 'The hollowing out of the public realm makes it difficult to cultivate solidarity and a sense of community on which democratic citizenship depends' (Sandel, 2009, p 267). Sandel concludes that 'a more robust public engagement with our moral disagreements could provide a stronger, not a weaker, basis for mutual respect ... it is a more promising basis for a just society' (Sandel, 2009, pp 268–9). The process of local residents debating what constitutes the common good is therefore an important aspect of developing citizenship, solidarity and social justice, and local authorities should be promoting such debate. Habermas's notion of a deliberative democracy provides an amplification of this view and will be discussed in Chapter Five.

Liverpool Come2gether

The Liverpool Come2gether campaign is about making Liverpool the UK's exemplar city for fairness. Their independent Fairness Commission, established by the City Council, is campaigning to encourage as many businesses and organisations in the city as possible to get involved by adopting the fairness principles and charter that the Commission developed. An annual fairness summit is planned, with the first meeting in the autumn of 2013, and there will be an annual fairness audit to measure progress on implementation (see: http://liverpoolfairnesscommission.com/come2gether.php).

Does the policy address recognition and emancipation?

So far, the emphasis has been on: fairness and distributive justice; positive liberty or freedom to choose one's own lifestyle; and the value of taking part in the democratic process, with everyone participating as peers to determine policies that affect them. But there is a further dimension to social justice: recognition, or the respect and disrespect that demonstrates how society values different people (Fraser, 2011a).

For Nancy Fraser, recognition is not about identity, but about fairness. It enables full terms of parity in participation. It is enhanced through emancipation, which opposes all forms of domination and oppression. So, the emancipation of slaves, the liberation of women and the opposition to caste societies all enhance recognition. She also raises the issue of refugees, who can be excluded from citizenship of a particular community, impairing their ability to participate as peers in social interaction.

Nancy Fraser (2011b) builds on Polanyi's analysis, discussed earlier. She supports much of his analysis but argues that he failed to see other injustices beyond those caused by a free market. As the solution to commodification, he promoted a form of social protection that did not reduce domination, particularly the domination of women. She argues that each of three movements – marketisation, social protection and emancipation – has benefits, but that any combination of two movements must be mediated by the third. So, free markets and full recognition and emancipation without social protection would lead to a society with no solidarity and no social/community regeneration – it would be without Sandel's 'common good'. Allowing smokers to pursue their habit in all locations has been justified in this context. It is therefore necessary to mediate these movements by considering social protection. Similarly, without emancipation, Polanyi's markets and social protection could embed domination. The new Universal Credit, while promoting work and social protection, fails to recognise the impact on second household earners, who are mostly women. The impact on women if benefits are paid only to the man in the household is also ignored. Finally, Fraser suggests that emancipation and protection on their own might endanger negative liberty, the freedom from interference by other people. They therefore need to be mediated by the market.

Fraser therefore makes the case for constraining markets, giving them a moral and ethical underpinning. She also provides a clearer guide to action, not only dealing with individual freedom and distributive fairness, but also emphasising the need for recognition and an emancipated version of social protection.

Local authorities have been leaders in promoting recognition since the early 1980s, as explained in Chapter Two, and continue to be very active in this area, working with their residents and public sector partners (see Russell et al, 2010). The Equality Act 2010 contained a new integrated Equality Duty on public bodies, bringing together existing duties (race, gender and disability) and extending them to cover age, sexual orientation and religion or belief. Its approach had, however, already been prefigured in the local authorities' **Improvement and Development Agency**'s (IDeA's) equality framework for local government (IDeA, 2009). This uses 10 dimensions of 'substantive freedom' and a wider definition of equality, based on the idea of equal life chances, to provide a framework for both monitoring and deepening the understanding of equality. It builds on the work of Doyal and Gough, and Sen, discussed earlier.

The equalities framework for local government: 10 dimensions of equality

- **Longevity** – including avoiding premature mortality.
- **Physical security** – including freedom from violence and physical and/or sexual abuse.
- **Health** – including well-being and access to high-quality health care.
- **Education** – including being able to be creative, to acquire skills and qualifications, and having access to training and lifelong learning.

- **Standard of living** – including being able to live with independence and security and covering: nutrition, clothing, housing, warmth, utilities, social services and transport.
- **Productive and valued activities** – such as access to employment, a positive experience in the workplace, work–life balance and being able to care for others.
- **Individual, family and social life** – including self-development, having independence and equality in relationships and marriage.
- **Participation, influence and voice** – including participation in decision-making and democratic life.
- **Identity, expression and self-respect** – including freedom of belief and religion.
- **Legal security** – including equality and non-discrimination before the law and equal treatment within the criminal justice system (IDeA, 2009).

Local authority councillors play a leading role in ensuring recognition and emancipation. Equality training is normally a central part of any councillor training.

Training elected members in Tower Hamlets

The Members' Diversity and Equality Group looked at all schemes in place and picked out the trickiest issues, which were largely ones that did not fit specific portfolios: preventing violent extremism; homophobic hate; and policies for refugees and new communities. One approach was to develop a scenario: 200 words on a postcard describing a particular situation – for example, a gay Muslim boy with problems at home and school. The group had to decide what the issues were for the local authority as a service provider. They had a specialist on hand to offer advice. Since then, a similar format has been used for member development in relation to the single equality duty (Russell et al, 2010, p 39).

Does the policy help professionals deal with day-to-day ethical problems?

An ethical framework should provide some guidance to those facing the day-to-day ethical choices in local government: 'Should I leave these children with their mother or take them into care?'; 'Should I cut services in the park or road maintenance?'; 'Should I recommend raising council tax or cut local authority services further?'. Public services are about social relationships: about both the political decision around *who* accesses the services and the quality of the relationship between the bureaucrat/professional and the citizen (Murray, U., 2012). Relationships should be about care and justice. Justice here involves both distributive justice and the recognition and understanding of difference. These elements were missing from the debate about the 'relational state' discussed in Chapter Three.

The incremental expansion of the private sector within public services and of contractual models of regulation are leading to a loss of collective notions of what constitutes the public interest and a lack of any ethical and moral meaning in the notion of the public service ethos (Murray, U., 2012). This point is also made by Hugman (2005, p 42), who argues that effective public service delivery requires the development of trust, while contracts lead to relations of mistrust, as both parties focus on the terms of the contract rather than negotiating the service relationship. He quotes Bauman in setting out how the response to 'the Other' cannot be limited by a contract or treated as a commodity. It should not be limited by who 'the Other' is or what they do. Bauman sees a business ethic, bureaucratic rules and hierarchy as making 'strangers out of people who should be able to see themselves as being in a relationship where discretion and moral responsibility go hand in hand' (Hugman, 2005, p 111).

Employees within the private sector can have a personal moral or ethical approach but it is not possible to instrumentally transfer a public sector ethos, as suggested by Aldridge and Stoker (2003, p 17, quoted in Murray, U., 2012, p 54) through commissioning. Aldridge and Stoker (2003, p 8) suggest that five criteria can be written into contracts: 'a performance culture, a commitment to accountability, a capacity to support universal access, responsible employment and training practices and a contribution to community well-being'. However, most basic public service continually raises complicated moral judgements. In supporting residents with mental health issues, for example, the social worker has to find the balance between the particular interest and universal need, the protection of individual rights and the promotion of public welfare. These are political issues, as are questions of the distribution and allocation of funds. The focus on business ethics elides the moral distinctions around care and justice:

> Rather than an essential public service ethos, that can be enshrined in abstract principles, in practice public service workers constantly have to negotiate boundaries between such general principles, their own values and the particularist requirements of service users and different kinds of community.... From the perspective of lived practice,

> what constitutes justice is not abstract and immutable, but has to be worked through case by case. (Hoggett et al, 2006, p 767)

The marketisation of the public sector fails to resolve value conflicts and pushes them onto employees in a way in which they then 're-emerge at the level of operations as impossible tasks adding to the already considerable complexities of day-to-day roles' (Murray, U., 2012, p 53). Such issues cannot be simply resolved by the professional or manager on an individual basis. They need to be resolved politically (Newman, J. and Clarke, 2009, p 133).

Many readers of this book who are professionals or councillors working in local government will be only too aware of the moral and ethical problems they face that have to be worked through on a case-by-case basis whilst considering the wider political context. The preceding discussion around the ethical framework for local government has identified a number of useful principles: the focus on need and distributive justice, both now and in the future; the importance of constraining the market and considering emancipation, recognition and social protection; and the centrality of participative discussion around justice and well-being. But public service, as Murray makes clear, is about social relationships and it is also essential to clarify 'the role for emotion, capacity for sympathy and care and the importance of the specific commitments, relationships and responsibilities we have to particular others' (Banks, 2001 [1995], p 54).

Hugman stresses that professional ethics must take account of compassion and caring because they involve recognition of the person, or situation, in a way that demands a moral response. But this approach is supplementary to a call for social justice. Care and compassion cannot be the main drivers of day-to-day ethics since: public sector workers also have to protect themselves from burnout; care can reinforce traditional relationships of domination; and professional roles are also about ensuring that individuals thrive in society. Professions have grown out of particular social power and control over the distribution of resources and this power can be abused, as we see again and again through scandals about children's homes, care for people with learning disabilities or care for the elderly. So, caring and compassion are crucial but need to be backed by an ethic of social justice and emancipation, and the professional needs to be accountable. Personal values have to be considered together with professional values that, in turn, require the performance of a job or task, all of which are set in the context of social norms. As Banks says: 'We need to recognise personal, professional, agency and societal values are interlocking, yet in tension' (Banks, 2001 [1995], p 113).

Hugman (2005, p 166) argues that the caring professions, in particular, need to develop conscious reflection and a discursive ethic that provides a way of openly talking about and applying ethics to ensure that their practices are congruent with their values and moral principles. Such a discursive ethic also supports learning from concrete experience. Although professional codes of practice are helpful (Hugman, 2005, pp 141–7), they are not substitutes for reflection and challenge involving discussion of a real incident in a particular context.

Principles in the code of practice for Social Workers

Banks identified five core principles for the British Association of Social Workers' code of practice: respect for persons; self-determination; promotion of human welfare; social justice (equality and distributive justice); and professional integrity (Banks, 2001 [1995], p 37).

Ethical education or debates on ethics should be visible and not confined to professionals or councillors. It is important to make them 'public' again so as to expose the political issues around power and justice that need to be addressed (Newman, J. and Clarke, 2009, ch 9). Following Sen, I would also argue for the need for input from those outside the normal group. Developing a discursive ethic based on *universal* values is of central importance in being able to deal with day-to-day ethical decisions.

Does the policy consider future generations and promote sustainability?

As indicated earlier, Polanyi's discussion about the problems created by an unrestricted market, which takes no account of social and environmental impacts, is particularly useful when looking at discussions about future generations. Within a market system, the price of a good does not reflect externalities, such as the impact on air or water quality or how production could increase the risk of environmental disaster. It does not reflect the amount of labour time or other resources that go into production, although it will reflect in some way the monetary price paid for these resources. The market value, therefore, distorts the value of natural resources and labour that goes into providing a product. Furthermore a market system aims to maximise the amount of the good that is consumed. Gross Domestic Product (GDP – the measure used to assess growth and closely related to Gross National Product) contains no assessment of distribution, of the resources used and the impact on future generations, and no assessment as to whether the growth actually leads to a better quality of life or an increase in happiness or well-being (Layard, 2005; Dorling, 2011).

Robert Kennedy's description of Gross National Product

Gross National Product counts air pollution and cigarette advertising, and ambulances to clear our highways of carnage. It counts special locks for our doors and the jails for the people who break them. It counts the destruction of the redwood and the loss of our natural wonder in chaotic sprawl. It counts ... nuclear warheads and armored cars for the police to fight the riots in our cities....Yet the gross national product does not allow for the health of our children, the quality of their education or the joy of their play. It does not include the beauty of our poetry or the strength of our marriages, the intelligence of our public debate or the integrity of our public officials. It measures neither our wit nor our courage, neither our wisdom nor our learning, neither our compassion nor our devotion to our country, it measures everything in short, except that which makes life worthwhile.[5]

Unrestrained capitalist production will always absorb any **surplus** funds in luxury production or in some form of investment that generates a return in our cities and natural environment. It is only within a system that controls the market that society can choose how it uses the surplus (Soper, 1991, pp 287–8; Harvey, 2011). We could, for example, use it to have more free time for family and community support or to enhance nature through organic production, through establishing new habitats or through inventing new technologies that reduce energy consumption.

The Right to the City

The Right to the City alliance (see: www.righttothecity.org) in the US emerged in 2007 as a response to the increased dominance of market-led development in shaping cities and the impact that this was having on poor and disadvantaged groups. David Harvey has argued that it is 'one of the most precious yet most neglected of our human rights' (Harvey, 2008, p 23). It can be seen as the predecessor of the Occupy movement and a reflection of the growing interest in collective rights, the third generation of rights, discussed earlier.

Harvey argues that urbanisation has played a major role in absorbing surplus product for capitalists. He describes a process of 'creative destruction' (Harvey, 2011, p 191), from Haussmann's clearance and reconstruction of Paris in 1853, to the recent financial crises. He argues that the property market has absorbed a great deal of surplus capital through regeneration, thereby stabilising capitalism by recycling some finance back into demand, but also ultimately creating a greater crisis through the expansion of credit institutions that are not backed up by genuine growth. Furthermore, the creative destruction and regeneration of the city is predominantly carried out in the interests of the capitalists who control the surplus rather than the residents and workers who live and work in the city.

It is this concept of 'place making', discussed in Chapter Two, which has come to dominate local authority planning policies. The successful cities provide new markets and new lifestyles, new forms of capital accumulation – street life, cinemas, waterside restaurants, shopping centres – as attractive ways of spending your money if you have spare funds. This is what urban sociologist Sharon Zukin (1995, p 28) has called 'pacification by cappuccino'. 'Places are therefore reconstructed, so that their visual and symbolic meanings are transformed in the interests of market-led development' (Raco, 2003, p 1883). The selling and branding of place becomes integral to how capitalism works (Harvey, 2011, p 203).

In its darkest form, this urban transformation is now leading to what Harvey calls 'accumulation by dispossession' (Harvey, 2008, p 34), where land and houses that have been lived in for many years by low-income households are taken from them to generate new surpluses for capitalists. As stated in Chapter Seven, some 80,000 poor households are having to move out of inner London from 2012 to 2015. Harvey gives similar examples from Seoul, Mumbai and cities in the US and China.

In response to this reshaping of our cities and lifestyles, Harvey suggests that we should demand 'greater democratic control over the production and utilisation of the surplus' (Harvey, 2008, p 37) and that this constitutes the Right to the City. The surplus has, after all, arisen from the work of employees, so the ordinary citizen, rather than the developer and the heads of industry, should control how it is spent. Currently, in England, business-led Local Enterprise Partnerships play the main role in allocating public investment funding. The Right to the City implies that such decisions should be controlled by ordinary citizens and workers in our cities.

What are the implications of this discussion for local authorities' approach to future generations? Sustainability is a normative concept that has underpinned much of the work of local authorities. Wilson and

Piper (2010, p 16) describe the principles within this concept as 'the principle of futurity (long-term thinking and owing a duty to future generations); the principle of equity for current generations; community engagement in these processes; and the concept of quality of life within environmental carrying capacities'. The duty to future generations has already been raised in relation to Doyal and Gough's discussion on basic needs. Distributive justice is as important in sustainability as it is in the other aspects of justice that have been discussed. Climate change and environmental management are moral issues that have unequal impacts (Wilson and Piper, 2010, p 129) – it is the poor that experience a higher risk of flooding or have to endure poorer air quality. Giving a voice to those who suffer from environmental injustice through community engagement, which addresses power inequalities and different people's ability to participate, will enable discussion of the alternative ways of using the surplus.

Finally, an ecosystem approach, which looks for ecological solutions and innovation to address an environmental problem (Wilson and Piper, 2010, p 42), helps develop sustainability and can also transform our aesthetic and cultural experience. Green infrastructure will improve air quality and biodiversity, as well as providing aesthetic and leisure opportunities. Restoring intertidal habitats, rather than building new sea defences, can provide natural flood protection and bird habitats that people enjoy. The right to roam, removing access to the countryside from the market, has improved the quality of life for many people and increased their understanding of nature. By controlling the market's use of nature and changing our policies, we can provide protection for the environment and enable people to realise their full 'essence' (Soper, 1991, p 283). So, an ecological approach can deliver on Fraser's protection and emancipation. It can provide an understanding of the limits of resource use that is essential for human well-being (Soper, 1991; Wilson and Piper, 2010, p 42). This is not to argue that nature should always be given priority. As we know, nature can be cruel and there are advantages in the ability to adjust natural forces and to make technological progress. Rather, the argument is that it is important for people to discuss how we invest both now and in the future and what types of lifestyle we would want to prioritise, rather than letting the market or experts make so-called rational decisions on the basis of utility models.

Local authorities have considerable scope to make a difference in this area. Bulkeley and Kern (2006, quoted in Piper and Wilson, 2010, p 102) outline four forms of governing that they can use: self-governing (eg minimising their own environmental footprint); governing through enabling (eg recognising power inequalities and promoting wide discussion of alternative forms of investment and behaviour, and how the surplus should be used); governing by provision (eg green spaces and habitats); and governing by authority (eg regulation).

Conclusion

This chapter has sought to establish an ethical framework for local government based on universal needs, incorporating the demands for rights and social justice. The framework has been developed as a set of challenges to enable policymakers to interrogate their decisions. The chapter has argued that rights–based practice and practice promoting social justice is more effective in reducing inequality, providing recognition, developing citizenship and delivering sustainable outcomes than recent approaches based on commodification and the market.

As Sen has argued, a complete prioritisation is not necessary, but policies must be able to stand up to rational scrutiny and address the responsibility of the state to reduce inequality and injustice and increase the opportunities for residents to lead flourishing lives. Both Sen (2009, p 13) and Sandel (2009, pp 187–8) give the example of the flute. If you have one flute, do you give it to the person that made it (do they have the right to fruits of their labour), or do you give it to the person who can play it well (because we value and honour good flute-playing) or to the poor child with no other toys (distributive justice)? I would agree with Sen that we do not need to fully answer this question in the abstract. But, for any policy issue, we do need an agreement, based on public reasoning about justice and values. This means that we do need to address the fact that, currently, the voices of the rich and powerful dominate the debate. Furthermore, those who are disadvantaged are constrained by dominant social norms in their capacity to see alternative ways of leading their lives and of making free choices between these alternatives. We therefore need to focus on how the local authority can widen capabilities (ability, freedom to choose and achievement) and how it can ensure that the debate addresses power differentials and the limits imposed by social norms and prejudice.

The chapter has argued that de-commodification and ensuring that the market is constrained by considering emancipation and social protection opens up opportunities. It increases solidarity as more people use public services; it enables us to think about relationships and ecology and how these can be developed for the common good; it provides social protection; and it removes stigmatisation and increases the self-esteem of those requiring support. This enables the disadvantaged to contribute to shaping policies and articulating their needs.

Throughout the discussion, the importance of participation has been emphasised. Decisions on policy should not only come from those with power: the current decision-makers. The chapter has made clear that social justice requires the development of capabilities – ability, freedom to choose and achievement. It has suggested that professionals need to reflect on their practice and work with users and citizens in discussing care and justice and what constitutes a 'good' service. Deliberation is central to clarifying policies; otherwise, it is all too easy to agree policies that further domination and reduce emancipation. As Sandel argued, robust debate is a more promising basis for a just society. Such a debate must start by addressing inequalities in power. Chapter Five turns to look at how local democracy can be reclaimed, building on the lessons drawn from the ethical framework that has been established here.

Notes
[1] Although Doyal and Gough attempt to develop a cross-cultural approach to basic need, it should be acknowledged that they are still influenced by a Western liberal approach and that personal autonomy and individual action would have less prominence in some cultures.

[2] Sen, however, sees justice as multidimensional (Sen, 2009, p 297). Although he promotes the concept of capabilities, he argues that justice is not reducible to one aspect (economic advantage, resources, utilities, well-being or capabilities) and that both equality and liberty must be seen as having several dimensions (Sen, 2009, p 317).

[3] Although some countries abstained from the original vote – notably, Saudi Arabia and some countries from Eastern Europe (Newman, K., 2012, p 49).

[4] Point 5, Vienna Declaration and Programme of Action. Available at: www. unhchr.ch/huridocda/huridoca.nsf/(symbol)/a.conf.157.23.en

[5] Robert Kennedy, University of Kansas, 18 March 1968. Available at: www.jfklibrary.org/Research/Research-Aids/Ready-Reference/RFK-Speeches/Remarks-of-Robert-F-Kennedy-at-the-University-of-Kansas-March-18-1968.aspx

FIVE

Reclaiming local democracy

Chapter Four has argued for an ethical framework constraining the market by focusing on emancipation, environmental and social protection and the promotion of social justice. The chapter emphasised process: the importance of public debate and discussion and the role of deliberation around the common good in developing citizenship. This debate is usually conducted through some form of democracy and politics, and it is to these concepts that this chapter turns.

The chapter starts by defining the concepts of democracy, accountability and participation. It argues that the current practice of democracy is dominated by a democratic elitism. This increases the power of business elites in relation to public policy. It also separates representative and participatory democracy, and attempts to depoliticise representative democracy. The dominance of democratic elitism has led to decentralisation and localism being consistently 'misframed' so that the links between local issues and national issues are not the subject of deliberation. This has an impact on both representative democracy and participation. The ward councillor role is seen as encouraging apolitical community engagement in the neighbourhood and little attention is given to how local demands can influence council-wide and national decision-making. There is a failure to understand the important role of the councillor in linking to the wider political project of furthering social protection, emancipation and social justice. Participatory democracy is also limited to residents as customers of services or local neighbourhood facilities.

If democracy is to be reclaimed, councillors will need to address power inequalities and to increase the capacity of individuals or groups to engage in the policy process. This is essential so that those without power can engage in meaningful deliberations about their needs and the common good, as advocated in Chapter Four. This chapter argues that a new version of local democracy is required that focuses on the relationship between different levels of government and civil society and what they are trying to do together. The chapter points to the ways in which councillors can enhance participation and explores in more detail the tensions between participation and rights and justice.

Defining democracy, accountability and participation

As Antony Arblaster (1991 [1987], p 6) makes clear, democracy used to be regarded as a 'bad thing', equivalent to the rule of the mob and fatal to individual freedom and civilised society. Since elected municipal corporations in 1835, it has been redefined to be consistent with the rule by elites and received general approbation, but the misgivings about wider democracy have not vanished.

Democracy comes from the Greek words 'demos', which is the whole citizen body living within a city state, and 'kratos', which means power or rule. Democracy therefore implies some form of popular power or popular rule, but these are not the same concepts. It is possible to have a system based formally on popular rule with a very unequal distribution of power and this could be claimed to be the case in many Western democracies today.

In the Greek city state of Aristotle, there was no division between the state and society. Ignoring for the moment the issue of the slaves and women, all those living in the city were citizens who governed themselves directly through active participation in politics. The Greek idea of 'citizenship' was an organic relationship like a human body. The state (or Polis) was the whole and the individual were the parts, like limbs dependent on the state and not self-sufficient (Arblaster, 1991 [1987], p 22). Participatory democracy here involves the individuals seeing themselves as part of the whole, with collective interests. This concept of democracy was built into the ethical framework discussed in Chapter Four by asking of any policy: 'Does the policy lead to a deeper understanding of citizenship and the common good?'

While modern states are too large to engage in an Aristotelian form of democracy, there are still aspects of this approach that are fundamental. The relationship between the individual and society has been widely accepted, with the notable exception of Margaret Thatcher, who claimed that 'there is no such thing as society'. Sandel's discussion of community and the importance of solidarity and common values are built on an Aristotelian understanding of the relationship between the state and the individual. Beetham, who devised the methodology for assessing democracy for the Democratic Audit in the early 1990s, argues that it is vital to return to the core principles developed by Aristotle if an assessment of democracy is to have any meaning (Beetham, 1993, p 6). The two core principles he identifies are *popular control* over the political process of decision-making within society and *political equality* in the exercise of that control. As Beetham (1993, p 4) recognises, 'in general, political equality becomes more difficult to realise the greater the socio-economic inequalities within society'.

The term 'democracy' must be distinguished from two other very important concepts. The first is the concept of 'accountability'. Accountability rests on the proposition that 'those who exercise public power in society should be answerable for the exercise of that power' (Stewart, 1992, p 4). Accountability involves giving an account of actions taken and being held to account for these actions. So, a local authority normally publishes information on how it has spent its income and distributes this to local residents and businesses. It is accountable to local stakeholders. Unlike 'democracy', 'accountability' separates out the state and society and can be exercised with no participation of citizens in the decision-making process.

Nor must participation be confused with democracy. On its own, participation does not imply any popular control. As Beetham (1993, p 8) argues, in the Soviet Union under communism, there was high participation in terms of voter turnout and citizen involvement in party life and public affairs but it was hardly democratic since the whole process was subject to control by the Communist Party leadership. There are various classifications of participation. Arnstein's (1969) ladder of participation is perhaps the best known, moving from manipulation on the bottom rung to citizen control at the top. The ladder implies that participation is promoted for very different reasons, from enabling the decision-making of experts to appear more legitimate, to devolving real power over policy. Barnes et al (2007) look at four different forms of participation: empowering participation, which is usually applied to a marginalised or disadvantaged community; participation as consumers, where views are sought by policymakers from citizens as customers of their services; participation as stakeholders, where participation is through partnerships of producers and recipients; and responsible participation, which is reflected in the calls for a 'Big Society' and where participation is sought to get communities to take responsibility for delivering their own services. They suggest that the four discourses are in tension but can coexist and that there are often confused reasons for promoting participation. In this chapter, drawing on Chapter Four, I am concerned primarily with participation that seeks to address power inequalities and to change the capacity of individuals or groups to engage in the policy process (transformative participation), as opposed to participation set up by experts to gather people's knowledge and views to support local government policies (instrumental participation) (see Newman, K., 2012, p 26). And I am interested in how such transformative participation can work with representative democracy to effect real change.

The concept of democracy demands the active involvement of diverse citizens in determining policy. It also demands institutions that address the current power inequalities that allow elites to dominate the policymaking process. It therefore involves both representative and participative democracy and this notion will inform the whole of this chapter. An effective democracy requires a sense of the common good or general interests that the citizens share and equality in the ability of different citizens to engage in and influence the outcomes. In this context, 'local' democracy is seen as the cornerstone of democracy. It is necessary both for prudential reasons (a check on centralised power, equal representation through the ballot box) and for developmental reasons (participation increases political understanding and equality and enables us to formulate shared concerns) (Phillips, 1996). Since local democracy can promote local participation and local needs against centralised power, it can respond more effectively than the nation state to local injustice and local claims for rights.

Democracy is not in terminal decline but the model of democratic elitism is dominant

Since the early 1990s, there has been a fear that 'the "local" element in our democratic mix has withered and is in danger of extinction' (Pratchett and Wilson, 1996, p 1). This concern is not limited to the UK, but is mirrored in many Western democracies and in the global South (Barnes et al, 2007, ch 2). The analysis in the UK is based on the declining power of local government (fragmentation, increasing numbers of quangos, declining financial independence and increasing power of the market), which, in turn, weakens residents' interest in local politics. The concerns include: declining electoral turnout (Rallings et al, 1996); moribund political parties that increasingly dominate the operation of local councils (Game and Leach, 1996); disdain from civil servants (Jones and Travers, 1996); and the growing unrepresentative nature of councillors, with 80% over 45 and 33% retired and the majority white, male and middle class (CLD, 1995, p 12). In November 1993, the Commission for Local Democracy (CLD) was launched to come up with proposals to counter the decline in the power of local government. It is interesting to note both how many of the recommendations of the CLD have been implemented and how little difference this has made to the dominant discourse of decline.[1] Mulgan and Bury (2006, p 8) produced a graph of the decline in local government autonomy. As Secretary of State for local government, Eric Pickles used the discourse of the decline of local democracy to justify the Localism Act 2011, arguing that: 'This government will restore local government to its former glory' (Rt Hon Eric Pickles MP, June 2011, quoted in PCRC, 2013, p 8). While there is plenty of evidence that local government is the most trusted tier of government and has more democratic legitimacy than central government (Studdert, 2013, p 20), the Big Society Audit (Civil Exchange, 2012, p 6) noted that only half a million people are now members of the three main political parties, compared to more than two million in the 1970s. Furthermore, 40% of people almost never trust governments of any party to place the needs of the nation above their own party, compared to 10% in 1987.

I would, however, argue that this overall story of democratic decline is a myth. Chapter Two has already tackled the argument about the decline in local government power and suggested that local government retains some creative autonomy. Newman, J. and Clarke (2009, p 1) warn against those who look back nostalgically to a golden era of social democracy or welfare that never existed. Rather, they suggest that there is a continual remaking of the relationship between public, private and personal. While representative politics has had a shrinking hold on public enthusiasm, engagement and trust, it is being supplemented by an ever-widening variety of forms of consultation, participation and 'citizen engagement' (Newman, J. and Clarke, 2009, p 3). They draw attention to the fact that the word 'public' is being attached to more and more concepts, like 'public value, public accountability, public scrutiny, public engagement, public empowerment and many others' (Newman, J. and Clarke, 2009, p 5). Barnes et al (2007, p 28) reveal that in 2001, each local authority used on average 10.5 different participation initiatives and some 14 million people took part in such exercises. So, as well as the decline in citizen interest in party politics, we have seen a proliferation of attempts to increase participative democracy.

The focus, therefore, should be on the nature of participative and representative democracy and how they relate to one another. I would suggest that the failure to gain public enthusiasm for representative democracy within local government results from the nature of representative democracy being pursued: the priority given to democratic elitism over political equality and the representative role in popular control.

Democratic elitism has been most closely associated with Joseph Schumpeter. His experience as a Czech and subsequently an Austrian finance minister and a German university professor who left Bonn in 1932 and wrote during the war, led him to have a very negative view of popular control or control by the masses. He argued that the mass of people were authoritarian and illiberal and 'to encourage participation by such persons would be to introduce into government ignorance and indifference in place of the expertise, however cynically motivated, of the professional politician' (quoted in Parry et al, 1992, p 5). Schumpeter saw democracy as a means to an end and as 'an institutional arrangement for arriving at political decisions in which individuals acquire the power to decide by means of competitive struggle for the people's vote' (Schumpeter, 1976 [1942], p 269). In this model, the citizen is the 'controller' (not the 'participant'), who exerts some checking influence on the leaders that are elected.

Schumpeter's view of democracy as a process of elite selection has influenced many political theorists and our concept of modern liberal representative democracy. Society is not seen as a whole, but as a variety of sectional interests. Bernard Crick, for instance, argued that society is 'diverse' and that there is no such thing as the 'popular will' (quoted in Arblaster, 1991 [1987], p 54). By competing for leadership, elites ensure that their rule is based on consent. Democracy becomes a means of getting a decision and ensuring that there is no 'tyranny of the minority by the majority'. The role of local government within this framework is to govern and to be the 'community leader'. While some who support democratic elitism see a considerable role for local people to be consulted and 'engaged' in debates about how resources should be allocated, the main role in governance rests with the elected representative, who is accountable to the electorate. Furthermore, in this model, central elites use low electoral turnout in local elections and a lack of interest in local issues compared to national issues (reinforced by the media) to justify the imposition of central government policy on local government.

While the CLD contains a significant amount of rhetoric about participation and about the importance of democratic politics (CLD, 1995, p 3), ultimately, in its implementation, it was dominated by a democratic elitist model. This, I would argue, is why the implementation of many of its recommendations has had limited impact on trust in representative government or on voter turnout.

The Labour government, which turned to its recommendations in 1997, placed responsibility for local government on Hilary Armstrong, who had been a Durham County Councillor between 1985 and 1987 and had a very low opinion of her fellow, mostly 'old Labour', male colleagues, whom she saw as maintaining male, traditional power. She encouraged the formation of the New Local Government Network; theoretically, an external independent think tank, but set up to support her radical proposals. Here, an inner circle promoted their elitist view of local democracy.

This is evident in the belief that central government had the right to prescribe and control local government action. It was also evident in the models for councils that were to underpin the Labour government's 'local government modernisation' programme. Local government was to have separate executives or cabinets and mayoral referenda attracting those representatives who were to be held capable of community leadership. Those not on the executive were held in low regard but a small role had to be found for them. In *Towards a new localism*, published jointly by the Institute for Public Policy Research (IPPR) and New Local Government Network in October 2000, it was suggested:

> We need to differentiate councillors' roles and to reduce the numbers, whilst increasing the involvement of the public and representatives through promoting neighbourhood governance or other forms of involvement where people can participate without signing half their lives away.
>
> Mayors and leaders should be able to bring in talented people from the voluntary and business sectors to take up a portfolio of responsibility within the cabinet, subject to approval by the council and **Nolan principles**. (Filkin et al, 2000, p 8).

Here, we see an un-evidenced concern about the quality of local councillors. They are assessed as not significantly different from the people who elected them and therefore part of the 'masses' who cannot be trusted with decision-making. This concern also goes back to John Stuart Mill, who thought that local councillors were of low calibre, regarding this as 'the greatest imperfection of popular institutions' (quoted in Sharpe, 2006 [1970], p 162). The ability of councillors had already been researched thoroughly in Wolverhampton in the 1960s (Jones, 1969). Jones concluded that there was no evidence of a decline in councillors' effectiveness and that the concern seemed to stem from the fact that councillors were becoming more outward-looking and engaging with their communities rather than concentrating on minimising rate increases. Yet, the denigration of councillors has been used since 1997 to promote a model where an elite take forward 'community leadership': the new role that is involved with everything that concerns the public locally, even if they have no direct responsibility for delivery. This elite often has close links with, and dependence on, the local business community, with the danger that 'Instead of the public sphere constituting a separate life domain, with its distinctive values, relationships and ways of operating, it has become an extension of the private market' (Beetham, 2011, p 21). The relationship between this elite and participative democracy remains unclear within this theory, except that it is to be developed through neighbourhood/ parish governance. This approach has persisted in the Coalition Government's promotion of the mayoral model and in their Local Enterprise Partnerships (led by business interests with membership from the elites in the public sector), which are now responsible for deciding on investment priorities with little or no participative input.

I am not suggesting here that there should be a return to the committee system or that these were more democratic than executive structures. However, I am arguing that New Labour's modernisation programme was based on a view that elites should be trusted with strategic decision-making. This model reinforced the separation of representative and participative democracy and strengthened the influence of business elites within local government. It is a model that has also seen the growth of the political career ladder: young political activists seeing the role of the councillor as a step towards becoming a national politician and a Member of Parliament (MP) and then maybe a director of a pharmaceutical, financial or defence company.

The majority of councillors do not seek election to further a career in national politics. There has even been one case of a national politician returning to local government (Peter Soulsby became Mayor of Leicester in 2011). New Labour also strongly promoted participative democracy and set up a Councillors Commission in 2006, chaired by Dame Jane Roberts, ex-leader of the London Borough of Camden, to look at strengthening representative democracy. In stark contrast to the elite view pursued earlier, this held that 'Councillors are most effective as locally elected representatives when they have similar life experiences to those of their constituents' (Councillors Commission, 2007, p 5). But the fundamental dominance of democratic elitism remains, causing a cleavage between representative democracy and participative democracy. This cleavage makes it much harder for councils to adopt the ethical framework outlined in Chapter Four and is explored further in the next section.

Representative and participative democracy

There has been a sustained attempt in the media to denigrate political representatives and promote participative democracy as an alternative. Some would argue that political representatives have brought public disdain on their own heads, with: the Poulson corruption in the 1970s; the Donnygate scandal, which ended in 2002 with a four-year sentence for Peter Birks, former chairman of planning in Doncaster following convictions of fraud of two former council leaders, two former mayors and 17 other Doncaster councillors; and, more recently, the MPs' expenses scandal; some councillor expenses irregularities and councillors offering consultancy services to property developers (*Daily Telegraph*, 2013). The Councillors Commission concludes: 'We have discovered the public's view of local government to be a dispiriting combination of poor awareness and understanding, distaste for organised politics and negative perceptions of councillors and their motives for seeking election' (Councillors Commission, 2007, p 7).

However, there is plenty of evidence that most councillors enter politics because they want to further the well-being of their communities. The general public disdain and cynicism about party politics is also not just a British phenomenon. The Norwegian *Study of power and democracy* (Norwegian Official Reports, 2003, referenced in the Councillors Commission, 2007, p 10) found the same signs of disengagement from conventional forms of political participation leading to a void between the public and their representatives and a decline in the influence of Norway's once-powerful local authorities. Similar trends can be found elsewhere. The disregard for councillors and the media's contempt for councils should be seen as part of the growing power of markets, individualism and consumerism and an attempt to limit the role of the state.

Newman, J. and Clarke (2009, p 21) argue that all public decision-making is political, but, increasingly, there is an attempt to take the politics and contestation out of public policy issues by making them the focus of technical judgements about the efficiency and efficacy of different solutions (Newman, J. and Clarke, 2009, p 25). As part of this process, attention is focused on civil society, community and voluntary organisations – 'ordinary people – and the good things they do' (Newman, J. and Clarke, 2009, p 66) – which are put forward as apolitical. While this may widen a restricted form of participative democracy, it can also limit the democratic processes of representative democracy.

Whitehead (2006) agrees. He sees representative democracy as primarily the way of deciding who gets what, when and how. He argues that political parties are fundamental to this process, quoting the Neill Committee (1998, p 27, s 2.23), which saw them as the means of recruiting people into decision-making positions at all levels of government, providing informed choice and accountability.

This conclusion was foreshadowed by George Jones, whose book on Wolverhampton in the 1960s concluded that political parties not only provide accountability, but also open up the policy process to influence and enable groups of individuals to devise and implement a clear programme: 'Parties have made the council more democratic and less oligarchic' (Jones, 1969, p 349).

Whitehead sees participative democracy as providing a crucial input to the policy process between elections and as complementary to the political process. But he argues: 'We are witnessing an unconscious division of political life into two strands: representative, in which party political candidates compete for office; and participative, from which political parties are excluded. At local level this can lead to some pathological outcomes' (Whitehead, 2006, p 8). First, those wishing to perform any non-elected role in public life begin to consciously avoid becoming involved in any political party because of the career-blighting impact of being seen as 'political'. For example, the Office of the Commissioner for Public Appointments treats political activity within the previous five years as a basis for disqualification from other public office (Councillors Commission, 2007, p 23). Second, political actors on the local stage are being forced into a political ghetto of party politics and away from 'real' community life because they are seen as politicising community discussion. Hostility to the concept of 'politics', as people understand it, acts as a deterrent to involvement. Whitehead concludes:

> We have to reconnect the notions of participation and representation. We cannot enjoy the undoubted benefits of a participative polity whilst at the same time, by acts of commission or omission, starving the representative functions of that polity and indeed, the functions that give any sense to the choices and options that participation throws up in the first place. (Whitehead, 2006, p 22)

The implication of the discussion so far is that if democracy is to be reclaimed, we need to engage in a set of related tasks. On the one hand, representative democracy must be strengthened by promoting a deeper understanding of politics. This, in turn, means wider engagement with the ethical framework developed in Chapter Four, so citizens see politics as something that is at the core of the society in which we live and to which we all contribute rather than the domain of a small elite. It also means that councillors need to be able to make a difference and act on agreed priorities, and this will be discussed further in Chapter Seven.

Finally, to achieve a wider understanding of citizenship, councillors' key role becomes to enhance political equality and enable participative democracy to be transformative.

Current practice has not been meeting these tasks. There have been active attempts to encourage local authorities to promote wider discussion of the common good and encourage active citizenship, as the following box illustrates. Significant progress was made. However, such initiatives were only partially effective (Barnes et al, 2007, p 184). For example, Chapter Three discussed the New Deal for Communities (NDC) programme and how participation and empowerment were constrained. Furthermore, in the current climate of expenditure cuts and outsourcing, radical attempts to increase empowerment through state funding have declined significantly.

Sustainable Community Strategies and Active Citizenship

Part I of the Local Government Act 2000 placed a duty on local authorities to prepare 'community strategies', 'for promoting or improving the economic, social and environmental well-being of their areas, and contributing to the achievement of sustainable development in the UK' (ODPM, 1999, para 4). The process of preparing these strategies was as important as the strategies themselves and was the means by which local people and organisations could be drawn into democratic decision-making. Community strategies were to 'allow local communities (based upon geography and/or interest) to articulate their aspirations, needs and priorities' (ODPM, 1999, para 10). Most local authorities set up public engagement exercises around community strategies. Many also funded community development and developed community empowerment networks to bring different voluntary and community groups together and enable them to input more effectively into the work of the local authority and the Local Strategic Partnership (LSP). In 2004, the Home Office funded seven Active Learning for Active Citizenship (ALAC) hubs to pilot various radical approaches to adult citizenship learning. This led to the Take Part Network (see: www.takepart.org) being formed in 2005 and a national Take Part Programme in 2008, in which local authorities worked with voluntary and community sector organisations to build active citizens. Furthermore, a network of 18 local authorities, the Network of Empowering Authorities (NEA), was established to develop learning and best practice (IDeA, 2010). All this activity has resulted in significant culture change within local authorities.

The difficulties are multiple and not just related to the impact of public expenditure cuts. Additional barriers are created by the democratic elitist view of a number of councillors and political parties who remain concerned about real mass participation and disruptive citizen protest that they cannot control (Copus, 2010). A further problem centres on the lack of confidence of many councillors. The top–down target culture has driven out innovation and independent action in some councils. Councillors and officers often wait for instructions from above and spend their time trying to make central government legislation or new initiatives work. But none of these problems are insurmountable and there are plenty of councillors who understand their role in relation to increasing participation and political equality, as the quotes from 1935 to the present day in the following box demonstrate.

How local politicians make a difference in their communities

When I first came to consider local government, I began to see how it was in essence the first-line defence thrown up by the community against our common enemies – poverty, sickness, ignorance, isolation, mental derangement and social maladjustment. (Winifred Holtby, Yorkshire's first woman alderman, 1935, from a letter to her mother, Alice Holtby, quoted in IDeA, 2007, p 2)

We represent very vocal, highly motivated, articulate residents; they can get a campaign up and running on the internet in 48 hours. Rather than leading, I see my role as an enabling one – helping to inform my constituents to find out what is happening and opening doors for them. (David Winskill, London Borough of Haringey, quoted in IDeA, 2007, p 11)

I have been a wheelchair user for more than 10 years following damage to my nervous system. Life on wheels does pose a few challenges for councillors in terms of energy and time, so I thought long and hard before I considered standing. The first thing I did when I was elected was to get to know the number of active grass roots groups in the area to get a feel for their priorities, challenges and aspirations. I try to be a link between the community groups, to be a bit of glue, putting people in touch with each other to share ideas and volunteers. (Chris Cheshire, Crawley Borough Council, quoted in IDeA, 2007, p 6)

However, a further problem is that the elitist model of democracy sees participation limited to the neighbourhood sphere and this impacts on the ability to strengthen participative and representative democracy.

Reframing local democracy

This section argues that local democracy is currently misconceived as localism and that this reinforces the separation of participative and representative democracy, obscures the relationship between empowerment and social justice, and limits local democracy. It is therefore important to recast the way local democracy is understood. In doing this, Nancy Fraser's (2009) notion of 'misframing' is helpful. A developed country in the global North can push development of a poor nation in the South onto that nation's government. If poverty is not reduced, the blame is placed solely on a failed state rather than looking at issues of trade policy, arms sales and market development models promoted through tied aid. Nancy Fraser argues that in this situation, transnational justice has been misframed as national justice. In a parallel analysis, I would suggest that national justice is often misframed as localism. Central government, which should be responsible for redistribution to meet basic needs, as argued in Chapter Four, pushes local development onto the residents of deprived neighbourhoods. Failures are then blamed on the 'undeserving poor'. If local democracy is to be regenerated, it has to be reframed or reconceptualised.

So, what is the problem with current concepts of decentralisation and localism and how have they evolved? The roots of decentralisation can be traced back to the 1960s and the area-based policies stemming from the war on poverty, together with the growing significance of locality (Gyford, 1991b), discussed in Chapter Two. There can be considerable variety in the reasons why councils pursue decentralisation objectives (Sullivan et al, 2001). The focus on decentralisation is not UK-specific and the past two decades have brought an unprecedented wave of radical decentralisation around the world (Mulgan and Bury, 2006, p 10). Decentralisation can be seen as the 'search for 'self-sustaining systems of improvement', based on increased choice for individual service users, and increased voice for neighbourhoods and local communities' (Benington, 2006, p 8), and Chapter Three criticised this as ultimately utopian (Harvey, 2000). Here, the concern is not with holistic approaches, but with decentralisation as the means to promote local democracy. In relation to democracy, decentralisation is usually promoted in order to foster more active citizenship, improve the accountability and responsiveness of the ward councillor (Lowndes, 1992, p 60), and provide new pathways for participation and partnership (Sullivan and Howard, 2005).

Early experiments with local authority decentralisation in England in the 1980s (in Tower Hamlets, Islington and Walsall) reflected radical attempts by local councils to bring local government closer to the residents. Most ended in difficulties, as costs escalated, fragmentation increased and professional expertise could not be spread effectively. However, decentralisation became particularly prominent under New Labour, when two agendas came together: the National Strategy for Neighbourhood Renewal, with its emphasis again on self-sustaining improvement through tackling social exclusion via neighbourhood governance; and New Labour's local government modernisation programme, with separate executives and non-executive councillors involved in community governance at ward level (Sullivan et al, 2001, p 4). Decentralisation was seen as way of providing a role on area committees for the disaffected 'backbench' councillors who were not in the cabinet.[2] Double devolution (a term promoted by David Miliband when he was the Secretary of State responsible for local government) suggested that central government would devolve powers to local government if local authorities in turn devolved power to neighbourhoods or parishes.

More recently, the Coalition Government has promoted localism (Clarke and Cochrane, 2013). Localis, the Conservative local government think tank, describes its 'philosophy' on its website as follows:

> We believe that power should be exercised as close as possible to the people it serves. We are therefore dedicated to promoting a localist agenda and challenging the existing centralisation of power and responsibility. We seek to develop new ways of delivering local services that deliver better results at lower costs, and involve local communities to a greater degree.[3]

While this may appear an uncontentious statement, with localism (and the similar European term 'subsidiarity') having a wide appeal and being seen as promoting active citizenship, there are two key problems.

Localism and redistribution, need and social justice

The first is the question as to whether localism is predicated on reducing redistribution from the centre. Localism – particularly where, as in the Localis model, it is linked with cost savings – implies a postcode lottery, with poor areas left to fend for themselves while wealth flows to the rich. Chapter Three evidenced how the cuts are impacting on the most deprived areas as distribution by need is replaced by per capita funding.

Subsidiarity has advantages, but these do not overrule issues of need and social justice, discussed in Chapter Four. Clearly, individual tutoring for children would be the most effective way of teaching literacy and numeracy and meeting an individual's different learning needs but it is not routinely provided because it would be incredibly expensive – as is most tailored neighbourhood service delivery. But there is a further reason too. Chapter Four discussed how being involved in public services develops solidarity and a sense of community on which democratic citizenship depends. Interaction at school builds social relationships and the social skills of cooperation and enables discussion around the common good. Social cohesion through joint use of services has to be in balance with the importance of subsidiarity and individual choice.

Addressing basic human needs and social justice, as advocated in Chapter Four, inevitably requires some check on the power of elites and some level of redistribution to provide services related to need and this, in turn, means a relatively strong central state. The call for a strong, redistributive, central state stems from the early days of the Labour Party and Sidney Webb's *Grants in aid* publication of 1911 (Travers, 2008). There is always going to be an issue about central–local relationships and local–neighbourhood relationships. The denial of this tension is a central weakness in the current concept of 'localism'.

However, a strong central state and a strong representative function within local government are still compatible with local empowerment. The issue is how *both* empowerment and redistribution can take place and models are required where *both* these priorities are addressed. Since meeting needs at the neighbourhood level involves addressing the causes of poverty and disadvantage at council-wide and national levels, participation should be promoted at all levels. Local neighbourhood demands for better local facilities and recognition should be linked to council-wide and national campaigns for rights and social justice. Local democracy also involves exploring how Whitehall could be made susceptible to bottom-up influence from those with little power rather than subordinated to an oligarchy of the wealthy and economically powerful (Beetham, 2011). If central–local and local–neighbourhood relationships are to be framed in the context of participation at *all* levels, it becomes clear that the 'relationship' and 'influencing' aspect of these relationships requires more attention. National government should be open to influence by bottom-up participatory democracy campaigning for different aspects of rights and justice alongside local authorities as advocated in Chapter Four.

Opening up national government to bottom-up influence

City Deals cannot be presented as bottom-up policymaking, but they do represent a small, first step in providing a route through to influence from the locality to central government. In September 2011, the government accepted a Core Cities Group Amendment to the Localism Bill for the eight core cities to be given greater freedoms to drive economic growth in their areas and deals were signed off by July 2012. City Deals are restricted to the economic growth agenda, with business interests prioritised. The offer requires cities to demonstrate 'strong, visible and accountable leadership and effective decision-making' (HM Government, 2011, p 2): a democratic elitist approach. The deals do not involve participatory democracy and are negotiated between local and national elites. However, the Partnership for Urban South Hampshire (PUSH), in negotiating an agreement under an earlier government initiative, highlighted the importance of an influencing relationship:

> Local partners also hoped that an agreement with the government would lead to a different relationship, so that negotiations did not proceed on an issue by issue basis but instead a single point of reference and a relationship based on mutual and shared objectives would assist PUSH in achieving its ambition. (Russell, 2010, p 24, Box 2.2)

The Political and Constitutional Reform Committee (PCRC, 2013) is calling for more fundamental change through a constitutional settlement between central and local government.

Within local government policymaking, local government has a legitimate role in targeting resources in deprived neighbourhoods and addressing need and councillors have to take decisions that may be unpopular with a majority of the constituent base. Democracy is thus enhanced by attempts to devolve, but, at the same time, it is essential to open up discursive space at council-wide level to discuss with citizens how they would do things differently to further the ethical framework outlined in Chapter Four.

How local politicians make a difference in their communities

I am also taking an active role in trying to save areas of special interest within a four mile greenfield site that is earmarked for development. It's ironic that I became a councillor because I was opposed to plans to build 2,500 homes on the land that I knew and loved, which is just at the back of my home, and now, a few years later, I'm having to take forward that very same planning application. I'm still trying to preserve the fundamental

> root of my objections to the development which are the shortage of
> green space in the area and the pressure that building many more homes
> would have on scarce resources such as water.... I'm working with local
> residents and with English Nature and English Heritage to identify areas
> that are of particular interest to local residents. It's all about balance. I
> now better understand about housing need. (Councillor Claire Denman,
> Crawley Borough Council, quoted in IDeA, 2007, p 8)

Localism: the depoliticisation and narrowing of democracy

The second problem with a localist framing of democracy is that
too often the localism model of democracy sees the community (a
community where there are no differences or conflict) as engaged
in relatively minor issues around the clean, green, safe agenda, or
more recently volunteering to run the local shop, library or youth
sports club. Although this can add a very positive dimension to local
decision-making, it cannot be seen as a total solution to widening
democracy. In this model, there has been a trade-off between the extent
of participation and the scope of control (Lowndes and Sullivan, 2008,
p 56). Participative democracy is frequently removed from influencing
the strategic level. Furthermore, representative and participative
democracy are separated. The strategic becomes the domain of the
executive of the council, while the ward role becomes depoliticised
and engaged in influencing relatively minor spending decisions. This
has an impact on both the participation and representative function.

In relation to representative democracy, the localist framing limits
the role of the non-executive councillor and full council. The non-
executive councillor's role is often seen in a narrow way of being only
a community leader in their ward. This is an important role but it is
equally important that learning and discussion from the ward is fed into
strategic decision-making. If the representative role of all councillors
is conceived more generally as promoting the ethical framework
outlined in Chapter Four, then politics takes centre stage. The focus
would switch attention to a discussion around how *all* councillors can
develop active citizenship to influence both local and strategic decision-
making for the purpose of promoting social justice. In this context,
the role of the full council, **overview and scrutiny committees**
and the political group should all gain greater prominence. In each of
these institutions, issues can be raised about how the councillor might
promote active citizenship and encourage discussion around issues of
social justice, social protection and recognition. Consideration should
be given to how the ward councillor can increase residents' influence

over the authority's decision-making processes: the routes by which change can be achieved. Councillors already recognise the importance of the political group in this process (Gardiner, 2006, pp 41–2). But the depoliticisation of decision-making, encouraged through the localist conception of politics, means that there is limited consideration and very little written on the importance of an effective political group and the manifesto. These wider political structures could ensure input from all councillors, greater accountability and a clear purpose based on inclusive debate and dialogue.

The councillor role and political parties are central to local democracy and democracy as a whole. It is the councillor, as the local representative, that can seek to forge some common purpose. As Newman, J. and Clarke (2009) argue, things become political because they are contested. Political parties mediate debates, help to clarify issues and mobilise people and build alliances so that policy change can be made. Trying to take the politics out of an issue and contain councillors in apolitical discussions about neighbourhoods removes the discussion about contested values. It reduces debate to a dry technical discussion about the most effective solutions, which are often seen as based on the market. In this way, the real causes of problems remain unexplored, policy deals with symptoms not causes, and debates about the common good, social justice, values, emancipation and social protection are suppressed. Newman, J. and Clarke support Jacques Rancière's (2006) view that, rather than denying politics, the councillor's role is to enlarge the public sphere by constructing issues, people, relationships and conflicts as public rather than private matters and to politicise debates in the public sphere by contrasting a democratic politics approach that seeks emancipation and protection with a depoliticised approach that prioritises the market (Newman, J. and Clarke, 2009, p 183).

In reclaiming democracy, therefore, we need more debate and more politics. But this should not be done by public school-type debates with petty point-scoring:

> A distinction, however, needs to be made between the language and tone of some political debate, which appears to be the source of public concern, and the importance of the political process. A reasoned defence, even a celebration, of the need for politics is required, at all levels of governance. (Councillors Commission, 2007, p 23)

The implications of adopting a wider approach than localism for local democracy

The preceding discussion implies that we need to reframe local democracy. Equating localism and local democracy: denies the need for redistribution and multi-level governance; separates out representative and participative democracy; and limits and depoliticises local neighbourhood politics. Local democracy needs to be reconceived as part of multi-level governance. Newman, J. and Clarke (2009, pp 40–1) suggest that multi-level governance should not be seen as a series of tidily nested Russian dolls within successively larger spatial containers. Instead, multi-level governance is more like a late Kandinsky painting (with organic shapes in bright colours linked together to form compositions), where a range of actors interact in ways that could make both empowerment and redistribution possible. Local councillors are concerned with improving the well-being of their residents and this is a political process. Their role is to promote debate and participation about the principles and values that should drive local decision-making. This involves bringing together representative and participative democracy and addressing political inequality. A lack of power over local government policymaking is bound to result in a lack of interest and involvement in representative democracy. Reclaiming democracy therefore involves councillors being far more active in promoting participative democracy, as discussed next.

How councillors can enhance participatory democracy

Opening up discursive spaces at the local level

A study of participation practices in contrasting English localities led to the development of the CLEAR model and suggested that participation will only be effective when the five conditions below are adhered to:

C an do – have the resources and knowledge to participate

L ike to – have a sense of attachment that reinforces participation

E nabled to – are provided with the opportunity for participation

A sked to – are mobilised through public agencies and civic channels

> **R esponded to** – see evidence that their views have been
> considered. (Pratchett et al, 2009, p 9)

Certainly, all authors on participation would agree with this list,
especially the need to respond. Encouraging participation without the
capacity to change policy in relation to the views expressed quickly
develops distrust and disaffection and makes participation unsustainable.
However, the preceding discussion suggests that it is vital to go further.

Deliberation around ethics, values and the common good

Local authorities need to open up discursive spaces and what Barnes
et al (2007, p 190) call 'sites of challenge and opportunity'. As argued
earlier, participative democracy needs to be seen as relevant to the
whole local authority and its decision-making processes. If the local
authority as a whole is to deliver on human need, the whole council
needs to engage with local residents in defining how it will further
social justice, increase capabilities and constrain the market.

The role of the full council

Braintree undertook a review of its decision-making processes during 2004/05
and set some guiding principles and outcomes for the role of the full council –
that it should:

- Be meaningful, accessible and accountable to citizens. Meetings are also held
  on a Monday to enable proceedings to be reported in that week's local
  newspaper.
- Debate major policy/issues.
- Hold the executive to account. The leader, chair of any committee, group or
  scrutiny panel can make a statement on key issues. Any other member can
  question these statements. They can also raise oral questions without notice
  to the leader and they can also use written questions.
- Decide the policy framework (Gardiner, 2006, pp 7–10).

Such a debate will take place primarily with the centre of the institution
(the executive councillors in the cabinet and the corporate management
structures) but ways need to be found to link with more detailed
debates on neighbourhoods, cross-agency issues (such as sustainability
and health) or emancipation (the way different groups are valued).
There is evidence that the key determinant of participation in public

policy is affiliation to a group (Parry et al, 1992, p 419). Thus, identity politics and single issue politics can often provide greater motivation for participation than locality. Many councils appoint community champions, who are non-executive members who represent specific themes or communities of interest, and this can enhance recognition and emancipation (Gardiner, 2006, p 17).

As discussed in Chapter Four, there is a need to have deliberation around fundamental values and their implications. Too often, community strategies start from 'motherhood and apple pie' vision statements about the locality being a place where everyone wants to live, with the best quality of life and the highest growth rate, and without endangering sustainability. Such deliberations do not tease out the very real choices that must be made if needs are to be satisfied and social justice addressed. Issues outlined in Chapter Four around human need, recognition and emancipation, and the desired level of social protection from the market are rarely, if ever, topics for discussion.

Habermas's (1984 [1981], 1990 [1983]) work on deliberative democracy is often cited in this context. Habermas was interested not only in how the state could improve the legitimacy of its own decision-making, but also in how debate and deliberation could be used to increase the potential for both challenge and cooperation (Barnes et al, 2007, p 36). He advocated a 'communicative' rationality, which involved 'free and equal participation in the public sphere in a deliberation about socio-political issues or practical issues' (Barnes et al, 2007, p 36). Such deliberation should be completely open, with everyone able to put forward their views or question other people's assumptions. Habermas distinguished between technical and practical rationality. Under technical rationality, local government tasks are understood as technical problems, solvable by technical means. Practical rationality emphasises conscious and enlightened reflection, which would clarify alternative goals and actions based on the widest possible communication and political dialogue (see Thompson and McHugh, 1990, p 30). The focus is therefore on the normative issues, as discussed in Chapter Four. His approach could be seen as a practical way of addressing Doyal and Gough's critical autonomy – the opportunity to engage in action and debate to change the moral norms and institutions of the country in which one is situated. Habermas saw it as having the possibility of transforming attitudes.

Wolverhampton City Council: Citizens' Juries

In May 2006, Wolverhampton's first ever Citizens' Jury was conducted, with the aim of getting the views of a representative 'jury' of citizens on two issues that were emerging from the Lyons Inquiry into Local Government (Lyons, 2005, 2007):

1. The relevance and potential of the 'place-shaping' approach in Wolverhampton?
2. Where responsibility for standard-setting and financial decisions should most properly sit – with central government, local government, local communities or a combination of these?

The findings of the Citizens' Jury can be summarised as follows:

- that Wolverhampton's citizens would like the council to concentrate on delivering appropriate, needs-led local services, which reflect and respond to the most pressing needs of the local population;
- that the council should concentrate on building a strong community spirit which would encourage communities to be a part of decisions that affect them, and that citizens should be actively encouraged to participate in decision-making;
- that there should be strong links between the council and other providers to ensure that all services are joined up, and that the council should provide leadership in these partnerships and be 'the voice of the people';
- that the council should take a lead on housing, transport, local environmental services and the assessment of need locally.

The Jury generally approved of the concept of 'place-shaping', although they were not enamoured of the term itself and thought definitions of the purpose of local government should be more rooted in the community. There was also a strong feeling that while central government should retain control of standards and budget setting for key national services, there should be a greater degree of local discretion as to how these standards are implemented at the community level.

The council concluded: 'The findings of the Jury, are useful, both in terms of informing our contribution to the debate on the future of local government and in shaping our future priorities and policy-making internally' (Wolverhampton City Council, 2006).

A second Jury was organised to involve residents in the budget decisions for the financial year 2009/10. At the close of the event, the jurors had ranked the 28 budget priorities in order of importance, giving the council a detailed and rigorous resource to use when allocating funding.

Barnes et al (2007, pp 35–42, 189) raise some issues with this approach, drawing on the work of Nancy Fraser (1997) and Iris Marion Young (2000). They argue that it is not possible to exclude power in this abstract way, that deliberations are inevitably framed by those setting them up and what people see as 'allowable alternatives', and that some people will be more capable of contributing while others will use styles of speech that will not be so persuasive. They suggest that power relationships and the impact of social positioning will need to be addressed and that other styles of speech – greeting, rhetoric, storytelling – must be valued. It is not possible to do this in one universal, single form of public discourse. Various debates that include affective, expressive and experienced-based forms of discourse are required (Newman, J. and Clarke, 2009, p 140). Councillors can draw upon participatory practice in development (see following box) to set up deliberations that will help to develop the ethical principles set out in Chapter Four, develop capabilities and provide clear guidance for council decision-making.

Participatory practice in development

Supporters of participation developed a wide range of tools and techniques to engage poor people in analysing their context, in sharing their information and knowledge, so that they could act on their analysis to transform their situation or condition. These tools involved 'visuals': large scale maps, calendars and matrices constructed on the ground using locally available materials and concerning a range of issues from health, to local services, to land tenure; theatrical methods (Boal, 1979); and various local art forms (song, dance, music, drama). More recently participatory practice has embraced new technologies including photography, video, radio, television and internet technologies. There has also been a growing focus on participatory or deliberative democracy with the inclusion of processes such as participatory budgeting, public hearings, debates and citizen juries. These approaches have also been integrated into long-term community organising and adult learning projects (such as *Reflect*: www. reflect-action.org). Manuals and training courses have been produced to support different participatory techniques, emphasising both the technical aspects of participation and the behaviour, skills and relationships needed to engage in community based participatory processes. (Newman, K., 2012, p 29)

Addressing power inequalities and working with social movements

If participation is to be transformative, it needs to closely address issues of power and to seek to understand how particular publics may be excluded, why some voices get marginalised and who sets the agenda, rules and norms of the debate. Local authorities may unwittingly set the limits of what it is possible to think and what choices can be made (Barnes et al, 2007, p 66). Discussions around 'troubled families' or 'anti-social behaviour' will constrain the terms and possible outcomes from the start:

> [By] exclude[ing] certain actors or views from entering the arena for participation in the first place ... [power] may be internalised in terms of one's values, self-esteem and identities, such that voices in visible places are but echoes of what the power holders who shaped those places want to hear. (Gaventa, 2003, p 11, quoted in Newman, K., 2012, p 33)

In the deliberations discussed earlier, local authorities have to think through their power and how the context and history have limited the power of other groups and the impact that this will have. The way the deliberation is set up should allow local authority power to be open to challenge.

But, even if local authorities try their best to have open deliberation, the reality is that most change comes from social movements or voluntary, community and trade union organisations challenging from outside the institutional framework (Barnes et al, 2007, pp 43–5; Wainwright, 2009a). These movements are usually claiming rights or they might constitute a group opposed to some local authority policy.

Protest and new social media

Protest organisations and individuals are becoming more adept at using social media in all kinds of creative ways. The Barnet Alliance for Public Services, discussed in the final chapter, is supported by four or more bloggers:

Mrs Angry at www.brokenbarnet.blogspot.co.uk analyses outsourcing

Mr Mustard at http://lbbspending.blogspot.co.uk/ is a lawyer who is primarily concerned with parking in Barnet.

Mr Reasonable at http://reasonablenewbarnet.blogspot.co.uk/ is a citizen of the London Borough of Barnet trying to get the council to be more transparent and accountable. He has sophisticated financial knowledge.

The Barnet Eye at http://barneteye.blogspot.co.uk/ involves guest bloggers.

These bloggers, and the campaign groups they support, are not only feeding into overview and scrutiny committees but also increasingly setting the agenda in the local press and reaching the national press and specialist magazines. Many councillors have yet to really learn how to engage with such campaigns in the social media and use them constructively.

Social movements, like the women's movement and the disability rights movement, have altered the way we think about people and their needs, and their significance extends well beyond any individual campaign directed at a particular policy area. These movements start as independent from the state, they are motivated, as Chapter Four explored, by a call to end injustice and they are bottom-up rather than top-down. But, ultimately, they have to relate to the state as progressive change cannot occur without engagement with the state at both the local and national level. A local authority can enhance democracy by responding to such social movements and voluntary and community organisations rather than by only establishing its own spaces for deliberative democracy.

However, a survey of councillors (Copus, 2010) revealed that they are resistant to this conclusion and to engaging with groups outside the council that want change. Councillors' perception was that groups outside the council who shared their views and wished to access decision-making in cooperation with them were more effective than those engaged in political protest (Copus, 2010). There is also the problem 'that "the people" can be intolerant, narrow-minded and prejudiced, especially when they are feeling defensive' (Goss, 2006, p 19). It is, however, all too easy to close down deliberative spaces by imposing frameworks of legitimate membership and controlling what can be discussed. Instead, the local authority should seek to promote social identification/solidarities, as it is through emancipation and recognition that some of the excesses of the market can be challenged.

It is important that voices are heard rather than denigrated as prejudiced, unrepresentative or the 'usual suspects'. Chapter Six will look in more detail at this issue, with the example of planning policy in Northern Ireland. Local authorities can also seek to encourage voluntary and community groups and social movements to ensure that they, in their turn, seek to maximise deliberative democracy with as wide as possible communication and dialogue. Participatory groups, and more formally constituted bodies like trade unions and the voluntary and community sector, very definitely also need to put their own houses in order.

Although it is not easy for local authorities and social movements to work with each other, it is clear that officials and councillors can often have the same values and goals as campaign groups outside the local authority and that such people can mediate across boundaries and support marginalised voices being heard, recognised and validated (Barnes et al, 2007, p 190; Wainwright, 2009a, ch 8). Distinctions between insiders and outsiders are more permeable than is sometimes suggested and there are dangers in creating too clearly delineated boundaries between councillors, public officials and opposition groups (Barnes et al, 2007, p 162).

Newcastle's Fairness Commission

Newcastle's Fairness Commission, set up by local councillors, is completely independent of the local authority, and is composed of local faith and black and minority ethnic (BME) groups, the voluntary and community sector, and education and health representatives. It produces a set of principles for fairness to guide the council's decision-making processes, providing tests against which to judge the fairness and impact of decisions (Studdert, 2013, p 38).

Local councillors can also play a key role in building social movements. At the moment, protest about the impact of the cuts on the poor and disadvantaged is fragmented. By feeding local information into national institutions, local social movements and voluntary groups, councils can help to build a national evidence base to support change.

Reflective practice and knowledge

Chapter Four discussed how day-to-day ethical problems could be addressed through conscious reflection on daily practice and discussions about ethics. Councillors can encourage their officers to engage in 'reflective practice' together with the residents that they are seeking to empower (Donald Schön, 1983). This would involve users, wider citizens and officers: reflecting on the practice of the professional; surfacing and criticising assumptions that have developed; and exploring how power has influenced what the professionals do. Finally, the group would explore who has gained and who has lost out through the professionals' actions and what impact this has on social justice. This opens up new ways of doing things that value the experience and knowledge of all those involved. It can seek to promote the recognition and emancipation that Fraser argued was essential. It is an approach that recognises the assets that the poor and disadvantaged bring to the policy debate and solutions to problems.

Joint learning and the development of a body of knowledge are seen by Wainwright as the way of coalescing disparate individualised disaffection and people who are claiming rights or protesting about some local authority policy into a 'public force with its own agenda of democratic control' (Wainwright, 2009a, p 370). She argues that knowledge is a social product that 'can be socially transformed by people who take action together – cooperating, sharing and combining different kinds of knowledge – to overcome the limits on the knowledge that they individually possess' (Wainwright, 2009a, p 93). In this way, new understanding about the world is generated and new possibilities are opened up. The process of building the knowledge creates a 'vested interest in democracy'. The development of knowledge and joint learning therefore has the possibility of changing institutions and the people involved in the process. It is part of the process of challenging traditional power and building capabilities.

South Lanarkshire

South Lanarkshire Council has encouraged innovation through a variety of processes, including regular team meetings, training, employee surveys, a suggestion box weighted towards suggestions from junior staff, an employee awards night and a staff appraisal process that values contribution to innovation (APSE, 2013, pp 24–6). The practice has yet to engage fully with residents and encourage participatory democracy but the following example evidences how the council's focus on bottom-up improvement and training and innovation has had wider community benefits.

South Lanarkshire Council was an early adopter of the radical changes to school catering brought about by the Scottish Executive's 'Hungry for Success' initiative, and regularly receives favourable comments from Education Scotland (HMI) for its positive approach.

South Lanarkshire's Facilities Management Service has an excellent track record: it was the first and only service in the UK to successfully retain in-house catering, cleaning and janitorial services within a school's Public–Private Partnership (PPP) at a time when this was considered impossible; it successfully retained external contracts for cleaning with Strathclyde Police and Strathclyde Fire and Rescue Services; and in 2009/10, it was listed by the Association for Public Service Excellence (APSE) as one of the top seven education catering performers in the UK. It established the Eddlewood Training Academy in 2009 in one of South Lanarkshire's areas of multiple deprivation. The Academy provides training for both council employees and local unemployed people in catering and cleaning. Staff cooking skills have improved, and the service receives very positive environmental health reports. The Academy has also contributed to the council's success in increasing the uptake of school meals (greater than the Scottish national average by 5% in the case of primary school meals and by 10.4% in the case of secondary school meals), and has generally promoted healthy eating through the provision of training events for pupils, parents and the general public. It is now used overnight as a centralised production facility, producing 41,500 cold salads and sandwiches each year for all South Lanarkshire's schools and corporate units, providing employment and saving £100,000 annually. (Taken from submission to APSE service awards 2012 in the best employment and equality initiative category.)

Rights and participation

It is important also to return to the tensions between participation and human rights. Chapter Four suggested that human rights and participation were both essential for social justice. Participation without rights tends to focus on service delivery within the existing framework, involving the local resident as a user, rather than taking on the broader discussion of what a local authority should be trying to do. It can result in a focus on the efficiency and effectiveness of the existing local services. At the neighbourhood level, it is often concerned with local service delivery or project work. It can fail to challenge inequality and power, to build capability, or to enable popular control. Meanwhile, legal rights with no participation soon fade as the existing power relationships and market interests dominate. The lack of participation will result in a failure to generate the momentum to innovate, strengthen government accountability or garner the necessary resources to ensure that the right is implemented in practice (Newman, K., 2012, p 62). The Equalities Act 2010 is gradually being whittled away as external social movements fail effectively to mobilise together with councils to protect it.[4]

Working with social movements to promote recognition and emancipation

While there is a considerable amount of work within local authorities to engage with external social movements and the voluntary sector to consolidate the culture of the Equalities Act 2010, much of the funding for bringing together external forums on the various equality strands is now being withdrawn. The London Borough of Islington's work on disability is an example of good practice of joint work with external organisations on rights, bringing participatory influences to bear on the council's policy. The council set up a Disability Reference Group (DRG) of 12 local disabled people, two from each of the six main impairment groups.[5] The council funds a local borough-wide organisation of disabled people to facilitate and manage the DRG. The DRG meets regularly with the council's Disability Equality Performance Group, which scrutinises performance on the disability equality scheme (Russell, 2011, p 31). It is not clear, however, if the council is engaged in positive action to ensure that this joint work also feeds into national campaigns.

Newman argues that by integrating participation and rights, the two concepts develop meaning and content, based on real contexts and experiences (Newman, K., 2012, p 273). Specific efforts need to be made to integrate work at the local, national and even international levels to enable poor people's perspectives to influence how work evolves at the other levels. But difficulties in achieving this integration in practice must be recognised. Participation can delay progress where quick decision-making is required. Partnership arrangements are usually between public institutions, whose key priority is efficient delivery rather than changing the way they approach processes and outcomes to allow the recipients of their services to have real influence. Often, those living in poverty do not have the capabilities (Sen's ability, freedom to choose and achievement) to campaign for their rights and are more concerned with dealing with an immediate issue. Meanwhile, local authorities may not have the officers who can work alongside social movements and residents in deprived areas and develop the links from local concerns to council-wide and national campaigns on rights. Appropriate training and support for officers is crucial (Mayo, 2006, p 25), as is action to build the capabilities of those in poverty.

So, it is not easy: success in bringing participation and rights together will depend on understanding the barriers and the trade-offs involved in day-to-day policy decisions (Newman, K., 2012, p 275). But there is evidence that a value-driven organisation that is committed to deliberative democracy can open up its practices to allow perspectives and voices from grassroots communities to impact on organisational learning and understanding and, ultimately, enable poor people's perspectives to influence wider policy debates (Newman, K., 2012, p 283).

Democracy in the workplace

Finally, participation and deliberative democracy tend to be seen in terms of empowering deprived residential communities. But citizens include those working for the local authority and participation should include opening up ways that trade unions and employees can influence public policy, and considering how democracy can be enhanced through different systems of internal management. The preceding discussion on reflective practice, and in Chapter Four on professional ethics, has already highlighted how professionals in local government have a crucial role in contributing to democracy. It is not only the professional, but also every employee, as citizens with particular expertise and experience, who should be able to influence the development of public policy.

The insidious nature of the New Right and New Public Management is demonstrated in the general acceptance of the view that 'the producer interest' needs to be limited in public policy. This ideology denies any concept of a 'public service ethos' and sees hierarchical management as essential to enforce a work ethic. Trade union power, it suggests, must be limited through the market, through breaking up public services and promoting local institutional industrial relationships, and through facilitating dismissal.

There are, in fact, many contradictions in the attempt to freeze out employee input in decision-making. An APSE report for **Unison** (APSE and Unison, 2010) shows how crucial trade union involvement and staff engagement are in service improvement. A subsequent report by APSE highlights how local authorities can encourage innovation among employees and harness ideas developed 'on the job' for service improvement (APSE, 2013).

Monmouthshire County Council in Wales and the Intrapreneurship School

Monmouthshire **County Council** (MCC) is looking to find creative solutions to deal with the growing expectations of public services. The first part of that process has been to create a culture in which staff can contribute, come up with new ideas and try things out without being afraid of failure. The Intrapreneurship School is a staff training programme that aims to foster this sense of empowerment, self-belief and purpose. The Intrapreneurship School equips staff with a set of tools and methodologies that they can apply to the 'day job' to help them think about how they can do things better. The School has developed an 'Intrapreneurship Cookbook', a collection of ideas, demonstrations, tools and techniques to show how staff can engage in innovative action and to document and codify the learning. Ideas range from giving staff the time to go and have a cup of tea with a service user to understand their experiences, to asking and reflecting with colleagues about their best and worst experience of using public services.

The council believes that innovation must be an inclusive process: not just for the chosen few. Furthermore, the only way that the council can stay relevant to its communities is to fully use the best asset they have: council employees (Peter Davies, Head of Innovation, MCC; see APSE, 2013, pp 29–31; Davies, 2013).

The importance of involving employees, however, goes well beyond service improvement. Employees are citizens and democracy in the workplace provides a crucial educative and ethical counterweight to the dominant elite ideology. There is evidence that democratic management can be economically successful and that the freedom and self-realisation it affords gives an experience of solidarity and working together that fosters a recognition of true citizenship.

Transformative participation

In Chapter Seven, two current initiatives are looked at in more detail to see if these provide some possibilities to further local democracy: the promotion of co-operatives and mutuals; and co-production. The preceding discussion on participatory democracy suggests that councillors need to ensure that the CLEAR model is supplemented by the following:

- opening up deliberative spaces at all levels of government;
- a wide concept of deliberative democracy that addresses power inequalities and discusses ethics, values and principles;
- reflective practice;
- a redistributive state working with social movements that challenge current practice;
- integrating participation with rights-based practice; and
- involving council workers as well as residents.

In these circumstances, there would be a real possibility of transformative participation and reclaiming democracy.

Note on councillors and representative democracy

Councillors do a vital and difficult job. Finding ways of enhancing representative democracy and reaffirming the importance of politics remains central to the project of reclaiming local democracy.

The Councillors Commission found that the average number of hours that councillors spend on their duties has risen over the years to 95 hours a month by 2006 (Councillors Commission, 2007, p 19). The discussion in this book implies that councillors should be in contact with their local community, meet their constituents, explain democratic processes to them, engage them in discussions on political issues, convey their views into the political process and report back to their constituents. The average remuneration of a councillor in England is £5,648 in basic allowances a year, with special responsibility allowances for leaders averaging £16,356. The ward councillor with no special responsibility is earning around £5.00 an hour. It is clearly very difficult for councillors to fulfil their role while doing a full-time job. The Councillors Commission acknowledged that those with a full-time job were 'grossly underrepresented in council chambers' (Councillors Commission, 2007, p 20).

The Councillors Commission was reluctant to argue for full salaries for councillors, suggesting that this might create a separate political class removed from their electors. Nor did it support legislation to guarantee paid time off for public duties, although it supported the promotion of good practice in this field. The All Party Parliamentary Local Government Group (Dungey, 2007), however, went further, calling for a review of the legal framework for councillors' rights to time off for public duties, for example, in comparison with the framework for jury service (recommendation 45). The more recent Communities and Local Government Select Committee report on councillors (Communities and Local Government Committee, 2012, para 82) suggested that councils (or local allowance bodies) should have the power to include a capped element to compensate for loss of earnings, as part of a councillor's allowance. This would encourage those at work to become councillors without providing an incentive for retired people to hold onto councillor roles. The debate remains open, but I would argue that the current system of most councillors earning below the minimum wage is ultimately untenable.

All reports also call for significantly more support for councillors if they are going to be able to do their job properly. The Select Committee argues that government must not accidentally undermine the authority of councillors, which it can do easily by limiting their ability to make a difference, pouring scorn on them and arguing for fewer councillors.

Conclusion

This chapter has argued that local democracy is not on the slope of irreversible decline; instead, local participative democracy has increased. However, many participatory mechanisms are tokenistic and misframed. In order to reclaim local democracy, participation needs to be developed so that it is transformative, and representative democracy needs to be enhanced and promoted so that involvement in politics is no longer scorned. These are not easy tasks and the chapter has highlighted the difficulties and tensions that exist. But real change requires social movements, political representatives and committed officers to work together in relation to an agreed ethical framework through which the concepts of social justice, rights, emancipation and social and environmental protection can be furthered. It involves looking at ways of making central policymaking more open, linking rights and participation, opening deliberative spaces for opposition and developing reflective practice. It necessitates clarifying how public policy decisions are political and require a consideration of who will benefit and who may be affected negatively. The decisions, as Sen, Habermas and others have argued, must be able to stand up to rational scrutiny and debate, involving a wider group of citizens, not just those involved directly as users of services. Policymaking must also involve consideration of alternatives that reflect the perspectives of those without power who are usually not heard.

There is one final point that is emphasised in a study of the state of local democracy in two Northern towns (Wilks-Heeg and Clayton, 2006). If local government does not have the power to make a real difference, local democracy is diminished. Chapter Seven of this book on the future will look at the reforms required to enable local democracy to improve the well-being of local residents and employees.

Notes
[1] Well over half the recommendations have been implemented, including: a mayor in London; council structures to include a separate executive; the duty to involve; procedures for declaration of interests; proportional representation in Scotland and Wales; postal ballots; remuneration of councillors; power to

hold local referenda; citizenship education; power of general competence; a community leadership role; less ring-fencing; directly elected police commissioners; transparent and independent public appointments processes; decentralisation; and parishes in London. The recommendations that have never been implemented include: elected regional assemblies; constitutional protection for local government through a legal framework in accordance with the European Charter of Local Self-Government; an increased number of councillors; proportional representation in England; a duty to prepare an annual democracy plan; direct control of training and enterprise services, fire authorities, all highways and Ofsted; a duty to consult staff on policy formation; and, crucially, financial independence.

[2] Some non-executive councillors have opposed decentralisation schemes, seeing them as widening community engagement and the influence of the executive in the ward and limiting the residual power and influence that their ward councillor role retains.

[3] See: www.localis.org.uk/page/53/About-Localis.htm

[4] The government has: cut the Equality and Human Rights Commission's (EHRC's) budget by 70%; removed the socio-economic duty in the Act that required public authorities, in deciding how to exercise their strategic functions, to have regard to how they can reduce the inequalities of outcome that result from socio-economic disadvantage; and removed clauses on gender pay-gap information and combined discrimination when someone has dual characteristics. In October 2012, the government confirmed that third-party harassment, discrimination questionnaires and the tribunal's powers to make wider recommendations to employers in discrimination cases will all be repealed.

[5] The six main impairment groups are: physical, visual, hearing, learning, mental and hidden/long term.

SIX

Recapturing discourse

This chapter looks at how language is used in local government. It explores whose interests are being served by particular **discourses**. It asks how discourses could be changed to make them serve the ethical framework developed in Chapter Four and the objective of reclaiming local democracy.

Chapter Five focused on how representative democracy can be strengthened by local councillors working to promote active citizenship and discussion around the ethical framework and routes of influence through the tiers of government. I argued for more political discussion and debate at all levels of government. But this debate occurs within a cultural framework. Social and cultural norms shape the way we see the world and how we then represent it in our own discussions and actions. It is important to raise awareness of who benefits and who loses and how the discourses constrain alternative courses of action. Understanding how discourses can impact on policymaking can strengthen the way councillors can promote participation. Councillors could also do more to contest the dominant discourses and so open up alternative possibilities.

The chapter starts by asking why language is important and how it can be used as a political resource. Three dominant discourses that constrain debate are then explored. In this way, the need for an alternative discourse is highlighted. The chapter finally looks at appropriate strategies through which such an alternative can be developed, building on the development of active citizenship and participation advocated in Chapter Five.

Is language important?

> Words are constantly being inflected and re-inflected with new meaning as they are used in different contexts and media, carried over into new spheres of discourse and deployed in arguments among people with conflicting beliefs and interests. (Cameron, 1994, pp 28–9)

The word 'wicked', for example, moved from its meaning of 'evil', to its use by children in the 1980s ('It's wicked!') to mean 'It's excellent!', to the concept of 'wicked issues', originating in the 1960s, but promoted by Rittle and Webber (1973) and Stewart (2003, p 12) to categorise complex problems that were ill-defined and resistant to resolution.

Raymond Williams noted the changing meaning of words, particularly 'culture', when he returned from the Second World War to Cambridge University in 1945 and it encouraged him to write his famous book *Keywords* (Williams, 1983). Keywords were defined as words that have different meanings in two areas of study that are thought of separately, such as 'culture', which has different meanings in *art* and *society*. These words cause problems when we discuss ideas and values with others because they have a range of meanings that have developed from their origins in different languages and these meanings continue to change over time.

Williams saw language as reflecting actual political, social and economic relationships. But he also argued that important social and historical processes occur within language (Williams, 1983, p 22). If you can persuade someone to see the world in a new way, you can open up a variety of new possibilities for action. Williams' aim was not to clarify difficult words so as to reduce disputes: 'I believe that to understand the complexities of the meaning of class contributes very little to the resolution of actual class disputes and class struggles' (Williams, 1983, p 24). Rather, he sought to raise consciousness about how language was used and critical awareness of whose interests were served when people insisted on the 'right' use of a term. This would increase understanding of how language is shaped and reshaped from different points of view: 'a vocabulary to use, to find our own ways in, to change as we find it necessary to change it, as we go on making our own language and history' (Williams, 1983, pp 24–5).

It is clear that those with power are more able to create a dominant discourse than the powerless. The ability of the Prime Minister compared to an unemployed worker to shape discourse around 'scroungers', for example, needs to be recognised. Bourdieu, a very influential French sociologist, highlighted how dominant groups impose censorship on those without power (Davies, 2011, p 118). It is also evident that changes in language on their own can achieve little (Davies, 2011, p 102). However, even Bourdieu argued that it is important to expose how language is used to reinforce social and cultural inequality, with the aim of helping people to develop more effective challenges (Mayo, 2000, p 35). So, the action of challenging discourses remains very important for councillors who are opposed to the inequality in the capability of different people to achieve the personal and critical autonomy that has been discussed earlier. And there is evidence that challenging discourse can contribute to the development of rights and social justice. The feminist movement has achieved some change in recognition and emancipation through challenging language. Calling female adults 'girls' reflects a set of assumptions about how society values and thinks female adults should be treated. Insisting on being called 'women' may not change men's attitudes dramatically, but it confronts established views, and demands being treated with respect, as an adult equivalent to 'men'.

How councillors can link challenges to dominant discourses with wider action for change: the views of Cllr Rachel Allen, Sevenoaks District Council

Domestic violence is a subject that I have personal experience of. It is very easy to think that it doesn't happen in a nice area like Sevenoaks, but it does. As a councillor, I wanted to use my position to raise awareness about the fact that one in four women and one in seven men experience domestic abuse and I wanted to improve support locally. I'm fierce about democracy. I didn't think I was being represented by someone who understood people like me; a single mother with four young children, one of whom is profoundly disabled. So, in 2003 I decided to stand for the ward where I live. I feel that I am cutting a new path for women. I've publicly challenged women councillors being called Miss or Mrs when male councillors are just referred to as councillor so and so. It's very important to get rid of these old Victorian ideas. I've breastfed in the scrutiny committee. It's not gone down too well but I'm the first one to do it. And a year after I started I got councillors an allowance which they can claim for babysitters. Not everyone has a husband or wife at home looking after the kids. (Quoted in IDeA, 2007, pp 20–1)

Rydin (2003) develops what she calls an institutional framework 'that allows both for the constraints placed on practice by the influence of discursive patterns and the potential for achieving change through discursive strategies' (Rydin, 2003, p 38). Her analysis involves looking at cultural context, norms and values, and how these are reflected in policymakers' everyday working practices. She explores how actors use discursive strategies to influence the direction of policy. In this way, she provides insights into how those involved in policy formulation and implementation construct stories and meanings around problems in order to persuade others to adopt the solution they want to pursue. These insights can question taken-for-granted assumptions and open up new opportunities for action.

As part of this analysis, one can explore how particular concerns become framed as public policy issues for those involved in policy formulation and how this concern might differ from the conception of the problem by those personally affected by it. Wright Mills (1959) argued that individuals need to have a 'sociological imagination'. He used this term to describe a form of self-consciousness or an understanding of how 'private troubles' relate to what is going on in their world and how the public policies of society shape individuals' own thoughts and consciousness. Without a sociological imagination, most individuals are unable to 'cope with their personal troubles in such ways as to control the structural transformations that usually lie behind them' (Wright Mills, 1959, p 12). The sociological imagination enables the individual to both understand everyday life and change it – to make a difference. It can help to explain how a policy issue shifts from being a 'personal trouble' to become a 'public issue' (Wright Mills, 1959, pp 7–9). Teenage pregnancy, for example, emerged as a public policy issue under New Labour. To understand why, one would need to look at the shift in middle-class and lower-income childbearing, adoption and abortion practices and the reasons for these. Then, one would interrogate the narratives that framed teenage pregnancy as a problem for state intervention, with a reduction in the numbers as a target for public policy. Finally, one would need to consider the discursive strategies of the teenage mothers themselves in contrast to those of the state to understand what policy outcomes each group sought and who managed to dominate the policy agenda. One could then consider if a deeper understanding of how their issue of motherhood had been turned into a public problem by society could lead to different discursive strategies by the mothers that could have shifted the agenda.

Rydin's approach can also be used to explore how rationality and a focus on evidence are used to justify political decisions based on values. Despite the fact that there is broad agreement that social science problems (and science problems) cannot be solved through empirical inquiry alone and that absolute certainty is elusive, there is still an attempt to present decisions as totally rational and to look for 'what works'. Thus, policy textbooks suggest that the policy analyst should go through a logical process: identify the problem; formulate goals and objectives that lead to the optimal solution; ascertain the range of options that meet the goals; analyse the costs and benefits of the options; and select the best option for implementation (Fischer, 2003, p 4). It is accepted that not all the necessary information will be available and sometimes rationality is therefore limited or 'bounded', but this approach still dominates how local government justifies and argues for particular policies. Fischer calls it a 'methodological fetish – that brings ever more rigorous quantitative analysis to bear on topics of narrower and narrower import' (Fischer, 2003, p vii). The approach constrains attempts to promote more democratic and socially just forms of policy analysis and policymaking because it ignores the basic values that are involved in policymaking. The way problems are narrowly defined in the rational process often excludes the social and political issues that are the fundamental causes of the problem. So, for example, the problem is defined as personal debt and the solution through rational policymaking might be seen as a credit union. Meanwhile, the issue of what causes the debt in the first place (poverty, the profit needs of credit card providers and weakly regulated short-term loan providers) is not addressed. Society's values in relation to income distribution, profligacy and the private profit of credit institutions are not explored. These are issues of politics and policymaking, and the rational model, by ignoring these factors, undermines the political process.

Newman, J. and Clarke (2009, p 25) provide a similar analysis, arguing:

> the rationality of what works is one that takes the politics out of public policy issues by rendering them not the site of contestation over competing values, or between different interests, but making them instead the focus of technical judgements about the efficiency and efficacy of different solutions.

Dean (2010, p 4) suggests that rationality is a cloak for the operation of power, with claims of rationality embodying certain assumptions regarding appropriate and logical action. Fischer concludes that we need to understand how the rational should be embedded in the normative. In presenting an ethical framework, I have sought to embed the rational within a normative context and argued that any framework must be able to stand up to scrutiny and rational debate.

Eco-towns

Wilson and Piper (2010) suggest that planning has been dominated by discourses that seek to legitimate state action through rationalist approaches. Such discourses emphasise the expertise of planners and their use of due process, and suggest that they use objective knowledge. But this approach hides the uneven distribution of power and uncertainties around science, knowledge and conceptions of the public interest (Wilson and Piper, 2010, pp 71–3). Wilson and Piper are clear that planning is a normative and ethical-based policy process. Discourse analysis can provide insights into how actors in policy formulation and implementation construct stories and meanings to further their interests. They give the example of eco-towns, which were promoted by a discourse coalition of the government and the Town and Country Planning Association (TCPA) as a solution to climate change. Eco-towns were new settlements with carbon-neutral housing that were promoted by the Labour government to expand house-building and address the shortage of new homes. They were eagerly seized on by the TCPA as furthering the garden city movement from which the organisation originated. However, such carbon-neutral housing could also have been built in existing settlements and near existing transport facilities, where they would have had a lower impact on carbon emissions, but this option was not considered because of the normative goals of the TCPA. Wilson and Piper (2010, p 84) conclude that 'to understand the complex arena of the spatial planning response to climate change requires a much more nuanced understanding of discourses, discourse coalitions, and the arenas for debate and promulgation of these discourses, than mere injunctions to better practice'.

An approach that starts from values, as promoted in this book, results in very different discursive strategies, as will be outlined later in the chapter. First, however, three current dominant discourses within local government will be investigated: economic and market discourse; responsibility discourse; and 'motherhood and apple pie' discourse. All three discourses seek to frame the policy debate in ways in which politics is downplayed and disadvantaged groups are disempowered. Councillors who want to open up alternative spaces for debate and promote participation, as outlined in Chapter Five, should be challenging these dominant discourses.

Economic and market discourse

Chapters Two and Three have already discussed the rise of the New Right and New Public Management (NPM). The New Right's aim was to limit the size of the state, open up public services to private competition and increase the profitability of the private sector. In legitimising this policy, the particular aspects of public service highlighted in Chapter One (the provision of public goods and services; the development of values of democracy and citizenship; and the realisation of justice and equity) were downplayed and the term 'consumer' or 'customer' as opposed to 'citizen' was increasingly used.

Needham (2007, pp 8, 197) shows that the term 'consumer' is the second most widely used keyword in local government after 'community'. It can refer to someone paying for a service, someone treated with respect or someone who makes a choice. The debate around the difference between 'citizen' and 'consumer' has been the subject of a wide range of literature (eg Rhodes, 1987; Stewart and Clarke, 1987; Hambleton, 1989; Gyford, 1991a; Stewart and Walsh, 1992; Marquand, 2004; Clarke, 2007a, 2007b; Needham, 2007). 'Citizen' is a keyword with a variety of meanings over time, but in France, in particular, it has been associated with claiming universal rights from the state (Bennett et al, 2005, p 31). While 'consumer' carries aspects of user agency, empowerment and anti-elitism (Needham, 2007, p 3), it ultimately constructs people as economic subjects who pursue their individual needs and wants like buyers, sellers, customers, clients and entrepreneurs. The term 'consumer' normalises a market relationship between the state and the individual (Newman, J. and Clarke, 2009, p 18). The discourse strategy that was pursued by the New Right in promoting 'consumer' and 'customer' over 'citizen' was to emphasise 'choice' for the consumer, arguing against unresponsive 'bureaucracies' that served producer interests and produced standard public services. Such a discourse clearly undermines universal public provision.

Newman, J. and Clarke (2009, p 79) note that choice has three meanings: there is the choice of a particular type of policy mechanism (eg the choice of schools); choice involving exchange (eg council house swaps); and choice as a value – the freedom to choose. Slipping between these three meanings has enabled policymakers to promote certain policies as value-driven and a 'good thing'. In fact, one of the roles of the public domain is to limit individual choice in certain areas so as to maximise general well-being (enforcing planning regulations, tackling anti-social behaviour or ensuring everyone drives on the left-hand side of the road). Clarke (2007a, p 162; 2007b, p 11) notes that New Labour pursued a similar discursive strategy to the New Right (with the slightly different rationale of obtaining service improvement by delivering equity – 'extending choice to the many not the few' – and responding to increased diversity in society): 'Choice acknowledges that consumers of public services should increasingly be given the kind of options that they take for granted in other walks of life' (Tony Blair, Foreword to Office of Public Services Reform, 2002, quoted in Clarke, 2007a, p 161).

Interestingly, Clarke's work shows the failure of both Conservative and Labour governments to establish this dominant discourse, with people still refusing to be seen as consumers or customers and preferring terms like 'patient' or 'member of the public'. However, he argues that the discourse has had a significant impact on the organisation of public services, with attempts to create choice and markets and to contract out services. He suggests that these attempts to get institutional change created 'impoverished forms of choice' (Clarke, 2007a, p 174), since choice can only be created with excess capacity in the system. In times of limited resources, the focus in public services is actually on reducing demand rather than increasing choice, whatever the rhetoric (Clarke, 2007b, p 7).

The attempt to create a market discourse in public services and to encourage those who deliver such services to see themselves as economic agents came across very strongly in the publications of the New Local Government Network (NLGN), and continues in Localis's publications. *Towards a new localism: a discussion paper* (Filkin et al, 2000) is full of private sector language: the 'virtual' local authority; choice and consumers; world–class procurement; supply markets; winning the e-revolution; competitive cities; and so on. It is noticeable that the words 'probity', 'public sector ethos', 'ethical', 'reliable', 'equity' or 'equal opportunities' and 'collaboration' never appear in the discussion paper despite its Labour Party provenance. Stoker (2005, p 11) puts it even more clearly in a later NLGN paper, arguing that the 'rationale for government at all levels is to be a client – choosing the level and quality of service; and a market-maker – ensuring that a market place of providers exists and the competition is fair and quality assured'. Such language tries to break down the discourse of professionalism, public sector ethos and basic needs. The market narrative hides the political choices that are being made and seeks to present decision-making as a technical process to maximise efficiency. It is a short step from this discourse to the discursive framing of the 2010 Coalition Government's Work Programme or other payment-by-results schemes, with talk about shifting risk, prime contractors, setting incentives and saving through private sector investment – all technical and procedural issues on how to contract most effectively, rather than discussing the basic social and political problems (Newman, J. and Clarke, 2009, p 78). In the *Open Public Services* report (HM Government, 2012a), the discourse remains the same, only becoming more forceful. It states that governments at all levels should increasingly become the funders, regulators and commissioners of services that are provided by the private and third sector: 'To improve quality for all, and particularly for the most vulnerable' (HM Government, 2012a, p 3). It states:

The purpose of removing barriers to choice, encouraging people to exercise choice, and seeking evidence on potential legislation for a 'right to choose' is to create and embed a culture in which people can expect and demand the opportunity to exert control over the service they receive by choosing the provider that best suits their needs. (HM Government, 2012a, p 4)

Yet, we know that choice favours those with educational and financial resources and that while citizens are critical of public services, they do not want them to be like private services. In general, they believe that public services are and should be fair, consistent, needs-based and responsive 'but not profit-driven' (Needham, 2007, p 193). Needham concludes that the discourse on choice is out of step with public preferences. People want better information about, and access to, services and want to be listened to and have a greater role in framing or co-producing services.

The NLGN discussion paper used the term 'community leadership' (Filkin et al, 2000, p 6) as a discourse to weaken the importance of direct service provision and to provide a discursive framing for New Labour's take on Nicholas Ridley's (1988) 'enabling' local state. The strategy was purely discursive: there was no evidence presented to show that direct service provision was incompatible with community leadership. As Chapter Two has argued, attempts to control local government in the Thatcher period had the perverse impact of demonstrating local government's scope for leadership and creative autonomy. In fact, there were, and remain, a number of strong arguments for combining both the community leadership and service delivery roles, as already indicated in Chapter Three. At the time of the NLGN pamphlet, I argued in a Local Government Information Unit (LGiU) briefing that:

The assumption that community leadership can exist without service delivery fails to deal with:

1) how local authorities 'learn' if they do not deliver services.
2) how a 'virtual' local authority can carry weight in negotiations over community leadership and 'tough decisions'.
3) how a local authority with no service capacity can respond to a disaster or crisis or major change, while achieving best value.

4) how a 'virtual' local authority can deal with fragmentation and joining up different contractors on highly specified contracts.

5) how accountability can be achieved in 'arms length' services.

6) how the public interest can override vested contractor interests within a contractual, outsourcing framework.

7) how the public sector can lead by example on employment issues and link the employment, quality and equality agenda, if it has limited direct employment.

8) how social inclusion issues and access for disadvantaged groups can be prioritised in a changing environment when services are delivered by the private sector.[1]

Chapter Seven will explore further the whole debate about direct service delivery.

'Place-shaping' is a keyword that can also be seen as part of market discourse, but its use remains contested. Although the final Lyons' report defined 'place-shaping' as 'the creative use of powers and influence to promote the general well-being of a community and its citizens' (Lyons, 2007, p 52) and Lyons never posited a contradiction between direct service delivery and community leadership, the choice of the term 'place-shaping' can fit neatly into the increased emphasis on the competitive city. The discussion of Rights to the City in Chapter Four raised the issues around how such a competitive city has little to do with bringing real benefits to those in need. Jane Roberts (2006, p 39) uses the concept in a very different way when she argues:

> It is the core business of all local authorities to understand the different localities that fall within their administrative boundary so as to ensure the highest possible quality of services is delivered and to facilitate a sense of belonging – a sense of place.

Stears (2012, p 41) also suggests: 'At its most straightforward, a shared identification with a particular place can generate powerful bonds of mutual loyalty. Connections with buildings, streets, neighbourhoods, towns and cities are often the vital precursors to deeper relationships between individuals.' Public place is important for local democracy, but not as part of the commodification of the city.

The final discourse I want to draw attention to here relates to the misframing of neighbourhood and decentralisation discussed in Chapter

Five (the following paragraphs draw on Newman, I., 1996). Within the decentralisation literature, two terms (tight–loose and front line–back line) have come to be regularly used, which have led to private sector management models limiting the understanding of the public sector. These terms are also currently being used in relation to contracting out and public expenditure cuts.

Tight–loose was taken from Peters and Waterman (1982), who argue that successful companies need to develop flexible workforces and devolved decision-making units. They describe companies as having simultaneous loose–tight properties and suggest that 'excellent' companies combine clear, central direction and the promotion of quality and objectives for the company as a whole with the maximum degree of individual and unit autonomy in operational matters. The model is replicated by Gaster and Hoggett, who state:

> We have consistently argued that decentralisation and devolution are the only effective route towards the development of a strong centre within large complex organisations.... The key point is that the devolved unit is left to decide how it will achieve its targets. So, because it frees the centre from absorption in administrative detail, it can provide the means for a tighter, leaner and more purposeful centre than in the past. (Gaster and Hoggett, 1993, p 136)

A similar discourse was used by the New Labour governments in their double devolution and localism discourse, while, at the same time, pursuing a stronger targets and outcome regime to control local government. Stacey (1993, p 371) has argued that loose–tight is a logical inconsistency and that in the private sector, power is delegated to use resources in predictable circumstances for predetermined purposes only. There are parallel limitations in the public sector and true democratisation, which Gaster and Hoggett seek to promote, as made clear in Chapter Five, depends on democratisation of the centre – a concept not discussed precisely because the private sector model, where the central goal of profitability or maximising shareholder value is assumed, has not identified this as a problem. If democratisation and facilitating contributions to the polity as a whole is a key function of local government, another approach is required. Instead of a tight–loose organisation where everyone has the same 'vision' of the goals of the organisation, we need to look for models of organising where there are discussions about alternatives at both the 'centre' and the 'neighbourhood'. The current 'localism' discourse also adopts a false tight–loose approach by asking those listening to the discourse to assume that tight financial control at national government level (over which there is no input from disadvantaged groups) can still allow real power at the local and neighbourhood levels.

The decentralisation literature also introduced the distinction between the front line and the back line of the local authority workforce (eg Burns et al, 1994, p 106). Again, the concept is taken from private sector management texts, where the sales force is seen as the 'front line' in touch with the 'customer' and the 'back line's' role is to support the front line in reaching its sales target. The concept is used in the recent literature on the relational state (Cooke and Muir, 2012, p 7), arguing that the private sector no longer uses NPM techniques, but 'instead driving decisions down to the frontline, encouraging learning and innovation and putting in place flatter management structures', and suggesting that the public sector could learn from this approach. This is the old argument about Fordism and post–Fordism discussed in Chapter Two. The transfer of the front line concept to the public sector is inappropriate. In the private sector, the power of the front line is controlled through tight sales or profit targets or, in restaurants like McDonalds, through rule books on staff behaviour in relation to the 'customer'. Those involved in facilitating the democratic process do not fit neatly into a front line–back line division. Where, for example, do you place the equal opportunities officer or the clerk who records the minutes of council meetings? When cuts have to be made, councillors come under pressure to concentrate these on the 'back line'; so, already in 1995, the Chief Executive of Sheffield was talking about 'cutting through bureaucracies to give front line staff greater freedom over how they deliver services' (Gordon, 1995). The 'back line' is damned by the pejorative use of the term 'bureaucracy' in this discourse. The values that support councils in promoting citizenship, democracy and 'bureaucracy' in delivering equality, accountability and good employment conditions for 'citizens' are all rendered invisible through this language.

There are clearly a range of functions in a local authority, from a receptionist to a human resources manager, which have different levels of external contact, but all the posts support the political process in one way or another. This is not to say that cuts can never be made, but the term 'front line–back line' hides the interdependence in the organisation and the fact that all are 'public sector' workers. It makes it easier to ignore the role of employees in supporting the political process and facilitates the privatisation of a section of public sector employment.[2]

Austerity and the front line/back line distinction

A councillor has discussed with me how many functions, which are classified as back line, are even more crucial to developing management for the public domain in a period of austerity. For example, Information and Communications Technology (ICT), human resource management and asset rationalisation are all crucial in developing the flexibility in the organisation to respond to new challenges. Councillors are aware that the public sector needs to develop a different managerial discourse. If an ethical framework is to drive the political process, they need to be careful that private sector management terms are not used inappropriately.

There are many such examples of the transfer of language from the private sector to the public sector that systematically undermine discourses on public sector ethos, probity, accountability and political choice and values. The dominant economic discourse starts by decrying the weaknesses of the public sector, it posits reform based on choice and competiveness as the only option, and concludes that 'what works' is increased outsourcing of local authority services and smart commissioning. It is important to keep challenging this discourse and demonstrating how the use of language, with hidden assumptions, seeks to legitimise the marketisation of public services while failing to present any real evidence about the benefits of marketisation for those who have unmet basic needs (see Whitfield, 2012, pp 216–18 and more generally).

Responsibility discourse

The concept of **responsibilisation** stems from Michel Foucault's concept of governmentality: the way in which governments try to shape citizens to suit their policies. The 2010 Coalition Government has made it clear that it wishes to cut back on welfare spending. It is therefore not surprising that in the context of trying to reduce demand for public services, there has been a systematic attempt to use discourse strategies to encourage, or force, people to take more responsibility for their own well-being. There has been an attempt to persuade people that social risks such as illness, unemployment and poverty are not the responsibility of the state, but are risks for which the individual should take responsibility, thereby transforming the issue into a problem of 'self-care' (Lemke, 2001, p 201). The government has even set up a 'nudge unit' to look at how it can influence behaviour. This policy is reinforced by discourse about the deserving and undeserving poor, decent families, vulnerable groups and the Big Society.

Big Society

In 2011, the Prime Minister described the Big Society project as his 'mission in politics' and pledged 'to fight for it every day, because the Big Society is here to stay'.[3] But as the Public Administration Select Committee (PASC) warned: 'The Big Society project is hampered by the lack of a clear implementation plan, leading to public confusion about the policy agenda.' The Committee complained that: 'Ministers have not set out clearly what success means for the Big Society project' (PASC, 2011, p 53).

The *Big Society audit* (Civil Exchange, 2012, 2013) sought to measure progress on the three medium-term aims for the Big Society articulated by the government in 2011 (community empowerment, opening up public services and social action) and on some long-term indicators of social health. The audit identified some problematic areas (impact on disadvantaged areas, decline in funding for the voluntary and community sector, and a commissioning framework that favoured the private sector and some big charities against the small and local) and made appropriate recommendations.

But these three aims are not the goals for a greater role for civil society held by local community groups. Local community groups are concerned with enhanced democracy and with the re-emergence of democratic control over the institutions both of government and the market. They are focused on: building on the strengths of current community-driven, collective action; promoting civil liberties, social justice and citizens' rights; and, finally, reducing poverty and inequality (New Policy Institute, 2012). It is these goals that have informed this book.

Katz (1989) argues that the discourse of the deserving and undeserving poor has been used for over two centuries in the US to limit the obligations of the state. He shows how in the 1980s, the concept of the poor was divided into the working class and the lower class or underclass. The latter were predominantly black teenage mothers or young, unemployed, black men and were a minority, 'small enough to be the object of effective help and, if assistance failed, to contain' (Katz, 1989, p 196). Their status was blamed on their behaviour rather than the sources of their poverty. Targeted approaches helped to reinforce stigma. Katz argues that the division of the poor into two sharply divided groups 'helps perpetuate their political powerlessness by strengthening the barriers that for so long have divided them against each other' (Katz, 1989, p 235). But Katz sees this as just one phase in the 'othering' of the poor and sees this vocabulary as limiting political imagination and negating need, entitlement and justice (Katz, 1989, p 3). He concludes:

> We can think about poor people as 'them' or as 'us'. For the most part, Americans have talked about 'them'. Even in the language of social science, as well as in ordinary conversation and political rhetoric, poor people usually remain outsiders, strangers to be pitied or despised, helped or punished, ignored or studied, but rarely full citizens, members of a larger community on the same terms as the rest of us. (Katz, 1989, p 235)

Katz saw the European experience, including moral outrage and a focus on human dignity, community and the realisation of democracy, as providing an alternative approach. Unfortunately, recent experience in the UK mirrors Katz's analysis. Brown (2011) shows how the term 'vulnerable' has been used to split the poor and to legitimise welfare reductions on the basis of fairness. The phrase, 'protecting "the vulnerable" from cuts', appeared a total of 13 times in the Spending Review (HM Treasury, 2010). It was used by the Education Secretary Michael Gove when he cut the Education Maintenance Allowance and introduced a reduced scheme. Chancellor George Osborne's Emergency Budget Speech began with the pledge that 'the most vulnerable' must be 'protected'[4]. The term 'the most vulnerable' appears 27 times in the Social Justice Strategy (HM Government, 2012b). Brown (2011, p 22) suggests that as currently used, the term diverts attention from structural issues towards difficulties experienced by individuals and serves 'on the whole to "otherise" rather than to "include"'.

Similarly, Patrick (2011) looks at welfare reform and disabled people, showing how they stand to lose some £9 billion in welfare and services during the 2010–15 Parliament alone. Patrick makes a distinction between the medical model of disability, which locates disability at the individual level and as a result of the individual's medical 'problems', and the social model of disability. The latter grew out of the disabled social movements, post-1970, and focused on the societal barriers faced by disabled people. Patrick argues that the massive cuts have been justified through the rhetoric of vulnerability and deserving and undeserving poor, which has used the individual, medical model of disability rather than the social model:

> [The Prime Minister] argues that 'fairness means giving people what they deserve, and what they deserve depends upon how they behave' ... with work continually characterised as the hallmark of deserving, responsible behaviour. Focusing on a behavioural and thus judgemental reading of fairness, the coalition continues to defend measures that reward the 'right' behaviour and, if not explicitly punishing, at least discouraging 'bad' behaviour such as non-work, addiction and behaviours leading to family breakdown. (Patrick, 2011, p 14)

The 2010 Coalition Government discourse is having a major impact. As Matt Barnes argued:

> the narrative of undeserving benefit scroungers has been cemented in the public mind. Three-quarters of us think that parents with an addiction (i.e. drugs or alcohol) are a key cause of child poverty today. About two-thirds think child poverty is a result of parents being unwilling to work. But these views simply don't reflect the statistical reality. (Barnes, 2012)

Recent analysis shows that there are more people in poverty in working households (6.1 million) than in households without work (5.1 million). Other research demonstrates a strong work ethic among people living in deprived areas. Most people in poverty want to work hard and get on.[5]

Similarly, a survey by the Centre for Social Justice quoted at the launch of the second *Breakthrough Britain* study found 'that 55 per cent of people – the equivalent of 25 million people across the land – say at least one of their local communities is plagued by broken families, crime and poor schools'.[6] Meanwhile, the evidence is that in the last 10 years, rates of violence in Britain have fallen by 11% and the fear of crime is greater than the reality (Institute for Economics and Peace, 2013). Overall crime rates in England and Wales in 2012 had halved since the peak in 1995 and were the lowest for 30 years.[7]

The welfare-to-work area demonstrates most clearly the political use of discourse to stigmatise those in need in order to enable market considerations to dominate the welfare debate and to undermine any political power of the poor and unemployed (Newman, I., 2011). The discourse encourages both individuals and society to see unemployment ultimately as the 'fault' of the individual (Dwyer and Ellison, 2009). Within current UK policy, job security is minimised. Those losing their job, or who are without work, are given low-level benefits and conditional support to access job opportunities and accept a 'reasonable' job. The underlying assumption is that those who do not take the vacancies on offer are benefit 'scroungers' who do not want to work. The dominant discourse that legitimises this policy is promoted by government ministers. Lord Freud, Minister for Welfare Reform, calls on the poor to abandon the 'lifestyle' on welfare (Seymore, 2012), echoing the view of the Chancellor, George Osborne, who talked of 'People who think it is a lifestyle to sit on out-of-work benefits' and continued: 'that lifestyle choice is going to come to an end. The money will not be there for that lifestyle choice' (Wintour, 2010). Iain Duncan Smith, Secretary of State for Work and Pensions, also decried the fact that 'up to three generations of the same family are now growing up with no work in their lives' (*Daily Mail*, 2010).

In fact, only 15,000 households in the UK in 2012 had two generations who have never worked. Families with three generations of worklessness are hard to find and there is no evidence of a culture of worklessness discouraging employment and encouraging welfare dependency (Shildrick et al, 2012). The government even realises that the supply of jobs is the key determinant of unemployment and only expected their flagship Work Programme to deliver a job for six months for 5.5% of those on the programme by November 2012 (BBC, 2012).[8] The discourse, however, helps to shape an economic policy that incentivises work. It legitimises coercive policies through which spending on welfare is reduced,[9] the unemployed are pushed into low-paid jobs and the general level of pay for unskilled jobs is reduced. The proportion of children in poverty who live in a working household has reached 61% (Aldridge et al, 2012) and is rising.

But the implications go further. The prevailing view of the welfare state impinges on the ability of the unemployed to mobilise or have a voice in relation to welfare-to-work policy (Giugni et al, 2009, p 135). Because of the low levels and conditional nature of benefits, around a million unemployed people in the UK no longer claim benefit, disappearing from the view of statutory organisations (Bivand, 2013, p 40). Royall (2009) shows how in Ireland, the voluntary sector organisations that used to advocate on behalf of the unemployed have moved into service delivery, with the unemployed as service recipients rather than activists: 'The unemployed themselves have become marginalised actors within the very structures that act in their name or on their behalf' (Royall, 2009, p 117). So, how are these groups to be engaged in the deliberations proposed in Chapter Five?

Councillors and officers trying to develop more active citizenship and promote social justice need to be fully aware of these problems. Language, like that contained in the *Quid pro quo* report (Newham London, 2011) discussed in Chapter Three, unintentionally reinforces the scrounger discourse and should not be used. Action needs to be taken to raise the self-esteem of those under attack by providing opportunities to contribute to society in ways other than paid work and by valuing their assets and what they do positively, rather than decrying their unemployment or needs. Ways need to be found to connect with those who have become invisible to statutory services and to hear their voices. All this is not easy, but if the ethical framework outlined in Chapter Four is to guide policy, it will be essential.

Responsibility discourses are powerful, as the public opinion surveys quoted earlier show, but Newman, J. and Clarke (2009, p 173) argue that they are not always successful. Instead of producing the 'responsible' person, the pressure they create may just produce the 'neurotic citizen' or the 'mentally ill citizen', who is unable to achieve their desires. As Dorling argued: 'The ostracism that such prejudice engenders further raises depression and anxiety in those made to look different.... In turn despair prevents us from effectively tackling injustice' (Dorling, 2010, pp 310).

Motherhood and apple pie discourse

There are keywords like 'modernisation', 'reform', 'community', 'cohesion' and 'social capital' that provide approbation. They are used in discursive strategies to cover disagreement and to gain approval. Many of these words were originally used to promote radical alternative approaches to public policy, but, over time, they have become meaningless.

Finlayson (2003) has looked particularly at the use of the term 'modernisation' by New Labour. Like motherhood and apple pie, you cannot be against modernisation. The local government reform programme pursued by New Labour from 1997 used the term 'modernisation' to justify reform of local government and to embark on a crusade to achieve change (see Morphet, 2008, p xi). The first White Paper, *Modern local government: In touch with the people*, called on local government 'to break free from old fashioned practices and attitudes' (DETR, 1998, p 2). Modernisation was linked to metaphors of nature – it was something you have to adapt to, you need to 'modernise or die'. But it was also a 'historic opportunity' to be tackled by 'New' Labour. Finlayson points out that there is a fundamental contradiction between these two uses of modernisation: how can modernisation be something you have to adapt to in order to survive and, at the same time, be an active innovative policy? The incoherence of the modernisation claim is further demonstrated in the following box.

If mayors are the answer, then what was the question?

Orr (2004) demonstrates the incoherence of New Labour's modernisation agenda by looking at the discourse that was used to promote mayors. He argues that a number of themes were confused around concern about voter turnout, accountability, leadership, responsiveness and efficiency, and that there was no clarity about which of these issues mayors would solve. The government deployed language linking strong leadership and reform of the political structures and argued that this would deliver greater clout to local government, more visibility in the media, greater accountability, greater dynamism, efficient decision-making and thereby higher voter turnout and more responsive services. Orr argues that the government never decided which model of mayor they were pursuing: a responsive mayor who decentralised and promoted participation or a decisive leader with authoritative dynamism. The discourse talked up the impact of the mayoral model and the ability of mayors to achieve change without any devolution of power or resources to local government by central government and, at the same time, used a discourse of threat and sanctions if local government did not 'modernise'. No thought was given to the response of the media and those interested in depoliticising local government and how they could play on the celebrity culture to lower the quality of political debate. Nor was consideration given to how local political elites could control the referendum campaign since there was no grassroots clamour for mayors (Rallings and Thrasher, 2001). Orr concludes: 'In the absence of more coherent resolution to the wider tensions and contradictions within "modernisation", or even clarity about the key questions, magical transformatory leaders are unlikely to flourish' (Orr, 2004, p 343). No lessons were learnt by the Coalition Government, who repeated the exercise, forcing major cities to have mayoral referenda in 2012, with only Bristol voting for a mayor.

Another key term that falls into this category is 'community'. Raymond Williams (1983, p 76) noted that it is a 'warmly persuasive word to describe a set of relationships'. Cochrane (2007, p 49) argues that community 'is like an aerosol can, sprayed on social programmes to give them a more progressive and sympathetic cachet'. Mayo (2000, pp 36–41) shows how widely the term has been used: community as locality being used in the context of romanticised notions of the past; gated communities preserving privilege and exclusion; faith communities; communities of interest and identity, with the concept of identity itself subject to challenge; and communities of those wanting radical change within various social movements. The communitarians see it as countering excessive individualism, but also reinforcing people's responsibilities; the Right see it as an alternative provider of services, currently exemplified by the Community Right to Challenge in the Localism Act 2011. Newman, J. and Clarke (2009, pp 36–7) suggest that the word has the positive effect identified by Williams because it is both a normative concept (a source of solidarity and belonging), a territorial concept (belonging to a locality) and a concept that designates a group assumed to share particular characteristics (the 'minority ethnic' community or the 'gay and lesbian' community). But the term has become more problematic, with: increased mobility undermining the notion of community as shared locality; increased diversity and migration undermining the notion of community as common identity; and divisions between generations undermining the notion of communities of identity (Mayo, 2000, p 2).

The term clearly remains problematic and contested. For some, this means that it has become meaningless or worse than meaningless, since it hides real conflicts that exist within communities and how policies impact on different interests. However, Mayo would argue that it is not 'whether' the term should be used, but 'how'. First, it is clear that community conflicts need to be analysed and cannot be resolved without going beyond the symptoms and tackling the underlying causes, which usually rest in long-standing inequality and oppression (Craig et al, 1998, p 79). Second, Mayo suggests that a community development worker, with a critical awareness of their own position and power, can work with groups of people to get them to question dominant discourses and to empower them to analyse their own needs and develop their own strategies. 'Cultural action for freedom', as Freire (1970) has expressed this type of approach, has been central to debates on social transformation both in Britain and elsewhere (Mayo, 2000, p 6).

A similar analysis can be made of the terms 'social capital' and 'community cohesion'. Calls for greater social capital or community cohesion are beguiling but hide an attempt to gloss over the impact of inequality. The social capital concept came from Robert Putnam (1993, 2000) in the US and was taken up by the World Bank (Mayo, 2005, p 46). As Ratcliffe (2011, p 20) explains, the problem of modern society was seen to stem from people becoming isolated from the sources of help and support, and most especially from those services that would *help them to help themselves*. The solution therefore lay in reconnecting such people to their local 'community', building social trust and bonding relationships vital for knowledge-sharing. This would then help build 'bridging capital', linking communities to external organisations and agencies, providing resources and services, and curing social inequality. The problems of poor, multi-ethnic neighbourhoods were therefore reframed so that solutions were seen by policymakers to flow from initiatives that built social capital. This led directly to the UK policy focus on community cohesion.

The term 'community cohesion' emerged following the riots in northern towns in England in 2001. The Home Office Minister blamed the social instability on the wrongly (Finney and Simpson, 2009) perceived fact that residents from different ethnic groups led parallel lives: they lived in separate localities, went to different schools, worked in different organisations and did not socialise together. The solution was seen to be to create 'community cohesion', building closer relationships between people 'from different backgrounds and a common vision and a sense of belonging for all communities' (Ratcliffe, 2011, p 23).

Both the terms 'social capital' and 'community cohesion' have been strongly contested (see Mayo [2005], which gives many other sources, and Ratcliffe and Newman, I. [2011]). All aspects of the discourse have been challenged: the benefits of bonding capital, which can be exclusive; the lack of evidence for the narrative of parallel lives; and the fact that political and social trust are not necessarily related. The key criticism has already been raised in Chapter Three, in the discussion of the relational state. This criticism is that evidence shows that the principal correlates of both a lack of social capital and the absence of community cohesion are deprivation, low socio-economic status and poverty, so it is 'deprivation that undermines cohesion, not diversity' (Laurence and Heath, 2008, p 47). So, rather than social capital or community cohesion being solutions to community tensions, inequality and deprivation need to be tackled before any progress can be made on good relationships (Ratcliffe, 2011). Otherwise, those with the most effective social capital (such as the press barons and bank directors) will be able to put their social networks to the most effective use.

Alternative discourse strategies

The dominant discursive strategies discussed earlier are used in different ways to support policies that further the marketisation of public services and to constrain the ability of the public to conceive of different options. The terms 'scroungers', 'troublemakers' and 'anti-social behaviour' move problems from the private sphere to the public sphere but limit the range of public policy options that are 'acceptable' to tackle the issues. Comfortable terms, like 'community', 'social capital' and 'cohesion', gloss over conflicts within communities, limiting debates and self-awareness of needs among those most disadvantaged, and allowing elites to elide their interests with those of the whole community. They smother deliberative democracy. They limit the voice of those without power or influence. Meanwhile, rational discourse around 'what works' removes 'the public' from public services, facilitates the commodification of relationships and the privatisation of public services and depoliticises debates.

Yet, the preceding analysis has also shown that the dominant discourse is contested. People still want high-quality public services that are fair and consistent. They are not enamoured with choice. Individuals, who are pushed too far by trying to make them responsible for their own welfare, suffer stress and fall back on the state with demands for health services or they disappear off benefits into the informal economy. Trade unions and other organisations continue to challenge the privatisation of services. Many of these contested terms provide opportunities to engage in a battle of ideas. As Mayo (2000, p 26, emphasis in original) argues (quoting Gramsci), people are not empty vessels steeped in false consciousness but 'communities, and individuals within communities, *are* experts on their own situation'.

The problem about challenging the dominant discourse is that simple rejection is not effective. The public opinion polls quoted earlier show how embedded discourses promoted by those in power can become, even if there is rigorous evidence to counter them. Those involved in myth-busting on race issues have found that repeating a myth to deny it can, in fact, reinforce it (Amas, 2008; Kitchin et al, 2009). A more comprehensive strategy is required.

Rydin's framework, discussed at the start of this chapter, is helpful in that it seeks to analyse how discourse and the cultural context are reflected in policymaking. This book has argued for a new approach to local government, insisting that its key function is to address the barriers that prevent the realisation of basic needs. It has argued that public goods and services, ecology, and social relations are not commodities that can be bought or sold in a market. How we produce these goods and distribute them depends on values and an understanding of our relationship to fellow human beings and should be decided through both participative and representative democracy and the political process. A discourse is therefore required that can help legitimate policies that seek to constrain markets and promote emancipation and social protection. Of course, the point needs to be made again that discourse can only get you so far. No amount of forceful narrative on the equal role of men in child-rearing will establish a universal care-giver model for gender equality unless arrangements for infrastructure and financial support are adjusted to facilitate the cultural change (Lister, 2007, pp 159–60).

The policy process that could be effective in this context first involves challenging the dominant discourse, but then moves on to the type of community development advocated by Mayo earlier. Freire's (1970) 'cultural action for freedom' involves disadvantaged groups gaining an understanding of the way society currently stigmatises and oppresses them. This understanding enables those without a voice to discover how to participate in society to change the world. Councillors and officers who have some power and are already involved in policy development can assist in this process by uncovering injustice and misconceptions, explaining their causes, and setting out how to eliminate them (Lovell, 2007). Together with the disadvantaged, they should develop Wright Mills' 'sociological imagination', referred to earlier. This means working with those that have 'personal troubles' to develop a persuasive narrative so that society more generally understands these troubles as a public issue from the point of view of those in difficulties. It is part of generating more politics, the case for which was made in Chapter Five.

It has been argued that change usually stems from social movements outside the formal institutions, through which groups with a common interest seek justice or claim their rights. Councillors and officers working with such movements will often have a role in discussing the demands with more powerful individuals and institutions and persuading them as to why an injustice needs to be addressed. They will be providing support to develop an understanding of the common good and a route through to those with influence.

Often, differences, particularly between different identity groups, will not be resolved, but it will still be possible to identify some common ground. Morrissey and Gaffikin (2006), in their study about action oriented towards mutual understanding through the use of language in Belfast, show how neutral, rational planning models lack the conceptual tools to deal with developing urban policy where there is ethnic conflict and mistrust. They advocate what they call 'smart pluralism' (Morrissey and Gaffikin, 2006, p 887), where you do not need to achieve a shared moral baseline (except for agreement to engage and negotiate with respect and that neither side will dominate all the time). Within this scenario, you identify the areas where one side needs to convince the other side of the joint benefits and merits of their proposals in order to get the outcome they desire. Here, the language of peace-building, good relationships and shared public space (not competitive place-making) is linked to an incentive structure facing actors involved in policymaking. Morrissey and Gaffikin (2006, pp 888–9) suggest that there should be financial and other incentives used to develop a *collaborative* advantage for co-operative applications for joint provision. Rydin (2003, p 73) sees these incentive structures as crucial backing to the effectiveness of promoting new policies supported by new discourses. She also argues that such strategies need to become norms and routines. It is not enough for them to be used on occasion and in specific, separated situations; there has to be regular contact if any sense of reciprocity and mutual interest is to be developed.

This is a very different approach from the policymaking process that is traditionally pursued. Here, the concepts of developing a narrative with those involved, collaboration and deliberative democracy are promoted rather than the concepts of competition and community leadership. The reflective practitioner (as promoted by Schön [1983] and discussed in Chapter Seven), or councillor who can facilitate this process, has a key role. Rather than posit solutions, the councillor needs to identify the right questions, asking what alternative actions are available and what implications these have for the common values that the group can generate. Rydin suggests that there is a need to analyse the 'action situation'. The reflective practitioner will look at the rules in use, clarifying what is normally expected of them in this situation, the existing power relationships and shared discourses. These will then be challenged with the groups who will be affected by the outcomes of the policy. The challenge will involve looking at their interests, the incentives and disincentives, and how these impact on the situation and decisions that need to be made. And within this process, different actors will use various discourse strategies to persuade others to support their view.

Consensus conference

Fischer (2003, pp 210–20) discusses the Danish consensus conference as an example of how citizens' local knowledge and normative interpretations can have an influence on policymaking. The consensus conference was developed in 1987 by the Danish Board of Technology (BoT) and had two goals: to input into Parliament and to stimulate public discussion. It is organised and administered by a steering committee appointed by BoT. Some 10–25 diverse citizens, who respond to an advert, are selected to discuss socially sensitive topics of science and technology. A facilitator helps the panel to gather knowledge over several months and the panel thereby generates their own understanding of the issues.

The formal session lasts three to four days, during which time the panel questions experts in open sessions; members of the public can also ask questions. A final report is presented in a highly visible public setting and submitted to Parliament. The methodology of this deliberative process has been taken up in other countries – Austria, Holland, New Zealand, Norway and Switzerland – and at a local level in the Citizens' Juries in the UK (Dungey, 1997). Fischer suggests that the consensus conference can broaden citizens' access to scientific knowledge and help to systematise their own local knowledge. While existing powerful interests may still dominate, it opens up issues to public discussion and supports co-operative relationships between citizens and experts.

Rydin suggests that there are three different types of discourse strategy that can be used: scientific discourse, economic rationality and communicative rationality. Let us take policymaking on reducing air pollution as an example. Scientific/professional discourse brings in particular expertise to identify options. It is useful in identifying sustainability constraints or limits and in measuring the impact of air pollution on health. Economic rationality would qualify the options, as the costs and benefits of alternatives, or the risks involved, are explored. Both of these discourses would be moderated by what she calls 'communicative rationality', which is drawn from Habermas's concept of communicative action or action oriented towards mutual understanding through the use of language. Using the language of rights and focusing on the unequal outcomes of any decision, communicative rationality would expose who benefits and who loses. In the air pollution example, it would show how air quality will impact mostly on the poor communities living on the side of the city where pollution is carried by the prevailing winds (the east in the UK). It would involve working with poorer people to develop their private troubles (eg asthma, bronchitis) into a persuasive narrative that would increase public understanding of the policy issues involved. It would challenge the way in which the economic decision is taken and confront the scientific discourse's claim of expertise. Instead, it would call for social justice and for wider participation by affected communities who have their own knowledge.

Communicative discourse is central to this book, but Rydin suggests that it is difficult to embed it as a form of policy rationality because it fails to engage with the market discourse that constructs policy issues and with the institutionally defined incentive structure facing policy actors, which is weighted towards business interests. She also suggests that deliberative participation is not always appropriate because of such power imbalances. Communicative rationality works where there is community control of resources and incentives and where there is community-level co-operative action. It is very useful, for example, in helping to define the policy of a community development trust. It can be used in deliberation on how actors construct ethical public policy and to support the development of the reflective practitioner. But where there is little community control of resources, the state needs to be involved and will have a role in balancing scientific, economic and communicative rationality. The linking of the three discourses ensures that 'what works' is not seen as an independent empirical study removed from issues of social justice and politics, but that the empirical is understood in relation to values and principles (Fischer, 2003, p viii). Communicative rationality is a precious resource that should not be wasted in superficial and token public participation exercises, where real power remains with dominant interests (Rydin, 2003, p 182).

There are parallels between Nancy Fraser's work, discussed in Chapter Four, and Rydin's approach. Rydin sees the need to negotiate between scientific, economic and communicative rationality and Fraser between social protection, the market and emancipation. While there are interesting parallels between the two writers, there are also some strong joint messages: 'At the centre of Fraser's politics is the commitment to both defining emancipatory goals – "the good life" – and to intervention to achieve it, only through the mediation of public dialogics: democratic debate, with full parity of participation' (Lovell, 2007, p 2). Rydin's work contains a similar commitment to the 'good life', with a focus on the environment: a commitment to building institutional arrangements that promote sustainable development, supported by a discursive justification based on a discussion of rights. Both seek to constrain markets and to recognise community expertise, as well as professional expertise, and to promote the reflective practitioner. While promoting dialogue, both would see a role for protest movements that assert rights, rather than deliberative democracy in all cases.

Conclusion

An alternative discursive strategy needs to start by challenging technical and market-based language in public policy, and revealing the hidden assumptions of such language and how it constrains the development of alternative approaches. This chapter has called on councillors to challenge the 'market', 'responsibility' and 'motherhood and apple pie' discourses, showing how they marginalise the interests of those most in need. Challenge is more effective when it is positive rather than negative. There are many advantages in engaging in a positive discourse around people's assets rather than starting with types of problems (homelessness, drug abuse), where dominant discourses reinforce assumptions about the range of solutions. The asset-based approach will be explored in more detail in Chapter Seven.

In looking at the active use of language in discursive strategies, it is often necessary to insist on using alternative terms that expose the hidden assumptions or emphasise the aspect of a keyword that one wants to promote: 'chair' rather than 'chairman'; the need for 'responsiveness to service users' rather than 'consumer' (Needham, 2007); 'voice' and 'collective choice' rather than individual 'choice' (Crouch, 2003); and 'public sector worker' rather than 'back line worker'. It is difficult, but possible, to try and recapture keywords, using them in progressive ways rather than in negative ways. The gay movement attempted this with 'queer' and the women's movement with 'witch'. In Turkey in 2013, Prime Minister Erdogan used the term *capulcu* (which means looters) to insult those protesting against the redevelopment of Gezi Park. The use of the term created an instant reaction among protestors, who rather proudly began to call themselves *capulcu*, the word this time gaining a positive meaning: those who fight for their rights (Oz and Eder, 2013). A word that is ripe for recapture is 'bureaucrat', which could be used positively to reflect the accountability, consistency and the public service orientation of public sector workers. A march of public sector workers proclaiming 'Public Bureaucrat and Proud' would be interesting!

Challenges are most effective where short catchphrases or new keywords are deployed and when humour is used. Stewart (1992) promoted the concept of 'new magistracy' as a challenge to the unelected elite who were taking over the functions of elected local government. The Occupy movement's 'We are the 99%' is another example of using discourse effectively to confront forms of domination. Keywords such as 'community', 'democracy', 'citizenship', 'social cohesion' and 'customer' need to be used with care. The discussion around them provides an opportunity for debate and for setting out, in relation to an ethical framework, how such terms should be used and with what implications for policy and practice. In this way, they become part of a discursive strategy: the building of a narrative or story to persuade others to see the world from an understanding of basic human needs. But they can also be used to smother debate. Clarity is essential.

The chapter has argued for an alternative discursive strategy embedded in a policy process that promotes participatory democracy and opens up alternative possibilities for social justice through discussion forums, as emphasised in Chapter Five. But it is clear from the discussion in this chapter that this is no easy task. It involves councillors and their officers seeking out the powerless, who have been denigrated by dominant discourses. They then need to be engaged in explaining their private troubles to the councillors. Facilitators, or reflective practitioners, need to try to find common interests with those with more power and develop persuasive narratives to make the private troubles emerge as public issues, the subject of council policies, shaped by those experiencing difficulties. In some cases, instead of aiming for full consensus, cooperation is pursued and policies or developments are proposed that benefit a number of diverse groups in need, as in the Northern Ireland planning example.

It is clear that the active use of language in discursive strategies needs to motivate those involved. On the one hand, there is what Rydin calls communicative rationality: building on the philosophy of rights and values, challenging injustice, claiming rights and seeking to establish duties for the state. In Fraser's theory, this is related to emancipation. On the other hand, there is the discourse of ecological and social safety, protecting the environment for future generations, and stopping child abuse – Fraser's notion of social protection.

As Chapter Five showed, the 'cultural action for freedom' can include a variety of ways of building narratives and reflections. Mayo (2000, pp 102–6) describes the work of Augusto Boal, who developed the ideas of his fellow Brazilian, Paulo Freire, by using interactive people's theatre, the Theatre of the Oppressed. A similar project involved Oxfam working with participatory uses of video for community development in Vietnam, giving people a voice. Mayo (2000, p 180) argues that, in these examples, cultural strategies were central rather than marginal to the process by which communities and social movements developed transformative alternatives. In many situations, a photograph or image can be more effective than words in challenging a dominant discourse.

However, Mayo's work also emphasises that little will change if these actions are one-off, short-term successes. She emphasises the need to go beyond the local and to link into wider social movements that protest against injustice and domination at the national and international levels and ultimately change the norms and rules of institutions. Rydin also argues that such strategies need to become everyday norms and routines. Here, councillors again have a crucial role. They have the power to change local authority culture and practices to ensure that real participation is not just a one-off event. They also have some power to facilitate routes through to influence within other organisations and other tiers of government, so supporting wider social movements. This is the progressive interpretation of community leadership as opposed to the democratic elitist model discussed in Chapter Five.

This chapter has supported Tony Judt's view that to 'recast our public conversation – seems to me the only realistic way to begin to bring about change' (Judt, 2010, p 171).

Notes

[1] LGiU Circular 135/00, 27 October 2000.

[2] This is well illustrated in Wainwright (2009a).

[3] 'PM sets out commitment to Big Society', Number 10 website, 14 February 2011. Available at: www.number10.gov.uk

[4] George Osborne's, the Chancellor of the Exchequer's, Emergency Budget Speech, 22 June 2010. Available at: www.publications.parliament. uk/pa/cm201011/cmhansrd/cm100622/debtext/100622-0004. htm#10062245000001.

[5] See: www.jrf.org.uk/welfare-reform?utm_medium=email&utm_ campaign=Weekly%20publications%20and%20blogs%20wb%201st%20 April%202013&utm_content=Weekly%20publications%20and%20blogs%20 wb%201st%20April%202013+CID_a3b35e2f22780e72d0bea9b89447e7e5& utm_source=Email%20marketing%20software&utm_term=JRF%20and%20 JRHT%20position%20on%20Welfare%20Reform

[6] See: www.centreforsocialjustice.org.uk/

[7] See: www.ons.gov.uk/ons/rel/crime-stats/crime-statistics/period-ending-sept-2012/stb-crime-in-england-and-wales--year-ending-sept-2012.html

[8] The target was missed, only 3.5% were in work for six months. One-year job outcomes have since improved but were still below **Department for Work and Pensions** (DWP) minimum performance levels, delivering a rolling average of around 13% of those on the scheme in the summer of 2013, with better outcomes achieved in areas with more jobs (eg Surrey, Sussex and Kent) (*Working Brief*, Issue 232, Summer 2013, pp 20–1).

[9] Jobseeker's Allowance (JSA; the main out-of-work benefit) levels have been dropping and were half of the government's (income) poverty line for single adults in 2009 (Kenway, 2009). JSA, at £4.91 billion in 2011/12, was only 3% of the benefit bill. The 2010 Coalition Government will reduce JSA in

real terms by a further 3%–5% between May 2012 and May 2015 depending on inflation.

SEVEN

The future

Bringing together the key arguments of the book

Local government's current preoccupation in England is to cope with the unprecedented level of public expenditure cuts imposed by central government. It therefore seems presumptuous to talk about reclaiming local democracy when councillors are being forced to reduce service levels and grants to the voluntary and community sector, a process opposed by almost all councillors of all political persuasions. Yet, this is precisely the time when it is most important to reflect with citizens around priorities and how the local authority is going to work with employees and residents to shape the future.

It would be all too easy for policymakers to make the hard decisions behind closed doors to avoid the inevitable protests. Such an approach is likely to bolster trends (outlined in this book) that reinforce the market's control of local government policymaking. Many councils are implementing the model of the enabling authority, with a focus on commissioning, efficiency and effectiveness. Sometimes, councils are pursuing privatisation because the scale of change is so overwhelming that it is easier to shift responsibility to the private sector than work with unions to find the best way forward, whatever the longer-term consequences of this approach. Sometimes, they are pursuing this option because of an ideological commitment to the New Right beliefs described in Chapter Two. Most frequently, I would suggest, they are caught by the dominant discourse of private sector efficiency looked at in Chapter Six: the need for increased responsibilisation and coercion to decrease demand for services, and the requirement to develop a competitive local area to attract more employment and growth. In those councils that are pursuing this agenda, very little attention is put into thinking through the wider implications of the policy or discussing alternatives and values with those in need, or reflecting on appropriate management strategies for the public domain. There is only limited engagement with local residents as users of council services or about neighbourhood facilities.

The book has argued that this approach increases inequality and reduces the well-being of all those living in the local area. It reinforces the separation between representative democracy and participative democracy, weakening the role of the councillor and leading residents to further distrust politics and local politicians. It strengthens the position of private sector managers, consultants and some public sector managers as policy decisions are depoliticised and turned into technical debates about 'what works'. And it leads to a decline in an understanding of citizenship, the common good and the need for universal services, as those in need are denigrated as scroungers and divided into the deserving and undeserving poor. The Introduction argued that our system of government must have the capacity to learn, respond, change and win public loyalty. The enabling authority is reducing this capacity.

However, this book has also argued that there *is* an alternative – in fact, that there are several alternatives and many are already being pursued by local authorities. The analysis of local government history in Chapter Two showed that councils do have some creative autonomy and can make a difference to their local residents' lives, even if they do not have the power to reverse the cuts. Chapter Four suggested that if councillors start by setting out an ethical framework that will drive their actions, they will develop alternative policies based on human need and very different processes in order to reclaim democracy. The book has affirmed the continuing importance of representative democracy and has argued for greater consideration of councillors' role and the support given to this role. It has also argued for councillors to promote participatory democracy and alternative discourses that engender collaboration, recognition and a wider understanding of common interests.

Local government (including parish and town councils) is the only elected democratic voice of a locality and its community leadership role is not in dispute. But the book has rejected the democratic elitist view of leadership and promoted a more progressive approach. Such leadership should be driven by purpose and values, be open to challenge and be facilitative. It is the council that has the legitimacy to ensure that policy is shaped by an ethical framework and to target spending, within a universal service framework, as must be done in a time of reduced resources. Such targeting can aim to provide social protection, emancipation and distributive justice, as well as the necessary efficiency and effectiveness. It is also the council that has the power to take up environmental protection schemes and ensure that the needs of future generations are not forgotten.

If local democracy is to be enhanced, councils need to pursue their leadership role by building on external social movements and formulating the types of alliances that can make transformative demands, both at local and national level. This requires councillors to re-engage in political debate and deliberation, opening up opportunities for local residents and workers to contribute to defining what kind of common good and future the authority should be seeking, and clarifying and debating their manifesto commitments. Currently, many local manifestos are handed down by the party at national level and have a few local issues added to them. Political parties would be stronger both nationally and locally if the local manifesto was built bottom-up by those seeking election and their electorate, and if it provided ways of building national political campaigns for change. Councils should respond to the demands of citizens and employees to have a greater involvement in policy and control over their own lives. Participative democracy enables citizens and employees to see themselves as part of society and enhances an understanding of interdependence, the needs of others and the benefits of collaboration. It is the councillor's role to foster such democracy, to create the conditions where new relationships between citizens can flourish (as outlined in the discussion in Chapter Five) and to build new narratives (discussed in Chapter Six) to persuade the community to have consideration for others. This will be the basic building block to a progressive future.

In concluding this book, I do not seek to formulate a comprehensive list of the demands that would make a transformative difference to local authorities or build the bottom-up campaigns that would influence the national agenda. The changes, which I suggest, build on the new approach that this book seeks to develop and are the most fundamental to reclaiming democracy. There are six sections: starting from an ethical framework; working for transformation with external social movements and influencing the national agenda; reclaiming capacity; reclaiming autonomy; democracy in the workplace; and supporting citizen agency.

Starting from an ethical framework

Chapter Four sought to establish an ethical framework for local government, guidance on a set of questions that could be used to challenge policy to assess whether it would shift society from 'how things are' to 'how they ought to be'. Drawing on the theory of basic needs, it argued that local authorities should be delivering collective services designed to meet these needs for current and future generations. It sought to go further and look at the concepts of rights and justice and how these establish a framework in which to debate what policies are required to satisfy basic needs.

All the theorists discussed in this section emphasised the requirement to tackle inequality to remedy injustice: Rawls through his veil of ignorance; Sandel stating that inequality makes it difficult to cultivate a sense of community and a discussion of the common good; Sen arguing that capabilities also generate obligations – the duty to reduce inequalities in the overall opportunities and advantages of individuals in society to enable them to lead flourishing lives; and Fraser seeing distributive justice, emancipation and social protection as essential to justice. As Judt (2010, p 184) concludes, inequality is corrosive, it rots society from within and 'the reduction of inequality must come first – because without it all other desirable goals become hard to achieve'. The example of the Islington Fairness Commission (2011) in the following box shows how one council has put this conclusion into practice.

Islington Fairness Commission

Despite its wealthy image, the London Borough of Islington is the 14th most deprived local authority area in England, with extremes of rich and poor. Following a Labour Party manifesto commitment in the 2010 local elections, the Islington Fairness Commission (IFC) was set up in June 2010 to look into how to make the borough a fairer place.

The Commission was inspired by the argument in *The spirit level* (Wilkinson and Pickett, 2009), discussed in Chapter Three, that inequality is bad for all, and the council asked one of the authors, Professor Richard Wilkinson, to jointly chair the Commission. The aim was to look at what could be done locally to narrow the inequality gap over the next four years. The Commissioners included 20 cross-sector and cross-party representatives. It conducted a year-long listening exercise, with seven public meetings across the borough, testimony from local residents, expert evidence, over 100 written submissions, a cross-departmental problem-solving team of council staff and discussions with community groups. An interim report was fed back for further comment and a final report, *Closing the gap* (Islington Fairness Commission, 2011), with 19 recommendations, was agreed in June 2011.

Successes include (Islington Council, 2012):

- Islington Council was the first local authority (alongside Lewisham Council) to become a Living Wage Employer. It is now concentrating on spreading this policy to other employers in the borough. The council also reduced the salary of the chief executive by £50,000, reducing pay differentials.
- Preventing debt has been a focus for action, with support to debt advice agencies, a new programme to improve the financial confidence of young people living in social housing in Islington, increased action against loan sharks and the promotion of the credit union.

- On employment, the council has set up a Single Employer Face (SEF) and is encouraging local companies through a Fair Islington kitemark to adopt a corporate social responsibility approach to get local people into work. The Fair Islington work experience scheme has been launched with ambitions of providing 70 three-month work experience placements in 2012/13 at the council for local people. Candidates receive mentoring and free training as part of their placement. Islington Council won a London Councils' apprenticeship award in 2012 for 'Best Work with Supply Chain to Create Apprenticeships' and was also shortlisted for a 'Best Manager' award.
- Through the **Health and Wellbeing Board**, the council is working on a strategy to improve services for the first 21 months of a child's life. It is trying to provide some affordable childcare.
- Islington Reads, with the voluntary and community sector, is driving improved literacy in schools, prisons and libraries.
- The council aims to support the recruitment, training and deployment of over 500 new volunteers in the borough by 2014 and to encourage council staff to volunteer.
- The council has engaged 40 residents groups in identifying all unused communal space in Islington, especially on estates, to free it up, make it accessible and use it.
- A single telephone number has been established for reporting anti-social behaviour, requiring collaboration between housing associations, Homes for Islington, Islington Police and the council. Attention is being given to victims and improving restorative justice.
- The council is trying to tackle overcrowding and plans to build 1,800 new affordable homes by 2014.
- Attention is being focused on health, increasing the number of healthy schools and encouraging residents to exercise.

Progress reports are submitted to the council's Communities Committee every six months and to the full council every year. The council believe that the Fairness Commission has provided clarity and increased accountability. There are now many more Fairness Commissions in local authority areas in the UK, several of which have been set up in association with local MPs.

An ethical framework goes beyond redistributive justice. In relation to future generations, it has been argued that an ethical approach would seek to constrain the market, and while not necessarily being anti-growth, it would not put business interests in capital accumulation as the top priority. Instead, consideration would be given to the needs of future generations and there would be a wider debate about how the benefits of growth are used. Social protection from market forces is central to human emancipation – enabling people to realise their full 'essence'. There are many ways in which local authorities are already acting on these conclusions. Some are supporting and encouraging local communities to develop new neighbourhood plans under the Localism Act: plans through which environmental and social considerations can be enhanced. As local government in England takes over responsibility for public health, the potential of new initiatives in this area is being explored. Some local authorities are working on the way we access nature – improving health and well-being and deepening understanding of and commitment to an ecological approach. Some, mirroring the work of the Victorian paternalists, are focusing on sustainable energy generation to tackle fuel poverty, to take community control over basic utilities and to generate income to use to further social justice. Some examples of the latter approach are given in the following box.

Tackling fuel poverty and sustainability

Local authorities have been leading on the generation of community-controlled, sustainable energy and also addressing distributive justice by reducing fuel poverty.

- *Woking Borough Council* pioneered the development of a network of over 60 local generators, including co-generation and tri-generation plant, photovoltaic arrays, and a hydrogen fuel cell station, to power, heat and cool municipal buildings and social housing. The generators are connected to users via private electricity wires owned and operated by Thameswey Energy Ltd – a company set up and partly owned by Thameswey Ltd, a municipal energy and environmental services company itself wholly owned by Woking Borough Council. Some businesses are also connected and residents in social housing get cheaper electricity as part of Woking Borough Council's fuel poverty programme (see: www.greenpeace.org.uk/MultimediaFiles/Live/FullReport/7468.pdf).
- In January 2012, *Bristol City Council* announced that it had received a £2.5 million grant from the European Investment Bank (EIB) citywide to kick-start the establishment of an energy services company to spearhead renewable energy and energy-efficiency projects worth up to £140 million, helping to create up to 1,000 jobs. The investment in solar energy is seen as levering in more investment and leading to cheaper energy bills for thousands of residents (see: www.bristol.gov.uk/press/business-bristol/bristol-secures-funding-develop-energy-services-company-%E2%80%93-uk-first-local).
- *Cornwall Together* is a collective buying scheme aiming to involve more than 20,000 residents, reducing their energy bills by 10–15% and saving Cornwall an estimated £3.7 million in fuel bills. A slice of the revenue generated from each

energy switch goes into a fund addressing fuel poverty. Everyone who buys through Cornwall Together is offered free loft and cavity wall insulation (see: www.edenproject.com/whats-it-all-about/people-and-learning/communities/cornwall-collective-energy-buying-scheme).

• *Powering Preston* is a major council wind energy scheme. The money generated will be re-invested and ploughed back into Preston (see: http://blogpreston.co.uk/2012/12/preston-wind-turbine-plans-attracts-interest-from-european-firms/).

Chapter Six argued for new discursive strategies where technical expertise and issues around what could be afforded are balanced with respect for other types of expertise, valuing voices that are not usually heard and creating spaces where mutual understanding can be developed. The example of planning in contested space in Northern Ireland was given. The use of language warrants more attention. The focus on an ethical framework also requires councils to consider a set of concepts such as probity, public sector ethos, public service, honesty, openness, human relationships, solidarity, politics, equity, fairness and equal opportunities, which are central to public services but have been hidden by market discourse. In the 1980s, local authorities changed attitudes to discrimination and emancipation with the support of a strong focus on discourse. Although this was later attacked as political correctness, it did lead to a significant cultural change. Perhaps the methods can be improved, but the same awareness now needs to be brought to bear on how the use of language can support or undermine the public sphere.

The discussion of the ethical framework and discourse emphasises processes and relationships. It is not just the initiative that is important, but the processes of generating alternatives and decision-making. How the professional engages with citizens in considering day-to-day ethical issues in delivering care services will be discussed further in the final section of this chapter on supporting citizen agency. The next section turns to how local authorities can work with wider social movements.

Working for national transformation with external social movements

Throughout the book, I have emphasised that change only occurs when the state works with local community and workers' organisations, welcoming feedback and challenge and embracing opposition rather than seeking to squash it. This conclusion can be evidenced across the world. Parnell and Pieterse (2010) draw on experience in South Africa, where the post-apartheid Constitution states that its intention is to establish 'a society based on democratic values, social justice and fundamental human rights' (Preamble[1]). The Constitution highlights interaction between national, provincial and local levels through the mechanism of co-operative governance.

However, such a constitutional provision can quickly become meaningless and needs constant bottom-up pressure combined with a state that has the capacity and is prepared to enact some form of redistribution and support collective rights (Parnell and Pieterse, 2010, p 150). Parnell and Pieterse's work on urban policy suggests that it is only when interest-based coalitions, which articulate a transformative agenda, are built across several institutional sites that include the state, the professions, non-governmental actors and even selective business interests that progress can be made.

Such a conclusion has implications for the campaign that the Local Government Association (LGA) has been running with Graham Allen MP, Chair of the Political and Constitutional Reform Select Committee (PCRC). In February 2012, the LGA published a consultation paper (LGA, 2012a) supporting the PCRC's proposal to codify (or formally write down) the principles and mechanics of the relationship between central and local government. The final report of the PCRC, with a draft constitutional proposal, was published in January 2013 (PCRC, 2013). This is an important initiative and reflects this book's call for a greater focus on the relationship between central and local government rather than continual reform of local authority structures. However, as the South African example shows, constitutional reform will only bring about change if it is backed up by wide social movements outside the government and linked to a programme of action to achieve progressive change.

In another international example, Geddes (2010) explains how the extreme experiments in neo-liberalism in Bolivia in the 1980s, followed by attempts to increase participation within the existing economic system in the 1990s, opened up progressive opportunities: 'A heterogeneous coalition of indigenous people, labour movements, impoverished urban residents and coca producers' (Geddes, 2010, p 167) were able to form a national government in 2005. Major progress has been made in addressing needs and on emancipation, providing evidence that the combination of a progressive state and social movements can make a real difference. There is a danger, more recently, that this progress will be undermined by the cult of the individual leader and a focus on infrastructure projects rather than rights and services.

The social movements will need to be regenerated and work together, and will need to continue to maintain pressure and to engage with the government, if this progress is to be sustained.

Marinaleda, Spain

Marinaleda in rural Andalusia in Spain is a small town of 2,600 inhabitants, which is entered through an arch with the words 'Otro Mundo es Posible' ('Another world is possible'). After Franco's death, the town organised around a new trade union, a new workers' party, a very active mayor and weekly mass meetings. Twelve years of direct action campaigns eventually won them the right to 1,200 hectares of land that had been owned by the Duke of Infantile but remained unused. The town, in 2012, had virtually full employment (in Andalusia, unemployment at this time was running at 34% and youth unemployment at 53%), communally owned land and wage equality. The residents have built 350 homes over the last 30 years and work collectively to improve the environment (Hancox, 2012).

This international experience has relevance for the UK. There is evidence of growing opposition at both the national and local levels to the local cuts and the enabling local authority model. Occupy were involved with local residents and library campaign groups in the successful campaign to keep Friern Barnet Library open (Flood, 2013). The TUC campaign for 'A Future that Works' (see: http://afuturethatworks.org/) was launched in October 2012. The campaign 'We Own it' (see: http://weownit.org.uk/) and the People's Assembly against Austerity[2] are trying to build a broad base of trade union and community organisations. There is further potential to engage business leaders through their concern with corporate social responsibility or through the passions of individuals, like Jamie Oliver's campaign on school dinners. Social media campaign groups like Avaaz, 38 Degrees and Change.org have demonstrated the impact of online campaigning and can provide ways of linking the local to the national or even international. There are examples of councillors working with local Unison branches (and bloggers as in the Barnet example in Chapter Six) to look at alternative approaches to privatisation, campaigning with tenant groups against the bedroom tax and using media effectively in their campaigns.

How local authorities react to external movements is important. They could ignore them, seek to blame the government for what is happening and turn inwards in sorting out local problems. Many argue that they can cope with the cuts, hoping in this way to reinforce the institutional power of the council, but, ultimately, increasing the blame the council receives as services are cut and visionary goals are not achieved (Fuller and West, 2013). But councillors and their local authorities can also oppose the impact of the cuts on the poor. To do this, they will need to attack the dominant discourses discussed in Chapter Six, explain the impact of the cuts and campaign in the media. They can then: seek to build alliances; develop a local commitment to a common good; put energy into the fragmented protests to give people confidence in the possibility of change; and create a national movement for a progressive future for local government.

Council leaders in Newcastle, Liverpool, Sheffield, Birmingham and Kent started to speak out against the cuts in 2013; 150 council leaders wrote to *The Observer* on 16 June 2013, stating, before the Spending Review, that they could not take more cuts without loss of vital services, and the LGA has been taking a more robust stance. COSLA (the Convention of Scottish Local Authorities or Scottish local government association) is running a campaign against the bedroom tax, providing evidence on how it is leading to rent arrears and higher costs for local authorities. The Welsh Local Government Association (WLGA) has drawn up a memorandum of understanding on how to meet the fiscal challenges in partnership with local authority employees and their trade unions and is committed to a political partnership across all levels of government that engages with citizens in support of change (WLGA, 2011, p 12). But local authorities across the UK have yet to form campaigning networks, like the Local Government Campaign Unit formed against rate capping in 1982 (discussed in Chapter Two), or the campaigns against the poll tax. To be successful, alliances need to be formed with national organisations, Members of Parliament (MPs) and progressive business leaders. A clear set of transformative demands needs to be agreed. This book has emphasised the role of local government in providing a route through to influencing the national agenda. Local government, particular councillors, with their links to national political parties, can and should play a real community leadership role by facilitating social movements, articulating their demands and helping to build local protest into national campaigns.

Reclaiming capacity

It is noticeable in the Islington example that several of the actions depend upon the council having staff, an in-house delivery capacity and the ability to join up services with other agencies. Through the council as an employer, Islington Council is setting an example on the living wage, opening up work experience and apprenticeships to local unemployed young people and encouraging volunteering. Through its education function, leisure services and parks department, it is tackling health inequalities. It has also accessed government community budgets funding to set up *Families First*, a one-stop support service, run with the charity Family Action, aimed at families with children aged 5–18. All these initiatives require a council with capacity to implement the policies that stem from their ethical framework.

Chapter Six showed how market discourse had been used to separate out a council's service delivery role and community leadership functions and to reduce discussion on service delivery to a technical debate on how to increase efficiency. The chapter already started to put the case that far from being in conflict, the community leadership role depends on retaining a strong in-house capacity. Such a capacity provides flexibility, the scope to respond to an emergency, learning and also the ability to lead by example and to carry weight in negotiations with other partners. Chapter Three also exposed the weakness of the efficiency argument for outsourcing. There is no evidence that major outsourcing or privatisation ultimately saves money or provides a better-quality service in the long term. Short-term savings are often made, particularly where private companies are prepared to enter a new market as a loss-leader and where conditions of employment are reduced, but long-term costs rise as multinationals gain control over the market and failures occur, with the public sector having to pick up the pieces. There are increasing examples of savings being made by bringing contracts back in-house (eg APSE, 2009, 2011). These arguments have been accepted in Scotland and Wales, where there is no national push for privatisation.

However, the main arguments against the 'enabling' and 'commissioning' council concern the impact on the legitimacy of local government and democracy. Judt (2010, p 116) argues that 'by eviscerating the state's responsibilities and capacities we have undermined its public standing'. The market focuses on the individual, not the collective, and Judt concludes by quoting Burke's *Reflections on the revolution in France*, suggesting that any society that destroys the fabric of its state must soon be 'disconnected into the dust and powder of individuality' (Judt, 2010, p 119). We no longer talk about the duty to provide goods and services just because they are in the public interest, but, instead, the discourse is about how services are no longer affordable and how, in the past, the state services were of low quality and showed no consideration of users' views. This denigration of past service delivery is also a means of delegitimising the state and is historically inaccurate, as Chapter Two sought to show. While there were clearly some weaknesses in public services, the fact that they were universal, rather than residual, held many advantages. Some aspects of the 1960s' council house-building programme may have left their scar on the landscape, but at least houses had Parker Morris standards, affordable accommodation was widely available and council housing attracted a wide range of households living together in mixed communities – and the New Towns have stood the test of time. Whatever the problems of earlier provision, the current situation is far worse, with: rising homelessness; residual council and social housing, which is stigmatised and creates ghettos of those most disadvantaged; young people unable to afford to buy a home; overcrowding in the private rented sector; and 80,000 households about to be forcibly moved away from friends, relatives and existing schools in Inner London. The residualisation of social housing has further helped to discredit state provision and weakened the campaign for more council housing. Meanwhile, accountability is fragmented between Arm's Length Housing Management Organisations (ALMOs), housing associations, voluntary sector organisations providing hostels, private landlords housing social tenants and even bed-and-breakfast hotel providers.

Some councils have followed Southwark's example (Independent Commission on the Future of Council Housing in Southwark, 2012) and maintained a housing stock and engaged in joint deliberation between local councillors, tenant organisations, community groups, trade unionists, voluntary sector providers and other partners about an alternative, council-led approach. Chapter Three explained how this approach is leading to a national campaign to remove restrictions so that councils can borrow finance to invest in the building of new council houses. Significant new council and social housing can meet some of the challenges in the ethical framework: it would address basic needs; it could be built sustainably;[3] it could support recognition by expanding the stock, so allowing families and friends to live close to each other, if they so choose; and it would meet the right to secure accommodation of satisfactory standard. By expanding the stock: there would be wider benefits to those seeking private ownership, as house prices would not be inflated through a lack of supply; jobs and training opportunities in construction could be expanded; and social housing allocation could be widened.

When the Coalition Government initially promoted switching 'the default from one where the state provides the service itself to one where the state commissions the service from a range of diverse providers' (HM Government, 2011a, p 29), several councils signalled their intention to become 'commissioning councils', with all their services outsourced (*Local Government Chronicle*, 2011, p 8). Suffolk County Council[4] went first but was closely followed by the London Borough of Barnet, Cornwall County Council and Somerset County Council. In each case, local councillors, both from opposition parties and from those in control, expressed concern that, over time, their power to amend the contract would diminish, the control over services by the private contractor would increase and savings may not be realised. In summary, their ability to deliver on local need as circumstances changed would diminish and their democratic role would be undermined. Major campaigns developed among residents concerned about the lack of accountability and private profit being made out of need and leaders and chief executives were forced out of their posts. Despite the failure of the judicial review, the experience in the London Borough of Barnet is likely to have significant consequences.

Opposition to outsourcing in Barnet

In 2008, the London Borough of Barnet brought in PriceWaterhouseCoopers to advise it on cost-cutting measures. They put forward a joint venture proposal called 'Future shape', through which the council, the National Health Service (NHS) and the police could jointly commission services. This proved impossible to implement, so Barnet Council proposed the creation of an 'EasyCouncil', which would provide basic minimum services but charge for any extras along the lines of EasyJet Airlines. This rapidly fell foul of legislation and lost the support of residents. The council then pursued the 'One Barnet' proposal: to outsource 3,000 jobs in administrative support to Capita at a cost of £320 million over 10 years, with a further contract to BT (Whitfield, 2012, p 137). This was subsequently negotiated into two contracts with Capita: one for 'customer and support services', including benefit administration, for £350 million over 10 years and a £130 million joint venture on regulatory services. The Capita bids were approved amid much protest from both opposition and some Conservative councillors and the Barnet Alliance for Public Services (a campaign group of local residents and the local Unison branch) in November 2012. However, local residents mounted a legal challenge, arguing that the council had failed to consult fully, had breached their equality duty, had no mandate to privatise services and had not proved that the bid was the best value option (see: www.guardian.co.uk/local-government-network/2012/dec/19/barnet-council-judicial-review-future).

John Sullivan, the father of the claimant in the legal challenge, argued:

> The Council has robbed Susan and her family of their democratic voice in failing to consult on what is a wholesale privatisation of local government. If this happened nationally, there would be outrage. Why should it be any

different for our beloved Barnet? The national contract failure rate is 25%. When these contracts collapse, who will be left to pick up the pieces? No one but the poor, the disabled and short-changed Barnet service users, residents and taxpayers.[5]

In the event, the legal challenge was lost on the technicality that the residents brought their challenge too late. However, £39.2 million has been spent between 2009 and 2013 on lawyers and consultants and the legal costs will escalate. The chief executive left in 2012. There is no evidence as to whether the council will save money on the deal with Capita or what risk assessments have been done to anticipate any failures in the contract or variations pushing up costs. No comparison with an in-house option has been presented because the council is hiding behind commercial confidentiality. By February 2013, more than 8,000 residents in Barnet had called for a referendum against the London borough's controversial outsourcing plan. Whitfield (2012, p 139) concludes that: 'One Barnet seems to be a cocktail of dogmatic adherence to neoliberal ideology and some senior management practices that are incapable of meeting the basic requirements of public management.'

A contrast to the Barnet case study is provided in Cornwall, and the differences between the two cases are instructive.

Cornwall Council's cooperation with the unions

Cornwall Council was a new **unitary authority** created from the county council and six **district councils** in 2007. Its Conservative leader, Alec Robertson, and new chief executive, Kevin Levery, sought to divide the council into business units. The council has proceeded to establish arm's length, wholly council-owned business units. There is an ALMO for social housing, a leisure trust, an economic development company and Cormac Solutions, with 1,200 full-time staff providing grounds and roads maintenance. But the union has ensured some safeguards on these structures. All staff, including new staff, are on council terms and conditions and can join the council superannuation scheme. Furthermore, under European Union (EU) procurement law, the council is using the **Teckal exemption** to guarantee council work for the new companies rather than go through competitive tendering processes.

The council also sought to outsource more than 1,000 jobs in a strategic partnership with the private sector and parts of the NHS. It adopted an open process in its attempt to gain a strategic partnership and involved trade union representatives in the procurement process. The trade union representatives were able to commission research on the proposals and feed information to all councillors and lobby the NHS managers involved. Trade unionists from local authority areas that had established similar strategic partnerships (eg Sandwell) were invited down by Cornwall Unison representatives to explain the problems to Cornwall councillors. There was a groundswell of opposition to the scheme, which ended in a vote of no confidence in the leader and both the leader and chief executive resigning. A much smaller scheme, roughly a quarter of the original proposal, known as BT-Lite, has been developed. This is a joint venture, with the NHS outsourcing a tele-health service involving 23 staff and the council outsourcing human resources (HR) services and some information technology (IT) services involving the transfer of 299 staff. Again, the union has guarantees on staff terms and conditions and although they do not welcome the scheme, they believe that the campaign has been successful. There is now no further appetite for privatisation and better relationships between management, councillors and employees.[6]

The evidence of opposition to the commissioning council model through growing alliances between councillors, residents and trade unionists to reclaim democracy is encouraging. Real change requires the next step of formulating demands around justice, emancipation and environmental and social protection based on further deliberation. The *We Own it* campaign is calling for a Public Services Bill to protect and promote high-quality public services, making public ownership of public services and infrastructure, or ownership by organisations with a social purpose, the default option rather than private ownership (We Own it, 2013). They are also calling for greater transparency and public control of services that are outsourced to the private sector. Social Enterprise UK is campaigning for similar reform and for the strengthening of the Public Services (Social Value) Act 2012, which currently requires commissioners to consider social value in the procurement process for public service contracts (Williams, 2012). They have welcomed reform to EU procurement laws that confirm that environmental and social considerations can be taken into account in the contracting process (for instance, encouraging providers to employ disadvantaged people or long-term job-seekers in delivering the contract). The EU laws also clarify that performance under previous contracts can be explicitly weighed up as part of the decision-making process in procurement decisions (Gregory, 2013, p 15).

Some services and some goods will always be purchased from the private sector but major outsourcing that reduces capacity and democratic control is not the route to enhancing local democracy. It is possible to effect major change through more democratic management processes and the involvement of citizens and council staff. But before looking at this approach in more detail, a further point needs to be made about capacity. Councils also require the resources to make a difference and the issue of local government finance is central to local democracy.

Reclaiming autonomy

While this book has not focused on possible changes in the structures or powers of local government, the reform of local government finance, particularly council tax, is essential if local democracy is to be reclaimed. Local government has recognised this fact for many years and contributed to national inquiries, from the Layfield Report (1976) to the Lyons Inquiry (Lyons, 2005, 2007). Most countries (see following box) have several local taxes and almost all retain a property tax. Such a tax clearly relates to living in a local area, is relatively easy to administer and is not subject to tax evasion since houses and places of work remain fixed in space and identifiable. Most EU countries ensure greater local fiscal autonomy than the UK (Loughlin and Martin, 2006, p 16).

Local taxes in other European countries

Sweden is an exception in that it has no property tax. However, it has a very high level of local income tax, with national income tax levied as an additional tax on higher earners. A 30% local income tax funds more than 60% of municipal income and about 80% of county council funding comes from income tax (Loughlin and Martin, 2004). Six EU countries – Belgium, Denmark, Finland, Italy, Spain and Sweden – have local income taxes, but most combine this with a property tax.

French local authorities (communes[7]) have a variety of local taxes, which are collected for them by the state. These are:

- a property tax on developed land and undeveloped land (with exemptions to promote agriculture and reforestation) chargeable annually to the owner of the property (*taxe foncière*);
- a residence tax chargeable to occupants of property whether they are owners or tenants (*taxe d'habitation*);
- a business tax (*taxe professionnelle*) in two parts, which nationally accounts for half of local authorities' locally derived revenue:
  - on fixed assets: property only for small enterprises and property and fixed capital assets for larger companies; and
  - an employment tax varying from 10% to 18% of wages.

In addition, communes operating a household refuse collection service may introduce a collection tax and there is a regional planning tax (Jones and Newman, 2006).

The LGA launched a campaign in 2013 – *Rewiring public services* – for financial reform (LGA, 2013). This is calling for: self-funded local government with local control over council tax, business rates and other taxes; a local government bond agency and freedom to borrow, as discussed in Chapter Three; and place-based public service budgets to integrate services. Graham Allen MP, Chair of the PCRC, has gone further, suggesting that HMRC (the UK tax authority, Her Majesty's Revenue and Customs) should send half the national income tax take back to local councils via an independent redistribution commission, without central government interference (LGA, 2012a, p 3). All these demands are important.

Turning first to business rates: since 1990, business rate levels have been set nationally and business rates ceased to be a real local tax. The rates are collected locally and the national non-domestic rate (NNDR) is redistributed to local authorities in proportion to the number of people living in each authority. The total grant distributed by central government to local authorities consists of their NNDR allocation and additional money distributed on a needs-based formula, which is subject to political change (Adam et al, 2007, p 18). From April 2013, under the Local Government Finance Act 2012, local authorities will be able to keep half of the proceeds of any growth in NNDR. While this reform is welcome, it falls far short of the general local government view that control of business rates should revert to local government. When local government last controlled business rate in the 1980s, businesses contributed more than a quarter of local government income (Adam et al, 2007, p 16). In 1990/91, when government funding to local government increased to mitigate the impact of the poll tax, business rates contributed 29% of income (Travers, 2006, p 5). The contribution fell dramatically and was only around 20% in 2011/12. Business should make a fair contribution to local services. Furthermore, if the accountability between local authorities and the business community were clearer, this would provide a better basis for discussions on local authority support for the economy and corporate social responsibility.

However, here I want to concentrate on council tax, which is the most urgent change required for local financial independence and social justice. Council tax is the only locally controlled tax in the UK and the only annual wealth tax. The UK had a property tax that was based on the income that could be derived from renting a property, but this was abolished when the community charge (or poll tax) was introduced in 1989/90. As explained in Chapter Two, this led to an immediate political crisis and council tax was introduced in 1993 and all houses in England were classified into one of eight bands coded by letters the A to H[8] on the basis of their assumed capital value (as of 1 April 1991). No revaluation has taken place in England and new houses are allocated a nominal 1991 value.

Council tax has now become the second most regressive tax after tobacco duty. It in no way accords with an ethical framework. The top band (H) covers capital values above £320,000 in 1991, with the result that someone in a castle or mansion outside London could pay the same council tax as someone in a council house in inner London. At the bottom end of the scale, the lowest valuation is £40,000 at a time when terraced properties in Salford were selling for below £10,000. Top-level council tax payers only pay around three times the level of tax at the bottom. Band by band, from B to F, average household income rises roughly in line with the rise in council tax (Kenway and Palmer, 2004, p 11). But band A needs to be split into two so that those in the lowest-value houses do not pay disproportionately, and band G also needs to be split, with several bands introduced above band H to ensure that those living in more expensive houses pay more. At the same time, automatic revaluation is required every five or 10 years to ensure that valuations are current. Regional banding should also be introduced, or those living in London in poverty will be subsidising the wealthy in the North.

Both the Liberal Democratic Party and the Labour Party have discussed a wealth tax on houses worth more than £2 million. This would still leave council tax as regressive. A reformed council tax would be easier to introduce and provide a fairer wealth tax but with the proceeds going to local rather than national government. While some central government funding of local authorities is required to redistribute tax income to areas of need, the proportion of income raised locally could rise from an average of 25% to 50% without in any way impeding national redistribution.

Local residents should have some control over the income of their local council and should be able to vote for councillors committed to higher taxes if they wish for a higher level of service. On current referenda,[9] if they vote to raise council tax, this becomes a tax on the poor. So, councils are being forced to limit local income generation to below inflation levels, imposing further real cuts in the public sector.

Councillors are elected to make a difference; they must have the scope to do this.

To ensure that council tax is a fair tax, Council Tax Benefit (CTB) also needs to be addressed. This was the conclusion of the Lyons (2007) report and of the various studies of the New Policy Institute (Kenway and Palmer, 2004, 2005). CTB was introduced in 1993. It is not a generous benefit and means that the working poor still contribute disproportionately to council finances (Kenway and Palmer, 2005). Yet, in the financial year 2012/13, CTB provided £4.1 billion worth of income-related support to 4.9 million households in England (Popper and Kenway, 2012). In April 2013, English local authorities began their own schemes of 'Council Tax Reduction Support' (CTRS) to replace the existing national scheme of CTB. The new schemes received 10% less funding from central government than CTB but legislation ensured that pensioners' benefit levels were not cut, which has meant that the national funding for working-aged households has been decreased by 19%. The cut will inevitably impact most in areas of high deprivation. Coming on top of the major cuts to local authority expenditure, this was a further blow. The government has effectively forced councils to re-introduce an average £140 a year poll tax (Bushe et al, 2013) for the very poorest working-age households.

The whole system of council tax and CTRS needs reviewing to provide a fair and firm basis for local authority funding. As Beetham (2011, pp 7–8) argues, an effective tax system is important to democracy in three ways: it delivers revenues for public services; it should share the costs fairly; and 'it gives recognition to the value of the public sphere and collective responsibility for sustaining it'. Reform of council tax still remains an easier and less controversial task than introducing a whole new local tax system or a wealth tax. As Lyons (2007, p 221) said: 'council tax is not "broken", and should be retained as a local tax either on its own, or alongside other local taxes'. The Labour Government ducked this reform in 2007. The 2010 Coalition Government, in the name of localism, has made the situation worse. A new crisis will emerge and the next government, whatever its political complexion, must have the moral courage to reform the system, which is currently unjust. Local government, through the associations, with the support of sympathetic MPs, trade unions, some business leaders and community organisations, should be exposing the injustice and campaigning for this change as a top priority.

Democracy in the workplace

New Public Management, with its focus on explicit standards, measures of performance, competitiveness and efficiency, has led to hierarchical management regimes. These focus on leadership and provide little autonomy, trust or scope for real innovation from more junior staff, who have to 'talk the talk' to climb the career ladder (Manson, 2012, p 4). If democracy is to be reclaimed, the internal organisation of the workplace must also be tackled. More democratic forms of organising could provide an educative role for democracy in wider society: providing some experience of solidarity and working together that would foster an understanding of social needs and recognition of true citizenship. Such internal democracy could also promote greater citizen engagement.

Chapter Five already discussed the case for democracy in the workplace and gave the example of Monmouthshire County Council's Intrapreneurship School to show how employee knowledge can contribute to innovation. The experience in Newcastle in the following box demonstrates how public sector managers, unions and supportive councillors can lead major change and innovation.

Public service reform

In 2000, the chief executive of Newcastle, faced with a 25-year-old IT system, financial pressure and departments operating in silos, proposed a joint venture. Led by the private sector, this would modernise the council's systems and would involve 650 existing staff. The plan was opposed by the union branch supported by the Centre for Public Services. Following a political campaign, which acknowledged that the status quo was not an option, the union persuaded the Labour group to consider an in-house bid and gained wide support from managers and the workforce. The in-house bid was developed through staff and management workshops and reaching out to the community and councillors. It was selected over the bid submitted by BT, the preferred bidder, in 2002. The in-house bid involved: voluntary redundancies; redeployment and retraining; £28 million net revenue savings (greater savings than the outsourced proposal would have provided) over 11 and a half years, with re-investment to improve the quality of services; and a stress on training and learning throughout the organisation. Jobs that were seen as engaged in routine tasks were redesigned, drawing on wider tacit knowledge. This both helped staff to feel empowered and resulted in those using council services being more satisfied. 'Sincere efforts to attract the commitment of the workforce' were developed through: a collaborative, problem-solving relationship with the unions; 'diagonal focus groups', which involved staff from every level brainstorming ideas for improvement; regular staff forums; and good communication. Democracy was always part of the culture, with: councillors active on the steering committee that led the transformation process; reports to the scrutiny committee; and relationships of collaboration and mutual respect developed with service users. The whole process was underpinned by an active thinking-through of public service ethics and values in all parts of the organisation (Wainwright, 2009b).

There are 13 other case studies of public sector unions working with councils featured in research by the Association for Public Service Excellence and Unison (APSE and Unison, 2010), including in Belfast, where unions have delivered more 'person-centred care' to residents and better job satisfaction for staff in care homes. In Sheffield, unions worked with the council to build Care4you, an award-winning service for older people. In Lincolnshire, the unions developed an in-house approach to sharing services (IT, HR, revenue and benefits, customer services and finance) within three district councils that led to a bid from Tribal being dropped. Yet, the encouragement from and support by councillors for in-house bids, where an external procurement process takes place, remains limited. Similarly, most local authorities retain very hierarchical management systems and there are relatively few examples of councils embracing full democratic management. As citizens in a democratic society, people are theoretically free to hold their own opinions, make their own decisions and be treated as an equal. As employees, they are often denied all these rights (Morgan, 1986, p 141).

The case for the wider purpose and benefits of public employment also needs to be continually made. As noted in Chapter Two, the Webbs saw the benefits of a public sector workforce. Local government led the way in the 1980s in promoting equal opportunities within their own workforce and tackling racial, sexual and disability discrimination. These policies have impacted on employment practice more generally. Local authority workers bring in tacit knowledge to their work as local residents and spend their wages locally, generating a multiplier effect, while private sector dividends and profits flow out of the local economy. Bramah et al (2007) argue that public employment has an important strategic purpose for public bodies: bringing effective leverage over local economies; helping to shape places; managing costs and transactions; sustaining democratic networks and accountability; and realising the potential of the local workforce.

> ### Learning in Barking and Dagenham
>
> The London Borough of Barking and Dagenham developed the Fitzlands Learning Centre as a multi-use classroom providing basic literacy, numeracy and computer skills, mainly for street-cleaning and refuse employees. The initiative tackled low literacy and numeracy in the borough and will impact on parental support in schools. It improved staff morale and led to higher resident satisfaction with street cleanliness (Bramah et al, 2007, p 24).

In July 2012, the Co-operative Councils Innovation Network[10] was established – a group of 21 Labour local authorities who are driving forward new co-operative approaches to transform the way local public services are delivered in their areas. There are certainly some problems with this approach. It is perfectly possible to set up a co-operative with almost no democratic control and in which management is not driven by the ethical framework set out in Chapter Four. In the famous case of Equitable Life, established as a mutual in 1762, in which both policy-holders and pensioners lost considerable amounts of money after a court ruling in 2000, the Penrose Inquiry stated that there had been 'ineffective scrutiny and challenge of the executive' and that the board had insufficient skills and was a 'self-perpetuating oligarchy amenable to policy holder pressure only at its discretion' (quoted in Birchall, 2011, p 87). My Civil Service Pension (MyCSP[11]), set up in 2012 and strongly promoted by the 2010 Coalition Government as a democratic management model, is a joint venture with the staff owning only 25% of the assets and with limited involvement for pensioners and policy-holders. It cannot be considered as a co-operative or mutual in the traditional sense.

Yet, the Co-operative Councils Innovation Network has resulted in some more democratic policymaking initiatives. These include an attempt to raise the amount of co-operative and tenant-run housing from the low level of 0.6% of all UK housing (Local Government Leadership, 2010, p 9), thereby promoting the development of active citizenship. The community trust school movement aims to increase stakeholder engagement within a 'stronger collective and egalitarian focus' (Local Government Leadership, 2010, p 15). It brings the stakeholders of a school or group of schools together as members of the trust and they elect trustees and hold them to account. The model can increase parental involvement but also allow the local authority, local residents around the schools and other partners to retain a say in them and promote cooperation between schools rather than focus on competition. Caring Support in Croydon provides homecare support for adult disabled and older people in South London. It is set up on the Italian model of a multi-stakeholder co-operative and includes users, care support workers, families and volunteers. It shows how local authorities can facilitate mutual obligation through universal provision. In Lambeth Council, the commissioning process is being stripped down to its first principles, and remade both to reflect the requirements of the people who live in the area and to try to award contracts to organisations that can demonstrate greater community control (Williams, 2012, p 11). The hierarchical directorate structures within the council are being replaced with a matrix model based 'on collective responsibility for the whole organisation and a default assumption that all services will be co-produced by the users and the commissioners' (Studdert, 2013, p 44).

However, within the current competition and procurement framework, these initiatives frequently open the door to privatisation. Even when a small co-operative of existing staff is successful in a procurement exercise, it faces the danger of being outbid in the future by a large private sector company that seeks to reduce competition and can afford loss-leaders. Successful mutuals will be under pressure to merge and expand operations, and ultimately, under current British law, they can demutualise, drifting ever further from their democratic base. Meanwhile, there is evidence that public sector management buyouts are not democratic, participatory, accountable or good employers (Whitfield, 2012, pp 179–88).

Robin Murray (2012, p 5) argues that the civil economy has the same ethical mission as the public sector, but cooperation is weak, with little mutual learning, and there remains a 'deep moat between the public sector and co-ops'. His solution to the tensions identified earlier is to deepen the relationship between the state and the co-operative movement, learning from Italian practice (as illustrated in the following box on Imola). This would involve: close working between trade unions, councillors and co-operatives; changing the way the public sector operates; developing democratic work practices within the public sector as well as within co-operatives; ensuring that local authorities support co-operatives that further public goals; and establishing public–social partnerships for service delivery, like the co-operative schools that remain in the local authority sector (Murray, R., 2012, p 6). This does start to offer an alternative way forward. Furthermore, the new EU procurement rules also enable public bodies to reserve the award of many health, social and cultural services contracts exclusively to social enterprises for a time-limited period. The UK is required to bring national laws into line with these new rules within two years (Gregory, 2013). This is welcome, but real progress requires legislative changes around asset lock to guarantee that co-operatives do not demutualise in the future and regulations around procurement and accountability to support these ideas, with less emphasis on the co-operative or mutual model per se and more on the democratic changes that are being sought. As Diamond argues:

> Transferring ownership to non-state community-based institutions is desirable, but alone it is rarely sufficient. The objective ought to be a state in which power is shared between citizens, service providers, and elected representatives, supported by public service guarantees which entrench rights of equity and access. (Diamond, 2011, p 12)

Real progress on cooperation in the workplace and in the community requires a major programme of legislative and cultural change and the establishment of new institutions like the Legacoop and regional banks in Imola. If this can be achieved together with a move to democratic work practices within local authorities themselves, then a start will have been made on reclaiming local democracy. In the meantime, the emphasis should be on furthering democratic management within the council, rather than new structures that could open the door to privatisation.

Co-operatives in Imola

Imola, a town of around 66,000 people, lies south-east of Bologna in the Emilia-Romagna region. Around half the residents belong to the town's 70 co-ops, which have over 74,000 members (several residents belong to more than one co-op), 7,121 employees and a turnover of €2,060 million, with €1,039 million of exports. The leading co-operative sectors are:

1. The industrial sector, with 11 co-ops, nearly 5,000 employees, 1,537 members and a turnover of €1,773 million. The sector includes some major companies in the ceramics industry, including the multinational company SACMI.
2. The agro-food industry, with five co-ops and a turnover of around €9.5 million. It includes a wine co-op.
3. The service sector, with 25 co-ops and nearly 1,000 employees, including construction, logistics and distribution.
4. The housing sector, with three co-ops and nearly 8,000 members. Local co-ops give cheap mortgages to their workers, the council provides the land,

local co-op banks supply the remaining finance and the construction co-op build or renovate the houses and flats.

5. Three retail co-ops, with over 53,000 consumer co-op members.

6. Nine cultural co-ops, covering such areas as catering, facilities management and recreational and cultural activities.

7. Fourteen social co-ops, with some 600 employees and 1,500 members. Il Sorriso (the smile) is a co-operative of drug addicts who choose to go to live for two years in the therapeutic community outside Imola rather than go to prison. It is an example of the social co-operatives that started in Italy in 1963 and were promoted in Spain, Portugal and France at the turn of the century (Zamagni and Zamagni, 2010, p 16). These have multi-stakeholder governance and can involve employees, service users, carers, public agencies and the wider community. The addicts in Il Sorriso work on a farm and the community generates much of its own funds, with some income from the local health department. It has moved from dealing originally with young men, to supporting women, families and transgender addicts. By December 2012, it had treated 1,025 people.

The town has recently suffered from the recession and public expenditure cuts but has remained relatively buoyant compared to other parts of the Italian economy. The co-operatives are supported by Legacoop Imola, a co-operative development agency, to which each co-op gives 3% of its annual profit, and the co-ops also invest a high proportion of any profit in research and development. They have built up considerable financial resources and are supported by co-operative banks.

The role of Legacoop Imola, the co-ops themselves and the trade unions are kept distinct. The union is there to represent all workers in the co-op. Employees are not automatically accepted as cooperators: they have a probationary period and then have to buy their share of the co-op, which is usually a relatively small sum equivalent to a month or two of their wages. The union's role is to: encourage the co-op to expand the number of co-operators; look at wages, conditions of work and health and safety; and negotiate any redundancies. Each co-op determines how it is run. However, all have a system of one member, one vote and regular meetings during which company policy is discussed and, if appropriate, management is elected. Many of the co-ops may look like conventional companies, with managers and a differentiated workforce, but the managers are dependent upon the support of the other cooperators and a strong community ethos permeates all the enterprises in the town.

The real strength of Imola's co-operative movement lies in the local networking and mutual support. There are strong political links between the town council, the Legacoop, the individual co-ops and the regional government, which has considerably more influence than the national government. The Legocoop is well aware that this political tradition must be embedded and over the last 11 years, some 3,700 local students have completed a programme called 'Experiment'. This has involved the students developing their own co-op proposals and some 262 business projects have been collected, some of which will result in new enterprises. The students are also encouraged to think about co-operative principles and values, particularly solidarity and sustainability (see: http://www.imola.legacoop.it).

Supporting citizen agency

It is appropriate to complete this book with a final look at the key issue of reclaiming participatory democracy. The book has argued that democracy requires the active involvement of citizens in deciding about policy directions, and Chapter Five dealt in detail with the councillor role in promoting participative democracy. It contained a list of the elements needed to drive transformative participation. Councils should be developing Sen's version of capabilities (ability, freedom to choose and achievement) to enable those without a voice to campaign for their rights and should be opening up institutional spaces for bottom-up participation and emancipation. In particular, I have suggested that there should be discussion about human need, recognition and emancipation and the desired level of social protection from the market, rather than single-issue consultation exercises where the desired outcome has already been specified by central government. Such discussions must address issues of power, inequality and conflict, and promote reflective practice. Chapter Five recognised that this task was not easy and that bottom-up empowerment could often be in tension with more top-down rights campaigns. Yet, integration of participation and rights is necessary to give these concepts meaning and content.

This is illustrated in the arena of personal services, where there is a growing demand for greater individual and collective agency in the delivery of services. Walsh (1989, p 67) suggested that the provision of services by a local authority 'involves a relationship between producer and consumer that is often intimate and personal', and therefore establishing quality requires a participative technique where the user/citizen is involved in determining the service or product. The user/citizen has therefore always been involved in producing the outcome: whether it is the child at school who does their homework or the patient who discusses with the doctor the regime of drugs, exercise and diet that will lead to better health.

How the demand for citizen agency is met is crucial. It could just lead to individual participation or it could lead to the kind of local democracy advocated in this book. The difference between these two approaches is exemplified by the debate over personalised budgets. Personalised budgets can just encourage individuals to buy off-the-peg solutions rather than being involved in designing their own solutions (New Economics Foundation, 2008). Personalised budgets are an individualised, consumerist approach that masks 'the opportunity to develop a more collective and collaborative system of social care which has mutual aid and reciprocity at its heart' (Slay, 2012, p 30). The evidence around personal budgets within social care is that, in many cases, issues of power have not been addressed and service users are still reliant on 'experts' rather than being seen as experts themselves (Needham, 2012, p 7). So, personalised budgets or attempts to engage the individual user in defining their service can merely be seen as compliance with an externally imposed regime, particularly in mental health (Needham and Carr, 2012 [2009], p 9).

The alternative approach of linking participation and rights to ensure that personalised budgets really deliver empowerment involves addressing three gaps within the personalisation agenda (Slay, 2012, p 32). The focus should first be on relationships with people rather than budgets. Budgets, which can involve bypassing professional staff and carers, can undermine these relationships. Chapter Four has emphasised that professionals working for local authorities need to develop conscious reflection and a discursive ethic involving their clients and wider citizens, through which they can ensure that their practice accords with their moral principles and values. The chapter emphasised that public services not only involve compassion and caring, but also have to address issues of distributive justice, emancipation and recognition. This means understanding the power that professional roles hold and engaging in reflective practice with local citizens to open up new ways of doing things that value the knowledge and expertise that citizens and users bring.

Second, it is important to focus on assets other than financial resources and explore how the resources of both citizens and the state can be *combined* to develop more effective support. An asset-based approach starts from a focus on what communities have (their social, cultural and material assets) and builds on these strengths as this helps communities to work together to address their needs:

> We can't do well serving communities ... if we believe that we, the givers, are the only ones that are half-full, and that

> everybody we're serving is half-empty ... there are assets and gifts out there in communities, and our job as good servants and as good leaders ... [is] having the ability to recognise those gifts in others, and help them put those gifts into action. (Michelle Obama,[12] quoted in Foot, 2010, p 7)

Here, the emphasis is on the citizen rather than the consumer. The focus is not on reducing the role of the state, but on building social relationships that constrain the market and support emancipation and citizen agency. It is a process of consciously building on, and supporting, the contributions of citizens.

The third gap that needs to be addressed is how peer support or wider citizen groupings can be brought into the process. Here, we move from participation to rights. Personalised budgets are developed within the context of collective decision-making about resource prioritisation, the reconfiguration of services and regulatory practice to meet basic needs and remove the barriers that are creating injustice. This involves looking at how networks of those most marginalised can be improved to give them a stronger voice and enhance capabilities. Outcomes might be: time banks; peer support networks; new governance structures involving user groups, social movements and citizens more directly in guiding service development or environmental regulation; or local cultural and social activity bringing citizens together to shape new services. Many of the outcomes will be outside the market or nationally or locally funded services and might help to constrain the market (Needham, 2009, pp 10–11).

Wigan Council's asset-based approach in adult and social care: People at the Heart of Scholes project

Like many other councils, Wigan Council is trying to move towards a service model in adult social care that taps into underused and unrecognised resources in the community. Wigan, as one of five Creative Councils supported by **Nesta** from May 2012 for two years, is working on a community-led project in the Scholes area to create a new model for social care. The emphasis is on having a new conversation with social care users to understand their needs and priorities more fully and building a new relationship within the wider community to encourage good neighbourly action, volunteering and enterprise development. The use of new technology and alternative currencies is being explored. One of the volunteers explains the scheme as follows:

> What we are doing with the council is finding out what people want, what they need, and what resources we have within the community to help

> meet these needs. It's not about replacing social care, but looking at it differently and, in many cases, moving away from what's traditionally been on offer. (Parker, 2013, p 66; also information supplied by Kathryn Rees, Change Programme Manager at Wigan Council)

Final thoughts

This book has sought to both stimulate all those involved in local government to question what they are currently doing and to offer a framework for a new approach. In doing so, it has necessarily covered many theoretical issues, seeking to bring clarity to the debate. But, ultimately, the aim is not merely to understand the world, but to change it. The central point is simple. Tony Judt put it beautifully despite, or perhaps because, he was facing death from motor neuron disease and struggled to write at all. As he said:

> Something is profoundly wrong with the way we live today. For thirty years we have made a virtue out of the pursuit of material self-interest: indeed, this very pursuit now constitutes whatever remains of our sense of collective purpose. We know what things cost but have no idea what they are worth. We no longer ask of a judicial ruling or a legislative act; is it good? Is it fair? Is it right? Will it help bring about a better society or a better world? These used to be *the* political questions, even if they invited no easy answers. We must learn once again to pose them. (Judt, 2010, p 1, emphasis in original)

Notes
[1] See: www.southafrica.info/about/democracy/constitution.htm#. UORSDm_eTLc#ixzz2GpgRFbbb

[2] See the letter from the founders of the Assembly in *The Guardian*, 5 February 2013. Available at: www.theguardian.com/business/2013/feb/05/people-assembly-against-austerity

[3] See the example of Peartree Way and Cotney Croft in Stevenage. Available at: www.hertslink.org/buildingfutures/content/migrated/feature/onebright1

[4] The original announcement for Suffolk in September 2010 is discussed by James Illman in the *Local Government Chronicle* on 23 November 2010 and

the announcement that it was abandoning its plans is discussed by Johnstone (2011).

[5] See: www.barnetunison.me.uk/?q=node/1092

[6] I am grateful to Stuart Roden, Regional Organiser from Unison, for this case study.

[7] Communes are the lowest tier of government in France. There are over 36,000 communes in France.

[8] The situation in Scotland is the same, while Wales and Northern Ireland are slightly different.

[9] Under the Localism Act 2011, Parliament approved a report on 8 February 2012 setting out requirements for referenda in those cases where proposed council tax increases for 2013/14 exceeded 3.5% for most principal authorities, 3.75% for the City of London and 4% for police authorities and single-purpose fire and rescue authorities. No equivalent principles apply to town and parish councils for 2012/13, but they may apply in future years (LGiU, 2012, pp 13–14).

[10] See: www.councils.coop/

[11] MyCSP will administer 1.5 million civil servants' pensions. It will be 25% owned by the 475 staff, 35% by the government and 40% by the pension and HR service provider Equiniti, which already looks after almost three million pensions.

[12] See: www.abcdinstitute.org/faculty/obama

References

Adam, S., Emmerson, C. and Kenly, A. (2007) *A survey of UK local government finance*, IFS Briefing Note no 74, London: IFS.

Aldridge, H., Kenway, P., MacInnes, T. and Parekh, A. (2012) *Monitoring poverty and social exclusion 2012*, York: JRF.

Aldridge, R. and Stoker, G. (2003) *Advancing a new public service ethos*, London: NLGN.

Amas, N. (2008) *Housing, new migration and community relations. A review of the evidence base*, London: Information Centre about Asylum and Refugees.

Andersson, L.M. and Anderson, N. (2012) 'Nordic know-how', *The C'llr*, June, London: LGiU.

APSE (Association for Public Service Excellence) (2009) *Insourcing: a guide to bringing local authority services back in-house*, Manchester: APSE.

APSE (2011) *Insourcing update: the value of returning local authority services in-house in an era of budget constraints*, London: Unison. Available at: https://www.unison.org.uk/upload/sharepoint/On%20line%20 Catalogue/20122.pdf

APSE (2013) *Innovation on the frontline: how engagement with the local government workforce can improve service delivery in austere times*, Manchester: APSE.

APSE and Unison (2010) *The value of trade union involvement to service delivery*, London: Unison.

Arblaster, A. (1991 [1987]) *Democracy*, Milton Keynes: Open University Press.

Arnstein, S.R. (1969) 'A ladder of citizen participation', *Journal of the American Institute of Planners*, vol 35, no 4, pp 216–24.

Atkinson, H. and Wilks-Heeg, S. (2000) *Local government from Thatcher to Blair: the politics of creative autonomy*, Cambridge: Polity Press in association with Blackwell Publishers Ltd.

Atkinson, R. (1999) 'Discourses of partnership and empowerment in contemporary British urban regeneration', *Urban Studies*, vol 36, no 1, pp 249–70.

Audit Commission (2011) *Tough times: councils' responses to a challenging financial climate*, London: Audit Commission.

Bacon, R. and Eltis, W. (1978) *Britain's economic problems: too few producers*, London: Macmillan.

Ballard, M. (2012) 'Cornwall Council opts for IT outsourcing after rejecting BT privatisation', *Computer Weekly*, Wednesday 12 Dec. Available at: http://www.computerweekly.com/news/2240174364/Cornwall-Council-opts-for-IT-outsourcing-after-rejecting-BT-privatisation

Banks S. (2001 [1995]) *Ethics and values in social work* (2nd edn), Basingstoke: Palgrave.

Barnes, M. (2012) 'An army of benefit scroungers? The evidence just doesn't stack up', *The Guardian*, 28 November. Available at: http://www.theguardian.com/commentisfree/2012/nov/28/benefit-scroungers-child-poverty-parents

Barnes, M., Newman, J. and Sullivan, H. (2007) *Power, participation and political renewal: case studies in public participation*, Bristol: The Policy Press.

Bassett, K. (1984) 'Labour, socialism and local democracy', in M. Boddy and C. Fudge (eds) *Local socialism?*, London and Basingstoke: Macmillan, pp 82–108.

BBC (British Broadcasting Corporation) (2012) 'Welfare-to-work: official figures show job target missed', 27 November. Available at: http://www.bbc.co.uk/news/uk-politics-20499836

Beetham, D. (1993) *The democratic audit of the UK – auditing democracy in Britain*, London: The Charter 88 Trust.

Beetham, D. (2011) *Unelected oligarchy: corporate and financial dominance in Britain's democracy*, Liverpool: Democratic Audit.

Benington, J. (1976) *Local government becomes big business* (2nd edn), London: CDP Information and Intelligence.

Benington, J. (2006) 'Reclaiming the neighbourhood', in J. Benington, L. de Groot and J. Foot (eds) *Lest we forget: democracy, neighbourhoods and government*, London: Solace Foundation Imprint, pp 8–18.

Benington, J. (2009) 'Creating the public in order to create public value?', *International Journal of Public Administration*, vol 32, nos 3/4, pp 232–49.

Benington, J. (2011) 'From private choice to public value', in J. Benington and M.H. Moore (eds) *Public value: theory and practice*, Basingstoke, Hampshire: Palgrave Macmillan, pp 31–51.

Benington, J. and Moore, M.H. (eds) (2011) *Public value: theory and practice*, Basingstoke, Hampshire: Palgrave Macmillan.

Bennett, T., Grossberg, L. and Morris, M. (2005) *New keywords: a revised vocabulary of culture and society*, Malden, MA, and Oxford: Blackwell Publishing.

Beveridge, W. (1942) *Report of the Inter-Departmental Committee on Social Insurance and Allied Services*, Cmnd 6404, London: HMSO.

Birchall, J. (2011) *People-centred businesses. Co-operatives, mutuals and the idea of membership*, Basingstoke: Palgrave Macmillan.

Bivand, P (2013) 'Can a programme achieve fewer jobs than would have happened anyway?' *Working Brief*, Issue 232, Summer 2013, p 40-41.

Blinder, A.S. and Zandi, M. (2010) 'How the great recession was brought to an end'. Available at: www.economy.com/mark-zandi/documents/End-of-Great-Recession.pdf

Boal, A. (1979) *Theatre of the oppressed*, London: Pluto.

Boddy, M. (1984) 'Local economic and employment strategy', in M. Boddy and C. Fudge (eds) *Local socialism?*, London and Basingstoke: Macmillan, pp 160–91.

Boddy, M. and Fudge, C. (eds) (1984) *Local socialism?*, London and Basingstoke: Macmillan.

Boyle, D. (2011) 'The pitfalls and perils of payment by results', *Local Economy*, vol 26, no 8, pp 627–33.

Bramah, M., Mcinroy, N., Jackson, M., Bradford, V. and Griggs, S. (2007) *Towards a future for public employment*, Manchester: APSE.

Brenner, N. and Theodore, N. (eds) (2002) *Spaces of neoliberalism: urban restructuring in North America and Western Europe*, Oxford: Blackwell.

Briggs, A. (1952) *History of Birmingham. Volume 2: Borough and city 1865–1938*, London: Oxford University Press for Birmingham City Council.

Briggs, A. (1963) *Victorian cities*, Berkeley, CA: University of California Press.

Brown, K. (2011) 'The prioritisation of vulnerable groups in the age of austerity', paper for the Social Policy Association Conference. Available at: http://www.social-policy.org.uk/lincoln2011/Kate%20Brown%20P4(2).pdf

Brown, L.D. and Jacobs, L.R. (2008) *The private abuse of the public interest: market myths and policy muddles*, London and Chicago, IL: University of Chicago Press.

Buchanan, J. and Tullock, G. (1962) *The calculus of consent*, Ann Arbor, MI: University of Michigan Press.

Burns, D., Hambleton, R. and Hoggett, P. (1994) *The politics of decentralisation, revitalising local democracy*, London: Macmillan Press.

Bushe, S., Kenway, P. and Aldridge, H. (2013) *The impact of localising Council Tax Benefit*, York: JRF.

Butt, R. (1981) 'Mrs Thatcher: The First Two Years', *Sunday Times*, 3 May 1981. Available at: www.margaretthatcher.org/document/104475

Calhoun, C. (2012) *The roots of radicalism: tradition, the public sphere, and early nineteenth-century social movements*, Chicago, IL: The University of Chicago Press.

Cameron, D. (1994) '"Words, words, words": the power of language', in S. Dunant (ed) *The war of the words. The political correctness debate*, London: Virago Press.

Campbell, F. (ed) (2010) *The social determinants of health and the role of local government*, London: IDeA. Available at: http://www.thaisocialhealth. net/sites/default/files/resources/%5BEXT%5D2010%20SDH%20 and%20the%20role%20of%20local%20government%20-%20 IDEA%20Fiona%20Campbell.pdf

Carpenter, M. and Speeden, S. (with Griffin, C. and Walters, N.) (2007) 'Capabilities, human rights and the challenge to workfare', in M. Carpenter, B. Freda and S. Speeden (eds) *Beyond the workfare state. Labour markets, equality and human rights*, Bristol: The Policy Press, pp 159–84.

Carter, M. (2003) *T.H. Green and the development of ethical socialism*, Exeter and Charlottesville, VA: Imprint Academic.

Children in Scotland (2011a) 'Early years briefing paper no. 7: how they did it: Slovenia and Norway's early childhood education and care policies'. Available at: https://www.childreninscotland.org.uk/ members/docs/CIS_EYF_Briefing_paper_7.pdf

Children in Scotland (2011b) 'Early childhood education and care: developing a fully integrated early years system'. Available at: www. childreninscotland.org.uk/docs/CIS_ECECSpecialReport2_001.pdf

Chote, R., Crawford, R., Emmerson, C. and Tetlow, G. (2010) 'Public spending under Labour; 2010 election briefing note no. 5 (IFS BN92)', Institute for Fiscal Studies, Nuffield Foundation. Available at: http:// www.ifs.org.uk/bns/bn92.pdf

Civil Exchange (2012) *The Big Society Audit 2012*, London: Civil Exchange, in partnership with Democratic Audit and DHA Communications.

Civil Exchange (2013) *The Big Society Audit 2013*, London: Civil Exchange in partnership with DHA Communications.

Clarke, J. (2007a) 'Unsettled connections: citizens, consumers and the reform of public services', *Journal of Consumer Culture*, vol 7, pp 159–77.

Clarke, J. (2007b) 'Citizen–consumers and public service reform: at the limits of neo-liberalism?', *Policy Futures in Education*, vol 5, no 2, pp 239–48. Available at: http://oro.open.ac.uk/18126/3/B080F27A.pdf

CLD (Commission for Local Democracy) (1995) *Taking charge: the rebirth of local democracy*, London: Municipal Journal.

CLG (Communities and Local Government) (2009) *Local government finance key facts: England*, London: CLG. Available at: http://webarchive.nationalarchives.gov.uk/20120919132719/http://www.communities.gov.uk/documents/statistics/pdf/1374609.pdf

CLG (2010) *Local government financial statistics England no 20, 2010*, London: Crown Copyright, CLG.

Cochrane, A. (1993) *Whatever happened to local government?*, Buckingham: Open University Press.

Cochrane, A. (2007) *Understanding urban policy: a critical approach*, Malden, MA, and Oxford: Blackwell Publishing.

Cockburn, C. (1977) *The local state*, London: Pluto Press.

Cohen, G.A. (2008) *Rescuing justice and equality*, Cambridge, MA: Harvard University Press.

Communities and Local Government Committee (2012) *Councillors on the frontline*, Norwich: The Stationery Office. Available at: http://www.parliament.uk/business/committees/committees-a-z/commons-select/communities-and-local-government-committee/news/councillors-report-/

Cooke, G. and Muir, R. (eds) (2012) *The relational state: how recognising the importance of human relationships could revolutionise the role of the state*, London: IPPR.

Copus, C. (2010) 'The councillor: governor, governance and the complexity of citizen engagement', *The British Journal of Politics and International Relations*, vol 12, no 4, pp 569–89.

Corry, D. and Stoker, G. (2002) *New localism: refashioning the centre–local relationship*, London: NLGN.

Councillors Commission (2007) *Representing the future*, London: DCLG. Available at: http://webarchive.nationalarchives.gov.uk/20080910134927/http://www.communities.gov.uk/documents/localgovernment/pdf/583990.pdf

Craig, G., Hill, N. and Mayo, M. (1998) 'Editorial introduction: managing conflict through community development', *Community Development Journal*, vol 33, no 2 pp 77–9.

Cribb, J., Joyce, R. and Phillips, D. (2012) *Living standards, poverty and inequality in the UK: 2012*, London: IFS. Available at: http://www.ifs.org.uk/comms/comm124.pdf

Crouch, C. (2003) *Commercialisation or citizenship: education policy and the future of public services*, London: Fabian Society.

Daily Mail (2010) 'An end to Brown's welfare trap', *Mail Online*, 30 July. Available at: http://www.dailymail.co.uk/news/article-1298830/Coalition-tear-welfare-Tax-credits-biggest-reform-decades.html

Daily Telegraph (2013) 'Councillors for hire who give firms planning advice', 22 March.

Dale, A.W.W. (1899) *The life of R.W. Dale of Birmingham* (2nd edn), London: Hodder and Stoughton.

Davenport, E. and Totterdill, P. (1986) 'Fashion centres: an approach to sector intervention', *Local Economy*, vol 1, no 1, pp 57–63.

Davies, J.S. (2011) *Challenging governance theory*, Bristol: The Policy Press.

Davies, P. (2013) 'Put people at the centre of positive change', *Municipal Journal*, 8 August, p 21.

Davis, A., Hirsch, D., Smith, N., Beckhelling, J. and Padley, M. (2012) *A minimum income standard for the UK in 2012*, York: Joseph Rowntree Foundation.

DCLG (Department for Communities and Local Government) (2012) *50 ways to save: examples of sensible savings in local government*, London: DCLG. Available at: https://www.gov.uk/government/uploads/system/uploads/attachment_data/file/39264/50_ways_2.pdf

DCLG (2013) *The cost of troubled families*, London: DCLG. Available at: https://www.gov.uk/government/uploads/system/uploads/attachment_data/file/68744/The_Cost_of_Troubled_Families_v1.pdf

DETR (Department of the Environment, Transport and the Regions) (1998) *Modern Local Government. In Touch with the People*, Cm 4014, London: Stationery Office.

Dean, H. (2010) *Understanding human need*, Bristol: The Policy Press.

Deloitte Consulting (2005) *Calling a change in the outsourcing market –the realities for the world's largest organisations*, New York, NY: Deloitte Development LLC. Available at: http://www.deloitte.com/assets/Dcom-Luxembourg/Local%20Assets/Documents/Global_brochures/us_outsourcing_callingachange.pdf

DH (Department of Health) (1997) *Health action zones: invitation to bid*, London: DH.

Diamond P. (2011) 'Mutualism and social democracy', in P. Diamond, T. Hunt, T. Jowell, A. Painter, M. Stephenson, G. McClymont, W. Davies, A. Westall and A. Lent (eds) *What mutualism means for Labour. Political economy and public services*, London: Policy Network, pp 7–14.

Dorling, D. (2010) 'Using the concept of "place" to understand and reduce health inequalities', in F. Campbell (ed) *The social determinants of health and the role of local government*, London: IDeA, pp 16–25. Available at: http://www.thaisocialhealth.net/sites/default/files/resources/%5BEXT%5D2010%20SDH%20and%20the%20role%20of%20local%20government%20-%20IDEA%20Fiona%20Campbell.pdf

Dorling, D. (2011) *Injustice: why social inequality persists*, Bristol: The Policy Press.

Doyal, L. and Gough, I. (1991) *A theory of human need*, Basingstoke: Macmillan Education Ltd.

Dryzek, J.S. (2005) *The politics of the earth: environmental discourses* (2nd edn), Oxford: Oxford University Press.

Dungey, J. (1997) *Citizens' panels: a new approach to community consultation*, London: LGiU.

Dungey, J. (2007) *All Party Parliamentary Local Government Group. The role of councillors: report of an inquiry*, London: LGiU.

Dunleavy, P. (1986) 'Explaining the privatization boom: public choice versus radical approaches', *Public Administration*, vol 64, no 1, pp 13–34.

Dwyer, P. and Ellison, N. (2009) 'Work and welfare: the rights and responsibilities of unemployment in the UK', in M. Giugni (ed) *The politics of unemployment in Europe: policy responses and collective action*, Farnham, Surrey: Ashgate, pp 53–66.

Eaglesham, J. (2008) 'Profile: George Osborne', *Financial Times*, 6 September.

Esping-Andersen, G. (1990) *The three worlds of welfare capitalism*, Princeton, NJ: Princeton University Press.

Esping-Andersen, G. (ed) (1996) *Welfare states in transition. National adaptations in global economics*, London: Sage Publications.

European Institute for Urban Affairs, Liverpool John Moores University; School of Government and Society, University of Birmingham; Local Government Centre, Warwick Business School, University of Warwick; Cities Research Centre, University of the West of England; SQW Consulting; Office for Public Management; and Centre for Local and Regional Government Research, Cardiff University (2010) *Long term evaluation of LAAs and LSPs: final report November 2010*, CLG. Available at: http://webarchive.nationalarchives.gov.uk/20120919132719/http://www.communities.gov.uk/documents/corporate/pdf/1923459.pdf

Filkin, J., Stoker, G., Wilkinson, G. and Williams, J. (2000) *Towards a new localism: a discussion paper*, London: NLGN. Available at: http://www.nlgn.org.uk/public/2000/towards-a-new-localism-a-discussion-paper/

Finlayson, A. (2003) *Making sense of New Labour*, London: Lawrence & Wishart.

Finney, N. and Simpson, L. (2009) *Sleepwalking to segregation? Challenging myths about race and migration*, Bristol: The Policy Press.

Fischer, F. (2003) *Reframing public policy. Discursive politics and deliberative practices*, Oxford: Oxford University Press.

Flood, A. (2013) 'Library campaigners save Friern Barnet branch for community', *The Guardian*, 5 February.

Foot, J. (with Hopkins, T.) (2010) *A glass half-full: how an asset approach can improve community health and well-being*, London; IDeA. Available at: http://janefoot.com/downloads/files/Glass%20half%20full.pdf

Francis, R. (2010) *Independent inquiry into care provided by Mid Staffordshire NHS Foundation Trust January 2005–March 2009*, London: The Stationery Office.

Fraser, N. (1997) *Justice interruptus: critical reflections on the 'postsocialist' condition*, New York, NY: Routledge.

Fraser, N. (2009) *Scales of justice: reimagining political space in a globalizing world*, New York, NY: Columbia University Press.

Fraser, N. (2011a) 'Recognition and multiculturalism', Multicultural Bites, Open University. Available at: http://itunes.apple.com/us/itunes-u/multiculturalism-bites-audio/id449122394

Fraser, N. (2011b) 'Crisis of capitalism, crisis of governance: re-reading Karl Polanyi in the 21st century', podcast of keynote speech given at the University of Warwick Critical Governance Conference. Available at: www2.warwick.ac.uk/knowledge/themes/02/crisis_of_capitalism/

Freire, P. (1970) *Pedagogy of the oppressed*, New York, NY: Continuum.

Friedman, M. (1962) *Capitalism and freedom*, Chicago, IL: University of Chicago Press.

Fuller, C. and Geddes, M. (2008) 'Urban governance under neoliberalism: New Labour and the restructuring of state-space', *Antipode*, vol 40, no 2, pp 252–82.

Fuller, C. and West, K. (2013) 'The possibilities and limits of urban contestation in times of turbulence and crisis', draft paper presented to the conference on Urban Crisis at De Montfort University, September. Available at: www.dmu.ac.uk/urbancrisis

Game, C. and Leach, S. (1996) 'Political parties and local democracy', in L. Pratchett and D. Wilson (eds) *Local democracy and local government*, Basingstoke: Macmillan Press Ltd, pp 127–49.

Gardiner, T. (2006) *Frontline councillors and decision making: broadening their involvement*, York: Joseph Rowntree Foundation.

Gaster, L. and Hoggett, P. (1993) 'Neighbourhood decentralisation and local management', in N. Thomas, N. Deakin and J. Doling (eds) *Learning from innovation; housing and social care in the 1990s*, Birmingham: Birmingham Academic Press, pp 123–44.

Geddes, M. (2010) 'Building and contesting neoliberalism at the local level: reflections on the symposium and on recent experience in Bolivia', *International Journal of Urban and Regional Research*, vol 34, no 1, pp 163–73.

Giddens, A. (2004) 'Did they foul up my Third Way?', *New Statesman*, 7 June. Available at: http://www.newstatesman.com/node/148130

Giugni, M. (2009) *The politics of unemployment in Europe: policy responses and collective action*, Farnham, Surrey: Ashgate.

Giugni, M., Berclaz, M. and Füglister, K. (2009) 'Welfare states, labour markets and the political opportunities for collective action in the field of unemployment: A theoretical framework' in M. Giugni (ed) *The politics of unemployment in Europe: policy responses and collective action*, Farnham, Surrey: Ashgate, pp 133-49.

GLC (Greater London Council) (1985) *London industrial strategy*, London: GLC.

Gordon, P. (1995) *Local Government Chronicle*, 26 July.

Goss, S. (2006) 'Rules of engagement for the community worker', in J. Bennington, L. de Groot and J. Foot (eds) *Lest we forget: democracy, neighbourhoods and government*, London: Solace Foundation Imprint, pp 19–21.

Green, A.E. (2012) 'Government policy and women in the labour market: the importance of public sector employment', *Local Economy*, vol 27, no 8, pp 804–15.

Gregory, D. (2013) *Out of the Shadows? The fall and rise of social value in public services: a progress report,* London: Social Enterprise UK.

Grey, C. (2005) *A very short, fairly interesting and reasonably cheap book about studying organizations*, London: Sage Publications Ltd.

Guardian Letters (2013) 'Benefit cuts and rhetoric undermine a bastion of civilised society', *The Guardian,* 27 March 2013, p 53.

Guarneros-Meza, V. and Geddes, M. (2010) 'Local governance and participation under neoliberalism: comparative perspectives', *International Journal of Urban and Regional Research*, vol 34, no 1, pp 115–29.

Gyford, J. (1985) *The politics of local socialism*, London: Allen and Unwin.

Gyford, J. (1991a) *Citizens, consumers and councils; local government and the public*, Basingstoke: Macmillan Education Ltd.

Gyford, J. (1991b) *Does place matter? Locality and local democracy,* Belgrave Papers no 3, Luton: Local Government Management Board.

Habermas, J. (1984 [1981]) *Theory of communicative action, vol 1: reason and the rationalization of society*, Boston, MA: Beacon Press.

Habermas, J. (1990 [1983]) *Moral consciousness and communicative action*, Cambridge: Polity Press.

Hall, S. (2007) 'Will life after Blair be different?', *British Politics*, vol 2, pp 118–22.

Hambleton, R. (1989) *Consumerism, decentralisation and local democracy*, SAUS Working Paper 78, Bristol: SAUS.

Hancox, D. (2012) 'The Spanish Robin Hood', *The Guardian*, 16 August, p 9.

Harvey, D. (2000) *Spaces of hope*, Edinburgh: Edinburgh University Press.

Harvey, D. (2005) *A short history of neoliberalism*, Oxford: Oxford University Press.

Harvey, D. (2008) 'The right to the city', *New Left Review*, vol 53, Sept/Oct, pp 23–40.

Harvey, D. (2011) *The enigma of capital and the crises of capitalism*, London: Profile Books Ltd.

Hasluck, C. and Green A.E. (2007) *What works for whom? A review of evidence and meta-analysis for the Department of Work and Pensions*, Department for Work and Pensions Research Report 407, Leeds: Corporate Document Services.

Hastings, A., Bramley, G., Bailey, N. and Watkins, D. (2012) *Serving deprived communities in a recession*, York: JRF.

Hayek, F.A. (1973) *Law, legislation and liberty. Vol. 1: rules and order*, London: Routledge and Kegan Paul.

Hayek, F.A. (1976) *Law, legislation and liberty. Vol. 2: the mirage of social justice*, Chicago, IL, and London: The University of Chicago Press.

Henke, S.H. (ed) (1989) *Privatization and development*, San Francisco, CA: International Center for Economic Growth/ICS Press.

HM Government (2011a) *Open Public Services: White Paper*, Cm 8145, Norwich: The Stationery Office.

HM Government (2011b) *Unlocking growth in cities,* London: Cabinet Office.

HM Government (2012a) *Open Public Services 2012*, London: Cabinet Office.

HM Government (2012b) *Social justice: transforming lives*, Cm 8314, London: Department of Work and Pensions.

HM Treasury (2010) *Spending Review 2010*, Cm 7942, Norwich: The Stationery Office.

Hoggett, P., Mayo, M. and Miller, C. (2006) 'Private passions and public good and public service reform', *Social Policy and Administration*, vol 40, no 70, pp 758–73.

Hood, C. (1991) 'A public management for all seasons', *Public Administration*, vol 69, Spring, pp 3–19.

Horner, L. and Hutton, W. (2011) 'Public value, deliberative democracy and the role of public managers' value', in J. Benington and M.H. Moore (eds) *Public value: theory and practice*, Basingstoke, Hampshire: Palgrave Macmillan, pp 112–26.

Hugman, R. (2005) *New approaches in ethics for the caring professions*, Basingstoke: Palgrave Macmillan.

Huitson, O. (2012) 'The public–private partnership: the privatisation of governance', in J. Manson (ed) *Public service on the brink*, Exeter: Imprint Academic, pp 67–91.

IDeA (Improvement and Development Agency) (2007) *Frontline councillor: how local politicians make a difference in their communities*, London: Improvement and Development Agency for local government.

IDeA (2009) *Key principles of the equality framework for local government*, London: IDeA. Incorporated into Local Government Association guidance and available at: www.local.gov.uk/equality-frameworks/-/journal_content/56/10180/3476575/ARTICLE

IDeA (2010) *Community engagement and empowerment: our resource*, London: Local Government Association. Some of this resource remains available on the LGA site at: www.local.gov.uk/localism-act/-/journal_content/56/10180/3510950/ARTICLE

Independent Commission on the Future of Council Housing in Southwark (2012) *Investing in council housing: options for the future*, London: London Borough of Southwark, with support of the Smith Institute.

Institute for Economics and Peace (2013) 'The United Kingdom peace index'. Available at: www.visionofhumanity.org/wp-content/uploads/2013/04/UK-Peace-Index-2013-IEP-Report.pdf

Islington Council (2012) *Islington Fairness Commission – The first year of delivery (2011-2012)*. Available at: www.islington.gov.uk/about/fairness-commission/putting-fairness-practice/what-we-are-doing/Pages/default.aspx

Islington Fairness Commission (2011) *Closing the gap: the final report of the Islington Fairness Commission June 2011*, London: The Islington Fairness Commission. Available at: www.islington.gov.uk/fairness

Jeffreys, S. (2012) *Shared business services outsourcing: progress at work or work in progress?*, Working Lives Research Institute Working Paper 11, London: London Metropolitan University.

Jessop, B. (1994) 'The transitions to post-Fordism and the Schumpeterian workfare state', in R. Burrows and B. Loader (eds) *Towards a post-Fordist welfare state*, London: Routledge, pp 13–37.

Johnstone, R. (2011) 'Suffolk council suspends mass outsourcing plan', *Public Finance*, 5 May.

Jones, A. and Newman, I. (2006) *Parish and town council clustering*, London: LGiU.

Jones, G.W. (1969) *Borough politics*, London: Macmillan and Co Ltd.

Jones, G. and Stewart, J. (1983) *The case for local government*, London: George Allen and Unwin.

Jones, G. and Travers, T. (1996) 'Central government perceptions of local government', in L. Pratchett and D. Wilson (eds) *Local democracy and local government*, Basingstoke: Macmillan Press Ltd, pp 84–105.

Jones, G., Stewart, J. and Travers, T. (2011) 'Genuine localism – the way out of the impasse', in C. Morales Oyarce (ed) *Redefining local government*, London: Public Policy and Management Association, CIPFA, pp 7–22.

Judt, T. (2010) *Ill fares the land: a treatise on our present discontents*, London: Penguin Books.

Karlsson, D. and Montin, S. (2013) 'Solving municipal paradoxes: challenges for Swedish local democracy', in W. Hofmeister (with M. Sarmah and P. Rüppel) (ed) *Local politics and governance*, an occasional paper in the Panorama: Insights into Asian and European Affairs series, Singapore: Konrad-Adenauer-Stiftung.

Katz, M.B. (1989) *The underserving poor: from the war on poverty to the war on welfare*, New York, NY: Pantheon Books.

Kenway, P. (2009) *Should adult benefit for unemployment now be raised?*, York: JRF.

Kenway, P. and Palmer, G. (2004) *Council tax, the answer?*, London: LGiU. Available at: http://npi.org.uk/publications/council-tax/council-tax-answer/Kenway, P. and Palmer, G. (2005) *Making it fair: Council Tax Benefit and working households*, London: LGiU. Available at: http://npi.org.uk/publications/council-tax/making-it-fair-council-tax-benefit-and-working-households/

Kessler, L. (2012) 'Public service. Why it is so difficult to ensure that places meet the needs of people, especially in areas of multi-deprivation', in J. Manson (ed) *Public service on the brink*, Exeter: Imprint Academic, pp 185–206.

Kitchin, H., Phillimore, J., Goodson, L., Mayblin, L., Jones, A., Pickstock, A., Weir, S. and Blick, A. (2009) *Communicating cohesion. Evaluating local authority communication strategies. Research summary*, Birmingham: Institute of Local Government Studies, University of Birmingham.

Lancaster, L.W. (1959) *Masters of political thought. Volume three: Hegel to Dewey*, London: Harrap.

Laurence, J. and Heath, A. (2008) *Predictors of community cohesion: multi-level modelling of the 2005 Citizenship Survey*, London: CLG.

Lawrence, R. (1982) 'Voluntary action: a stalking horse for the Right?', *Critical Social Policy*, vol 2, no 6, pp 14–30.

Layard, R. (2005) *Happiness: lessons from a new science*, London: Penguin.

Layfield Report (1976) *Local government finance*, report of the Layfield Committee, Cmnd 6453, London: HMSO.

Leitner, H., Peck, J. and Sheppard, E. (2007) *Contesting neoliberalism: urban frontiers*, New York, NY: Guildford Press.

Lemke, T. (2001) '"The birth of bio-politics": Michel Foucault's lecture at the College de France on neo-liberal governmentality', *Economy and Society*, vol 30, no 2, pp 190–207.

LGA (Local Government Association) (2011) *The LGA quick guide to local government*, London: LGA. Available at: www.local.gov.uk/health/-/journal_content/56/10180/3510763/ARTICLE

LGA (2012a) *Independence from the centre; does local government's freedom lie in a new constitutional settlement?*, London: LGA.

LGA (2012b) *Provisional local government finance settlement 2013–14 and 2014–15*, LGA Briefing 19, London: LGA.

LGA (2013) *Rewiring public services – financial sustainability*, London: LGA.

LGiU (Local Government Information Unit) (2012) *The Localism Act: an LGiU guide. Updated September 2012*, London: LGiU.

Lipsky, M. (1980) *Street level bureaucracy*, New York, NY: Russell Sage Foundation.

Lister, R. (2007) '(Mis)Recognition, social inequality and social justice. A critical social policy perspective', in T. Lovell (ed) *(Mis)Recognition, social inequality and social justice. Nancy Fraser and Pierre Bourdieu*, Abingdon: Routledge, pp 157–76.

Local Government Chronicle (2011) 'LGC outsourcing: innovative approaches to service delivery', 31 March, Emap Ltd, London. Available at: www.lgcplus.com/Journals/3/Files/2011/3/30/LGC_March2011_Outsourcing_Supplement.pdf

Local Government Leadership (2010) *Co-operative communities: creating a shared stake in our society for everyone*, London: Local Government Leadership.

London Edinburgh Weekend Return Group (1979/80) *In and against the state* (2nd edn), London: Pluto Press. Available at: http://libcom.org/library/against-state-1979

Loney, M. (1983) *Community against government: the British Community Development Project 1968–78*, London: Heinemann.

Loughlin, J. and Martin, S. (2004) 'Local income tax in Sweden: reform and continuity', paper prepared for the Balance of Funding Review, School of European Studies, Cardiff University, and the Centre for Local & Regional Government Research. Available at: http://campaigns.libdems.org.uk/user_files/axethetax/LIT_in_Sweden.pdf

Loughlin, J. and Martin, S. (2006) 'Options for reforming local government funding to increase local streams of funding: international comparisons', prepared for the Lyons Inquiry into Local Government Funding, School of European Studies, Cardiff University, and the Centre for Local & Regional Government Research. Available at: http://campaigns.libdems.org.uk/user_files/axethetax/International_comparisons.pdf

Lovell, T. (ed) (2007) *(Mis)Recognition, social inequality and social justice. Nancy Fraser and Pierre Bourdieu*, Abingdon: Routledge.

Lowndes, V. (1992) 'Decentralisation: the potential and the pitfalls', *Local Government Policy Making*, vol 18, no 4, pp 53–63.

Lowndes, V. and Sullivan, H. (2008) 'How low can you go? Rationales and challenges for neighbourhood governance', *Public Administration*, vol 86, no 1, pp 53–74.

Lukes, S. (1974) *Power: a radical view*, London: Macmillan Press.

Lyons, M. (2005) *Lyons inquiry into local government: consultation paper and interim report*, Norwich: Her Majesty's Stationery Office.

Lyons, M. (2007) *Place-shaping: a shared ambition for the future of local government*, London: Crown Copyright, The Stationery Office.

Mackintosh, M. (1992) 'Partnership: issues of policy and negotiation', *Local Economy*, vol 7, no 3, pp 210–24.

Mackintosh, M. and Wainwright, W. (eds) (1987) *A taste of power: the politics of local economics*, London: Verso.

Manson, J. (2012) *Public service on the brink*, Exeter: Imprint Academic.

Marmot, M. (2010) *Fair society, healthy lives: a strategic review of health inequalities in England post-2010*, London: The Marmot Review. Available at: www.ucl.ac.uk/marmotreview

Marquand, D. (2004) *Decline of the public*, Cambridge: Polity Press.

Marris, P. and Rein, M. (1972) *Dilemma of social reform; poverty and community action in the United States*, London: Routledge and Kegan Paul.

Marshall, T.H. (1950) *Citizenship and social class and other essays*, Cambridge: Cambridge University Press.

Matka, E., Barnes, M. and Sullivan, H. (2002) '"Health Action Zones": creating alliances to achieve change', *Policy Studies*, vol 23, no 2, pp 97–106.

Mayo, M. (2000) *Cultures, communities and identities: cultural strategies for participation and empowerment*, Basingstoke: Palgrave.

Mayo, M. (2005) *Global citizens: social movements and the challenge of globalization*, London: Zed Books.

Mayo, M. (2006) 'A trained, professional workforce is key', in J. Bennington, L. de Groot and J. Foot (eds) *Lest we forget: democracy, neighbourhoods and government*, London: Solace Foundation Imprint, pp 24–5.

Mayo, M. (2014, forthcoming) *Accessing justice*, Bristol: The Policy Press.

Meynhardt, T. (2009) 'Public value inside: what is public value creation?', *International Journal of Public Administration*, vol 32, nos 3/4, pp 192–219.

Miliband, R. (1969) *The state in capitalist society*, London: Weidenfeld and Nicholson.

Moore, M.H. (1995) *Creating public value: strategic management in governance*, Cambridge, MA: Harvard University Press.

Moore, M. and Hartley, J. (2010) 'Innovations in governance', in S.P. Osborne (ed) *The new public governance? Emerging perspectives on the theory and practice of public governance*, Abingdon: Routledge, pp 52–71.

Morgan, G. (1986) *Images of organisation*, Beverly Hills, CA: Sage.

Morphet, J. (2008) *Modern local government: in touch with the people*, London: Sage.

Morrissey, M. and Gaffikin, F. (2006) 'Planning for peace in contested space', *International Journal of Urban and Regional Research*, vol 30, no 4, pp 873–93.

Mulgan, G. (2011) 'Effective supply and demand and the measurement of public and social value', in J. Benington and M.H. Moore (eds) *Public value: Theory and practice*, Basingstoke, Hampshire: Palgrave Macmillan, pp 212–24.

Mulgan, G. (2012) 'Government with the people: the outlines of a relational state', in G. Cooke and R. Muir (eds) *The relational state: how recognising the importance of human relationships could revolutionise the role of the state*, London: IPPR, pp 20–34.

Mulgan, G. and Bury, F. (eds) (2006) *Double devolution: the renewal of local government*, London: The Smith Institute.

Murray, R. (2012) *The new wave of mutuality: social innovation and public service reform*, London: Policy Network.

Murray, U. (2012) 'Local government and the meaning of publicness', in J. Manson (ed) *Public service on the brink*, Exeter: Imprint Academic, pp 41–66.

NAO (National Audit Office) (2013) *Case study on integration: measuring the costs and benefits of Whole-Place Community Budgets*, report by the Comptroller and Auditor General HC 1040, London: The Stationery Office.

Needham, C. (2007) *The reform of public services under New Labour; narratives of consumerism*, Basingstoke: Palgrave Macmillan.

Needham, C. and Carr, S. (2012 [2009]) *Co-production: an emerging evidence base for adult social care transformation*, Research Briefing 31, London: Social Care Institute for Excellence.

Neill Committee (1998) *The fifth report of the Committee on Standards in Public Life: The Funding of Political Parties in the United Kingdom*, Cm 4057–I, Norwich: The Stationery Office.

New Economics Foundation (2008) *Co-production: a manifesto for growing the core economy*, London: New Economics Foundation.

Newham London (2011) *Quid pro quo, not status quo: why we need a welfare state that builds resilience*, London: London Borough of Newham.

Newham London (2013) *Resilience making it happen: an update on delivery*, London: London Borough of Newham.

Newman, I. (1986) 'Greater London Enterprise Board: vision and reality', *Local Economy*, vol 1, no 2, pp 57–67.

Newman, I. (1996) 'Discourse and the public sector', *Local Government Policy Making*, vol 23, no 2, pp 52–9.

Newman, I. (2011) 'Work as a route out of poverty: a critical evaluation of the UK welfare to work policy', *Policy Studies*, vol 32, no 2, pp 91–108.

Newman, I. (2012) 'Community Budgets Research Report', Warwick: Warwick University Local Authorities Research Consortium. Available at The Knowledge Hub 'Total place, community budgets and other place based activity' group library: knowledgehub@local.gov.uk

Newman, I. and Mayo, M. (1981) 'Docklands', *International Journal of Urban and Regional Research*, vol 5, no 4, pp 529–45.

Newman, J. (2012) 'Making, contesting and governing the local: women's labour and the local state', *Local Economy*, vol 27, no 8, pp 846–58.

Newman, J. and Clarke, J. (2009) *Publics, politics and power: remaking the public in public services*, London: Sage.

Newman, K. (2008) 'Annex 1. Understanding rights', in J. Sumberg, V. Johnson and K. Newman (eds) 'Universal access to modern energy services: potential of a rights-based approach', a report to Practical Action by the New Economics Foundation, unpublished.

Newman, K. (2012) 'Challenges and dilemmas in integrating human rights-based approaches and participatory approaches to development: an exploration of the experiences of ActionAid International', unpublished PhD thesis, Goldsmith College, University of London.

Newman, M. (1993) *Harold Laski: A Political Biography*, Basingstoke, Hampshire: The Macmillan Press Ltd.

Newman, M. (2002) *Ralph Miliband and the politics of the New Left*, London: Merlin Press.

New Policy Institute (2012) *Poverty and the Big Society: views from the community sector*, London: NPI. Available at: http://npi.org.uk/publications/income-and-poverty/poverty-and-big-society-views-community-sector/

Nicholson, P.P. (1985) 'T.H. Green and state action: liquor legislation', *History of Political Thought*, vol 6, pp 517–50.

Niskanen, W. (1973) *Bureaucracy: servant or master?*, London: Institute for Economic Affairs.

Nozick, R. (1974) *Anarchy, state and utopia*, New York, NY: Basic Books.

ODPM (Office of the Deputy Prime Minister) (1999) 'Preparing community strategies: government guidance to local authorities'. Available at: http://collections.europarchive.org/tna/20090106142604/odpm.gov.uk/index.asp?id=1133742

Office for Budget Responsibility (2013) *Economic and fiscal outlook, December 2013*, Cm 8748, The Stationery Office.

Olmedo, A., Grimaldi, E., Lundahl, L., Santa Cruz Grau, L., Holm, A.-S., Lundström, U., Erixon Arreman, I. and Alexiadou, N. (2012) 'The privatisation in and of education in European countries: the cases of Italy, Spain, Sweden and England', paper submitted to the European Educational Research Association. Available at: http://www.eera-ecer.de/ecer-programmes/conference/6/contribution/17541/

O'Riordan, T. and Voisey, H. (eds) (1997) *Sustainable development in Western Europe: coming to terms with Agenda 21*, London: Frank Cass & Co.

Orr, K. (2004) 'If mayors are the answer then what was the question?', *Local Government Studies*, vol 30, Part 3, pp 331–44.

Osborne, S.P. (ed) (2010) *The new public governance? Emerging perspectives on the theory and practice of public governance*, Abingdon: Routledge.

Oxford Economics (2012) *Open access: delivering quality and value in our public services*, London: CBI.

Oz, O. and Eder, M. (2013) 'Urban crisis Beyoglu: conflicts over demolition of the Emek movie theater and Gezi Park in Istanbul'. Draft paper submitted to the Urban Crisis conference at De Montfort University, September. Available at: www.dmu.ac.uk/urbancrisis

Paine, T. (1791/92) *The political writings of Thomas Paine: secretary to the Committee of Foreign Affairs in the American Revolution: to which is prefixed a brief sketch of the author's life* (vol 2), Google eBook.

Parker, S. (2013) 'Connected localism and the challenge of change', in Local Government Information Unit (ed) *Connected localism: a blueprint for better public services and more powerful communities*, London: LGiU.

Parnell, S. and Pieterse, E. (2010) 'The "right to the city": institutional imperatives of a development state', *International Journal of Urban and Regional Research*, vol 34, no 1, pp 146–62.

Parry, G., Moyser, G. and Day, M. (1992) *Political participation and democracy in Britain*, Cambridge: Cambridge University Press.

PASC (Public Administration Select Committee) (2011) 'The Big Society', 17th Report of Session 2010–11, 7 December.

Patrick, R. (2011) 'Deserving or undeserving? The Coalition, welfare reform and disabled people', paper presented at the Annual Conference of the Social Policy Association, University of Lincoln, 5 July. Available at: www.social-policy.org.uk/lincoln2011/Patrick%20 symposium%20P4.pdf

Paull, G. and Patel, T. (2012) *An international review of skills, jobs and poverty: implications for the UK*, York: Joseph Rowntree Foundation.

PCRC (Political and Constitutional Reform Committee) (2013) *Prospects for codifying the relationship between central and local government, third report of session 2012–13, volume I: report and appendix, together with formal minutes*, London: The Stationery Office Limited.

Pearce, N. (2012) 'Under pressure: the drivers of a new centre-left statecraft', in G. Cooke and R. Muir (eds) *The relational state: how recognising the importance of human relationships could revolutionise the role of the state*, London: IPPR, pp 45–6.

Pearson, R. and Williams, G. (1984) *Political thought and public policy in the nineteenth century: an introduction*, London: Longman.

Peters, T. and Waterman, R. (1982) *In search of excellence: lessons from America's best run companies*, New York, NY: Harper and Row.

Petersen, O.H., Hjelmar, U., Vrangbæk, K. and La Cour, L. (2012) *Effects of contracting out public sector tasks: a research-based review of Danish and international studies from 2000–2011*, Copenhagen: AKF, Danish Institute of Governmental Research. Summary available at: www.akf. dk/udgivelser_en/2011/5111_ohp_udliciteringsrapport/

Phillips, A. (1996) 'Why does local democracy matter?', in L. Pratchett and D. Wilson (eds) *Local democracy and local government*, Basingstoke: Macmillan Press Ltd, pp 20–37.

Piven, F.F. (2006) *Challenging authority: how ordinary people change America*, Lanham, MD: Rowman and Littlefield.

Piven, F.F. and Cloward, R.A. (1977) *Poor peoples' movements, why they succeed, how they fail*, New York, NY: Pantheon Books.

Polanyi, K. (2001 [1944]) *The great transformation: the political and economic origins of our time* (2nd ed), Boston, MA: Beacon Press.

Pollitt, C. (1990) *Managerialism and the public services: the Anglo-American experience*, Oxford: Basil Blackwell.

Popper, S. and Kenway, P. (2012) *Localising council tax support: a briefing note on local authorities' plans*, London: NPI.

Pratchett, L. and Wilson, D. (eds) (1996) *Local democracy and local government*, Basingstoke: Macmillan Press Ltd.

Pratchett, L., Durose, C., Lowndes, V., Smith, G., Stoker, G. and Wales, C. (2009) *Empowering communities to influence local decision making: evidence-based lessons for policy makers and practitioners*, London: CLG.

Public Accounts Select Committee (2013) *Department for Communities and Local Government: financial sustainability of local authorities. Third report of session 2013–14*, London: Stationery Office Limited.

Putnam, R.D. (1993) 'The prosperous community: social capital and public life', *The American Prospect*, vol 4, no 13, pp 35–42.

Putnam, R.D. (2000) *Bowling alone: the collapse and revival of American community*, New York, NY: Simon & Schuster.

Queensland Audit Office (2013) *Contract management: renewal and transition*, Report to Parliament 10: 2013–14, Brisbane: The State of Queensland, Queensland Audit Office.

Raco, M. (2003) 'Remaking place and securitising space: urban regeneration and the strategies, tactics and practices of policing in the UK', *Urban Studies*, vol 40, no 9, pp 1869–87.

Rallings, C. and Thasher, M. (2001) 'Mayoral race draws level', *Local Government Chronicle*, September.

Rallings, C., Temple, M. and Thrasher, M. (1996) 'Participation in local elections', in L. Pratchett and D. Wilson (eds) *Local democracy and local government*, Basingstoke: Macmillan Press Ltd, pp 62–83.

Rancière, J. (2006) *The hatred of democracy*, London: Verso.

Ranson, R. and Stewart, J. (1989) 'Citizenship and government: the challenge for management in the public domain', *Political Studies*, vol 37, no 1, pp 5–24.

Ratcliffe, P. (2011) 'From community to social cohesion: interrogating a policy paradigm', in P. Ratcliffe and I. Newman (eds) *Promoting social cohesion: implications for policy and evaluation*, Bristol: The Policy Press, pp 15–39.

Ratcliffe, P. and Newman, I. (eds) (2011) *Promoting social cohesion: implications for policy and evaluation*, Bristol: The Policy Press.

Rawls, J. (1971) *A theory of justice*, Cambridge, MA: Harvard University Press.

Rawls, J. (2011 [1982]) 'The basic liberties and their priority', in S. McMurrin (ed) *The Tanner lectures on human values III*, New York, NY, and Cambridge: Cambridge University Press, pp 1–88.

Rhodes, R.A.W. (1987) 'Developing the public service orientation or let's add a soupcon of political theory', *Local Government Studies*, vol 13, no 3, pp 63–73.

Rhodes, R.A.W. (1988) *Beyond Westminster and Whitehall*, London: Unwin Hyman.

Rhodes, R.A.W. (1997) *Understanding governance: policy networks, governance, reflexivity and accountability*, Buckingham: Open University Press.

Rhodes, R.A.W. and Wanna, J. (2007) 'The limits to public value, or rescuing responsible government from the platonic guardians', *The Australian Journal of Public Administration*, vol 66, no 4, pp 406–21.

Ridley, N. (1988) *The local right; enabling not providing*, London: Centre for Policy Studies.

Rittel, H.W.J. and Webber, M.M. (1973) 'Dilemmas in a general theory of planning', *Policy Sciences*, vol. 4, no 2, pp 155–69.

Roberts, J. (2006) 'The root of the matter is all about a sense of place', in J. Bennington, L. de Groot and J. Foot (eds) *Lest we forget: democracy, neighbourhoods and government*, London: Solace Foundation Imprint, pp 9–40.

Roots, B. (2009) *The Roots review: review of arrangements for efficiencies from smarter procurement in local government*, London: Department for Communities and Local Government. Available at: http://www.actionsustainability.com/documents/downloads/Roots%20Review.pdf

Royall, F. (2009) 'Political challengers, service providers or service recipients? Participation in Irish pro-unemployment organisations', in M. Giugni (ed) *The politics of unemployment in Europe: policy responses and collective action*, Farnham, Surrey: Ashgate, pp 117–32.

Russell, H. (2010) *Research into multi-area agreements: long-term evaluation of LAAs and LSPs*, London: Department for Communities and Local Government. Available at: http://www.ljmu.ac.uk/EIUA/EIUA_Docs/Research_into_Multi_Area_Agreements.pdf

Russell, H. (in conjunction with Lepine, E., Newman, I., Dickinson, S., Meegan, R., Lawrence, R., Luanaigh, A.N., Swift, J., Grimshaw, L. and Chapman, R.) (2010) *The role of Local Strategic Partnerships and Local Area Agreements in promoting equalities*, Research Report no 63, Manchester: Equality and Human Rights Commission.

Rydin, Y. (2003) *Conflict, consensus and rationality in environmental planning: an institutional discourse approach*, Oxford: Oxford University Press.

Sandel, M.J. (2009) *Justice: what's the right thing to do?*, New York, NY: Farrar, Straus and Giroux.

Sandel, M.J. (2012a) *What money can't buy: the moral limits of markets*, New York, NY/London: Farrar, Straus and Giroux/Allen Lane.

Sandel, M.J. (2012b) 'What isn't for sale?', *The Atlantic*, 27 February. Available at: www.theatlantic.com/magazine/archive/2012/04/what-isnt-for-sale/308902/

Schlosser, E. (1998) 'The prison–industrial complex', *Atlantic Magazine*, December. Available at: http://www.theatlantic.com/magazine/archive/1998/12/the-prison-industrial-complex/304669/1/

Schön, D. (1983) *The reflective practitioner*, New York, NY: Basic Books Inc.

Schumpeter, (1976 [1942]) *Capitalism, socialism and democracy*, London: Allen and Unwin.

Sen, A. (2009) *The idea of justice*, London: Penguin Books.

Seymore, R. (2012) 'The welfare reform minister's lament about the risk-averse poor is simply a rationalisation for a policy of deep cuts', *The Guardian*, 23 November. Available at: www.guardian.co.uk/commentisfree/2012/nov/23/lord-freud-welfare-poor-risk?INTCMP=SRCH

Sharpe, L.J. (2006 [1970]) 'Theories and values of local government', *Political Studies*, vol 18, no 2, pp 153–74 (online).

Shildrick, T., MacDonald, R., Furlong, A., Roden, J. and Crow, R. (2012) *Are 'cultures of worklessness' passed down the generations?*, York: JRF.

SIGOMA (The Special Interest Group of Municipal Authorities within the LGA) (2013) *A fair future? The true impact of funding reductions on local government*, Barnsley: SIGOMA.

Slay, J. (2012) 'Co-production and personalisation: two sides of the same coin or worlds apart?', in E. Loeffler, D. Taylor-Gooby, T. Bovaird, F. Hine-Hughes and L. Wilkes (eds) *Making health and social care personal and local: moving from mass production to co-production*, Birmingham: Governance International, pp 28–33.

Soper, K. (1991) 'Greening Prometheus: Marxism and ecology', in P. Osborne (ed) *Socialism and the limits of liberalism*, London: Verso, pp 271–93.

Soros, G. (1998) *The crisis of global capitalism: open society endangered*, United States: Public Affairs.

Stacey, R.D. (1993) *Strategic management and organisational dynamics*, London: Pitman.

Stears, M. (2006) *Progressives, pluralists, and the problems of the state: ideologies of reform in the United States and Britain, 1909–1926*, Oxford: Oxford University Press.

Stears, M. (2012) 'The case for a state that supports relationships: not a relational state', in G. Cooke and R. Muir (eds) *The relational state: how recognising the importance of human relationships could revolutionise the role of the state*, London: IPPR, pp 35–44.

Stephenson, M.-A. (2012) 'Unravelling equality: the combined impact of spending cuts on women', *Local Economy*, vol 27, no 8, pp 859–63.

Stewart, J. (1992) 'The rebuilding of public accountability', paper presented to the European Policy Forum in Westminster, 9 December.

Stewart, J. (2000) *The nature of British local government*, Basingstoke, Hampshire: Macmillan Press Ltd.

Stewart, J. (2003) *Modernising British local government: an assessment of Labour's reform programme*, Basingstoke, Hampshire: Palgrave Macmillan.

Stewart, J. and Clarke, M. (1987) 'The public service orientation: issues and dilemmas', *Public Administration*, vol 65, no 2, pp 161–77.

Stewart, J. and Walsh, K. (1992) 'Changes in the management of public services', *Public Administration*, vol 70, no 4, pp 499–518.

Stiglitz, J.E. (2001) 'Prize lecture: information and the change in the paradigm in economics', 2 May. Available at: www.nobelprize.org/nobel_prizes/economics/laureates/2001/stiglitz-lecture.html

Stoker, G. (2005) *What is local government for?*, London: New Local Government Network.

Studdert, J. (2013) *One nation localism: how Labour councils are delivering fairness in tough times*, London: LGA Labour Group.

Sullivan, H. and Howard, J. (2005) *Below the LSP, issues paper*, National Evaluation of LSPs, London: ODPM.

Sullivan, H. and Skelcher, C. (2002) *Working across boundaries: collaboration in public services*, Basingstoke: Palgrave Macmillan.

Sullivan, H., Root, A., Moran, D. and Smith, M. (2001) *Area Committees and neighbourhood management: increasing democratic participation and social inclusion*, London: Local Government Information Unit.

Talbot, C. (2009) 'Public value – the next "big thing" in public management?', *International Journal of Public Administration*, vol 32, nos 3/4, pp 167–70.

Talbot, C.R. and Talbot, C.L. (2011) 'Local government strategies in an age of austerity', in C. Morales Oyarce (ed) *Redefining local government*, London: Public Policy and Management Association, CIPFA, pp 69–76.

Thompson, P. and McHugh, D. (1990) *Work organisation: a critical introduction*, London: Macmillan.

Townsend, P. (1987) 'Deprivation', *Journal of Social Policy*, vol 16, no 2, pp 125–46.

Travers, T. (2006) *Would it be possible to re-localise the NNDR? The technicalities of achieving reform*, London: LGA.

Travers, T. (2008) 'Revitalising politics: the eclipse of local government as the root of a problem', paper for Hansard Conference. Available at: www.astrid-online.it/I-nuovi-pr/Studi--ric/travers_academic-paper_Hansard-conference_05_11_08.pdf

Treasury Select Committee (2013) 'Quantitative easing: written evidence'. Available at: www.publications.parliament.uk/pa/cm201314/cmselect/cmtreasy/writev/qe/qe.pdf

TUC (Trades Union Congress) (2011) *Open Public Services White Paper: a response from the Trades Union Congress*, London: TUC.

Turok, I. (1989) *Developing planning and local economic growth: a study of process and policy in Bracknell New Town*, Oxford: Pergamon Press.

Tyler, C. (2011 [2003]) 'Thomas Hill Green', in Edward N. Zalta (ed) *The Stanford Encyclopedia of philosophy*. Available at: http://plato.stanford.edu/archives/sum2011/entries/green/

Unison (2011) *Factsheet #26: privatising local government*, London: Unison. Available at: https://www.unison.org.uk/upload/sharepoint/On%20line%20Catalogue/19581.pdf

Van der Wal, Z. and Van Hout, E.Th.J. (2009) 'Is public value pluralism paramount? The intrinsic multiplicity and hybridity of public values', *International Journal of Public Administration*, vol 32, nos 3/4, pp 220–31.

Vickery, L. (2012) 'Deepening disadvantage in housing markets for women', *Local Economy*, vol 27, no 8, pp 796–803.

Wainwright, H. (2009a) *Reclaim the state: experiments in popular democracy* (rev edn), London and Calcutta: Seagull Books.

Wainwright, H. (with Little, M.) (2009b) *Public sector reform … but not as we know it!*, Hove: Picnic Publishing for Compass and Unison.

Walsh, K. (1989) *Marketing in local government*, Harlow: Longman in association with LGTB.

Webb, S. (1891) *The London programme*, London: Swan Sonnenschien.

We Own it (2013) *Better in public hands: why we need a Public Services Users Bill*, Oxford: We Own it. Available at: http://weownit.org.uk/

Whilby, P. (2012) 'Philip Hammond has seen the light over privatisation. Sadly, the government hasn't', *The Guardian*, 18 August, p 34.

Whitehead, A. (2006) *Anti-politics and political parties: the case for state funding*, New Politics, No 3, London: New Politics Network. Available at: http://www.alan-whitehead.org.uk/pdf/Anti-pols.pdf

Whitfield, D. (2010) *Global auction of public assets: public sector alternatives to the infrastructure market and public–private partnerships*, Nottingham: Spokesman.

Whitfield, D. (2012) *In place of austerity: reconstructing the economy, state and public services*, Nottingham: Spokesman.

Widdicombe Report (1986) *Report of the Committee of Inquiry into the Conduct of Local Authority Business*, Cmnd 9797, London: HMSO.

Wilkinson, R. and Pickett, K. (2009) *The spirit level; why equality is better for everyone*, London: Penguin Books Ltd.

Wilks-Heeg, S. (2009) 'New Labour and the reform of English local government, 1997–2007: privatising the parts that Conservative governments could not reach?', *Planning Practice and Research*, vol 24, no 1, pp 23–40.

Wilks-Heeg, S. and Clayton, S. (2006) *Whose town is it anyway? The state of local democracy in two northern towns*, York: The Joseph Rowntree Charitable Trust.

Williams, R. (1983) *Keywords: a vocabulary of culture and society* (2nd edn), London: Fontana Paperbacks.

Williams, Z. (2012) *The shadow state: a report about outsourcing of public services*, London: Social Enterprise UK.

Wilson, E. and Piper, J. (2010) *Spatial planning and climate change*, London: Routledge.

Wilson, T., Morgan, G., Rahman, A. and Vaid, L. (2013) *The local impacts of welfare reform: an assessment of cumulative impacts and mitigations*, report commissioned from the Centre for Economic and Social Inclusion by the Local Government Association, London: LGA.

Wintour, P. (2010) 'George Osborne to cut £4bn more from benefits', *The Guardian*, 9 September. Available at: www.guardian.co.uk/politics/2010/sep/09/george-osborne-cut-4bn-benefits-welfare

WLGA (Welsh Local Government Association) (2011) *WLGA manifesto for National Assembly elections 2011–2016: Responding to the challenge*, Cardiff: WLGA.

Wolverhampton City Council (2006) 'Lyons Inquiry citizens' jury – topline summary of findings', Wolverhampton City Council Open Executive Information Item, 28 June, Agenda item 10(e).

Wright Mills, C. (1959) *The sociological imagination*, New York, NY: Oxford University Press.

Young, I.M. (2000) *Inclusion and democracy*, Oxford: Oxford University Press.

Young Foundation (2009) *Sinking or swimming*, London: The Young Foundation.

Zamagni, S. and Zamagni, V. (2010) *Co-operative enterprise: facing the challenge of globalisation*, Cheltenham: Edward Elgar.

Zukin, S. (1995) *The cultures of cities*, Oxford: Blackwell.

Index